THE MURDER OF
PROFESSOR SCHLICK

The Murder of Professor Schlick

THE RISE AND FALL OF THE VIENNA CIRCLE

David Edmonds

PRINCETON UNIVERSITY PRESS

PRINCETON AND OXFORD

Published by Princeton University Press
41 William Street, Princeton, New Jersey 08540
6 Oxford Street, Woodstock, Oxfordshire OX20 1TR

press.princeton.edu

Library of Congress Cataloging-in-Publication Data

Names: Edmonds, David, 1964– author.
Title: The murder of Professor Schlick : the rise and fall of the Vienna Circle / David Edmonds.
Description: Princeton : Princeton University Press, [2020] | Includes bibliographical references and index.
Identifiers: LCCN 2020018766 (print) | LCCN 2020018767 (ebook) | ISBN 9780691164908 (hardback) | ISBN 9780691185842 (ebook)
Subjects: LCSH: Vienna circle—History.
Classification: LCC B824.6 .E36 2020 (print) | LCC B824.6 (ebook) | DDC 146/.42–dc23
LC record available at https://lccn.loc.gov/2020018766
LC ebook record available at https://lccn.loc.gov/2020018767

British Library Cataloging-in-Publication Data is available

Editorial: Rob Tempio and Matt Rohal
Production Editorial: Kathleen Cioffi
Text Design: Lorraine Doneker
Jacket Design: Karl Spurzem
Production: Danielle Amatucci
Publicity: Maria Whelan and Amy Stewart
Copyeditor: Anne Cherry

Jacket image courtesy of the Austrian National Library, Picture Archives and Graphics Collection

This book has been composed in Arno Pro text with Parisian display

Printed on acid-free paper. ∞

Printed in the United States of America

10 9 8 7 6 5 4 3 2 1

CONTENTS

PREFACE

AS A TEENAGER, I had a rather low opinion of God (it was quite possibly reciprocated) and was contemptuous of the ethical judgments of my elders. Perhaps that's why I raced through the first book of philosophy that was ever thrust at me, and it hooked me on philosophy for life. A. J. Ayer's *Language, Truth and Logic* dismisses statements about God as meaningless. It rejects the idea of "objectivity" in morals. It has a wonderful, bravura style, free of doubt. It scorns philosophical predecessors: problems that have beset philosophy for two millennia, such as questions about God and ethics and aesthetics, are decisively laid to rest.

I didn't fully appreciate at the time that the ideas in this book had essentially been recycled. They originated not in Oxford, England, but in Vienna, Austria. They'd been lifted almost (but not quite) whole from a group of mathematicians, logicians, and philosophers called the Vienna Circle.

A quick note on terminology. Members of the Circle were logical empiricists, sometimes called logical positivists. Positivism is the view that our knowledge derives from the natural world and includes the idea that we can have *positive* knowledge of it. The Circle combined this position with the use of modern logic; the aim was to build a new philosophy. But the term *logical positivism* was only introduced in an American journal in 1931, and I will follow the practice of most scholars of the Vienna Circle in talking about "logical empiricism." Labels aside, logical empiricism was for a time, starting in the early 1930s, the most ambitious and fashionable movement in philosophy. Many of its central tenets have now been discredited, but its impact is still felt today. Analytic philosophy—the dominant form of philosophy in Anglo-American philosophy departments with an emphasis on the analysis of language— would not exist in its current form without the Circle. The Circle might not have had all the answers, but they posed most of the right questions—questions with which philosophers continue to grapple.

There have been some magnificent works of scholarship devoted to the Circle. This book aims to be of more general interest—to explain who the members were, what became of them, why they were significant, and, in particular, to understand them within the milieu in which they thrived.

The Vienna Circle was a philosophical group. But it cannot be understood in isolation. It arose in a city in which art and music and literature and architecture also flourished. The Austrian capital is a principal character in these pages. A birthplace of modernism, it was home to psychoanalyst Sigmund Freud and composer Arnold Schoenberg, journalist Karl Kraus and architect Adolf Loos, novelist Robert Musil and playwright Arthur Schnitzler. The Circle's ideas complemented or competed with others circulating around Vienna.

Then there were politics and economics. The backdrop to the Circle was economic catastrophe and the rising political extremism to which the Circle itself would eventually fall victim. I want in this book both to give a sense of the revolutionary and evangelizing nature of the Circle's philosophy *as well as* the troubled times in which the Circle operated. I've come to believe that whatever its scholarly merits the Circle's project, especially its attack on metaphysics, made it inescapably political, creating powerful enemies on the Far Right who were bound, in the end, to destroy it.

Vienna's always held a peculiar fascination for me. Much of a previous book, written with John Eidinow, *Wittgenstein's Poker*, was set in Vienna. In the personal sphere, my mother is half Viennese. My grandmother, then Liesl Hollitscher,[1] studied law at the University of Vienna roughly at the same time as the younger members of the Circle were studying there too. My family, like many in the Circle, was middle-class, assimilated Jewish, and, like many in the Circle, blind to the extreme turn that politics would take.

Writing the book has posed some challenges. One is the philosophy. The reason that there have been so few accessible texts on the Circle is because the philosophy is so complex. I have given only a schematic description of the Circle's philosophical positions and the various philosophical disputes in which members were embroiled, both within the

Circle and between the Circle and its opponents. But I also include, without apology, some (sometimes difficult) philosophy; an account of the Circle without covering philosophy would be like a history of an orchestra without mentioning music.

Then there are the characters. The Vienna Circle contained some fascinating figures, including several who merit (and some who have been awarded) full-length biographies in their own right. Inevitably, some of these figures have loomed larger than others—such as the extraordinary Otto Neurath, virtually unknown outside philosophy. It would need a book five times as long to do equal justice to them all.

We live during a time where phrases like *post-truth* and *fake news* are bandied around. In this environment, empiricism is more relevant than ever. And my hope is that this work will do something to revive interest in a brilliant set of thinkers who thrived in a vanished world and with whose intellectual spirit it's easy to sympathize.

David Edmonds
@DavidEdmonds100

ACKNOWLEDGMENTS

SORRY, I have a lot of people to thank. I will start with those to whom I owe the most.

I had already been researching this book for several years before I approached Thomas Uebel, one of the world's leading experts on the Vienna Circle. I had some questions I wanted to put to him and asked if I could visit him in Manchester, where he is a professor. It turned out that he is frequently in London and we met, as people discussing the Vienna Circle ought to meet, in a gemütlich coffee shop. It was the first of many long caffeine-fueled sessions in which he put me right on various matters Viennese. He also read the entire manuscript, correcting errors. He is not responsible for my interpretation of the Circle nor for the mistakes that no doubt remain. But thank you, Thomas, for being so incredibly generous with your time and knowledge. The book would have been much worse without you.

Several people read part or the whole of the manuscript and made helpful comments. They include Liam Bright, Christian Damböck, Josh Eisenthal, Nathan Oseroff, David Papineau, Ádám Tuboly, and Cheryl Misak, who also sent me in manuscript form her superb biography of Frank Ramsey. The director of the University of London's Institute of Philosophy, Barry Smith, gave me incredibly useful feedback on the book. John Eidinow, a good friend with whom I've written three books, read the manuscript not once but twice and made numerous helpful suggestions. Neville Shack always reads my books in manuscript form and is my comma czar. Edward Harcourt commented on the chapter on psychoanalysis. Many thanks to Friedrich Stadler, who alongside Thomas Uebel is an international authority on the Vienna Circle, and who also read the book. On the final lap, just before the manuscript was dispatched to the copyeditor, Christoph Limbeck-Lilienau read the whole thing and caught quite a few errors others had missed. Hannah Edmonds tidied up the whole text.

Some experts gave me private tutorials, including David Papineau and Christian Damböck, on the philosophy of science and Rudolf Carnap respectively, and the historian Edward Timms, who invited me to his home to discuss Viennese culture. Professor Timms, a great authority on Austria, died in 2018. Several pleasant hours were spent with Friedrich Stadler in the Café Landtmann, close to the University of Vienna, and he patiently answered many further questions by email. (He also provided many of the photos used in the book.) Steve Gimbel kindly emailed me a complete list of transcripts of interviews he'd conducted with relatives of Circle members. Peter Smith put me right on Tarski, and Elisabeth Nemeth helped out with Zilsel. Ádám Tuboly sent me some very useful articles on Neurath.

There were two anonymous referees who were supererogatory in sending in pages of detailed comments. I cracked their identity with some Poirot-esque sleuthing, but will not break convention by naming them here. You know who you are. Thank you.

During the course of research, I stumbled across, and became rather obsessed with, one character, Miss Simpson. The chapter on Miss Simpson is drawn from a BBC program I then presented—which was brilliantly produced by my friend and ace producer Mark Savage. This material then reappeared in a 5,500-word article published by *The Jewish Chronicle* and its editor, Stephen Pollard.

I need to thank helpful archivists and librarians. Much of the literature was read in the British Library, a marvelous public resource marred only by overpriced, book-advance-guzzling food. It has been oddly comforting to work in a building whose architect (Colin St John Wilson) was inspired by Wittgenstein. I made use of several archives—in the London School of Economics (both the Popper archive and the archive on the British Federation of University Women); the Warburg Institute, also in London; the Bodleian Library in Oxford (thanks to Sam Lindley and Rosie Burke); and collections in Konstanz, Minneapolis, and Pittsburgh. A special shout-out to Brigitte Parkenings at the University of Konstanz, who politely and efficiently responded to several requests about Moritz Schlick, and to the ever-friendly Lance Lugar at the University of Pittsburgh. Two Joshes, Josh Eisenthal and Josh Fry, undertook some archival research on my behalf in Pittsburgh. Sara Parhizgari sent me dozens of letters from the Herbert Feigl archive at the University of Minnesota. For a couple of previous books I have relied on the paranoid pursuit of leftists in postwar America, and I must once again acknowledge my debt to the FBI's assiduous investigations of harmless intellectuals, as they provided me with files on several Circle figures.

Several people helped with translations from German and Dutch. Thanks to Daniel Cohen, Hannah Edmonds, and Tim Mansel.

A special thank-you to the Uehiro Centre of Practical Ethics, and to Julian Savulescu, Miriam Wood, Deborah Sheehan, Rachel Gaminiratne, and Rocci Wilkinson. I've had a part-time link with the Centre for over a decade now, and it's been an inspiring place to think and has nourished my love of philosophy.

I am grateful to my agent at David Higham, Veronique Baxter, and all the team at Princeton University Press, most particularly Robert Tempio, Matt Rohal, Kathleen Cioffi, and Anne Cherry (and Al Bertrand too, before the apostate moved to a different press).

There are many other people I need to thank. I put out several appeals for anybody who had met Circle members. One was transmitted through Leiter Reports, a philosophy website. Others were channeled through US universities. Dozens of people got in touch. Many other people also provided me with information or pointed me toward useful papers and books. I fear there are bound to be people I've forgotten— and to these people I apologize—but I would like to acknowledge my debt to the following:

Albert Aboody, Laird Addis, Joseph Agassi, Thomas Allen, Bruce Aune, Harold Barnett, Mike Beaney, Bernhard Beham, Robert Bernacchi, Jeremy Bernstein, Albert Borgmann, Robert Borlick, Alisa Bokulich, Liam Bright, Karen Briskey, Paul Broda, Sylvain Bromberger, Panayot Butchvarov, David Casacuberta, David Chalmers, Robert Cohen, Susan Cohen, John Corcorol, Vincent Cushing, Richard Darst, Freeman Dyson (now deceased), Gary Ebbs, Evan Fales, Lorraine Foster, Liz Fraser, Curtis Franks, John Gardner, Rick

Gawne, Rebecca Goldstein, Leonie Gombrich, Robert Good, Irving Gottesman, Adolf Grünbaum, Alex Hahn, Phil Hanlon, Henry Hardy, Gilbert Harman, Rom Harré, Colin Harris, Alan Hausman, Miranda Hempel, Peter Hempel, Michelle Henning, Herbert Hochberg, Gerald Holton, Mathias Iven, Charles Kay, Anthony Kenny, Mead Killion, William Kingston, Richard Kitchener, John Komdat, Georg Kreisel (now deceased), Matt LaVine, Christoph Limbeck-Lilienau, Hugh Mellor (now deceased), Daniel Merrill, Elisabeth Nemeth, Ines Newman (for her amazing toil on her grandfather's, my great-grandfather's, diary), Nathan Oaklander, Van Parunak, Michael Parish, Charles Parsons, Alois Pichler, George Pieler, Ann Plaum, Mika Provata-Carlone, Douglas Quine, Irv Rabowsky, Sheldon Reaven, Harold Rechter, Maria Rentetzi, Wayne Roberts, Lawrence Rosen, Felix Rosenthal, David Ross, Markus Säbel, Albie Sachs, Adam Sanitt, Kenneth Sayre, Scott Scheall, Reinhard Schumacher, Eugene Sevin, James Smith, Peter Smith, Raymond Smullyan, Alexander Stingl, Markus Stumpf, Thomas H. Thompson, Alexandra Tobeck, Ádám Tuboly, Joe Ullian, Frederick Waage, Brad Wray, John Winnie, Stephen Wordsworth, Leslie Yonce-Meehl, Michael Yudkin, Anton Zettl.

A final appreciation to the people who've had to tolerate the most in the long period it's taken me to write this book—Liz, Saul, and Isaac.

THE MURDER OF
PROFESSOR SCHLICK

1

Prologue

GOODBYE, EUROPE

DEPENDING ON how you look at it, the timing was either fortunate or
ill-fated.

The Fifth International Congress for the Unity of Science met at Harvard from 3–9 September 1939. On 1 September 1939, German tanks had crossed into Poland: Britain and France had treaties with Poland guaranteeing its borders. Two days after the German invasion, Poland's two Western allies responded by declaring war on Germany. The Congress opened, then, just as World War II began.

On the evening of the first day, the delegates listened to President Franklin D. Roosevelt's radio address from the White House. He assured listeners that he did not intend the United States to become involved in hostilities. "I have said not once but many times that I have seen war and that I hate war. I say that again and again. I hope the United States will keep out of this war. I believe that it will. And I give you assurance and reassurance that every effort of your Government will be directed toward that end."

Given the enormity of the events that were unfolding, a conference on the philosophy of science must have felt inconsequential, if not downright inappropriate. But for some of the participants, the staging of the conference that week was both lucky and life-changing—in fact, life-saving.

The scientist and philosopher Richard von Mises, whose brother was another renowned academic, the economist Ludwig von Mises, had traveled to Boston from Turkey. He did not go back. The Polish logician Alfred Tarski also stayed on, having embarked on the last ship to leave Poland before the German invasion. Apparently oblivious to the imminence of the threat to his homeland, he had the wrong visa (it was for a temporary visitor) and no winter clothing. Rather more important was that he was now cut off from his family in Warsaw. But had he not accepted the invitation to participate in the Congress, he would most likely have shared the fearful destiny of three million fellow Polish Jews.

Other speakers at this Harvard conference had left Europe in previous years. There to greet Tarski as he disembarked from the boat in New York was German-born philosopher Carl Gustav (Peter) Hempel. Hempel had been a student of the philosopher of science Hans Reichenbach, who had arrived in America in 1938 and was also present for the Congress. Rudolf Carnap, gentle in personality, colossal in stature—and about whom we'll be hearing much more—had left for the US in December 1935. Philipp Frank, physicist and philosopher, had been based in the States for a year, after moving from Prague. Edgar Zilsel, considered a sociologist of science, had still been in Austria at the time of the Anschluss, the takeover of Austria by Germany in 1938, and was able to bring eyewitness testimony of the savagery the Nazis had unleashed. So too was the philosopher of law Felix Kaufmann. Because he had financial resources, Kaufmann had, naïvely, felt shielded from anti-Semitism, and left his escape until the last moment. Meanwhile, the most colorful character of them all, Otto Neurath, had arrived from The Hague, where he had recently taken up residence after fleeing Vienna in 1934. A contemporary *Time* magazine article painted him as a "bald, booming, energy-oozing sociologist and scientific philosopher."[1] Although his friends urged him to stay in the US, his immediate priority was to return to the Netherlands, and to the woman who would become his third wife.

In all there were some two hundred participants. The first sessions of the conference were focused on whether the sciences could be unified: What did the natural sciences, such as physics, have in common with the social sciences, such as psychology and sociology? Could they be placed on the same foundations, and how firm were these foundations? Beyond these issues, an eclectic range of other topics was discussed, including probability, truth, psychology, infinity, logic, the history and sociology of science, and the foundations of physics.

Much of the groundbreaking work in these areas had originated in Europe, specifically from Vienna. The conference had been organized by Neurath and Charles Morris, a Chicago-based philosopher with close links to the Vienna Circle and an enthusiast for bringing its ideas to the United States. American philosopher W.V.O. Quine wrote of the gathering in Harvard that it was basically "the Vienna Circle, with accretions, in international exile."[2] He himself was a vital accretion.

The Vienna Circle—and its so-called logical empiricism—had come to occupy a commanding position in the world of philosophy in general and in the philosophy of science in particular. The Circle had had a bold project. It had tried to marry an old empiricism with the new logic. It had wanted to carve out a role for philosophy in assisting science. It believed scientific propositions could be known and meaningful, and that this was what distinguished genuine propositions from pseudo-propositions; this was what demarcated science from metaphysics. It had included many brilliant thinkers, including Kurt Gödel, widely acknowledged to be the most significant logician of the twentieth century, and was linked to many others, including two of the most important philosophers of the twentieth century, Ludwig Wittgenstein and Karl Popper.

As the Harvard conference got under way, Europe was accelerating its descent into barbarity, with every day bringing acts of violence and cruelty that over the next six years would become routine. On 3 September, in the village of Truskolasy, in southern Poland, dozens of peasants were rounded up and shot. Just fifty miles away, twenty Jews were forced to assemble in the marketplace. Among them was sixty-four-year-old Israel Lewi. "When his daughter, Liebe, ran up to her father, a German told her to open her mouth for 'impudence.' He then fired a bullet into it."[3] The execution of each of the other Jews followed soon after. On the day the conference drew to a close, 630 Czech political prisoners were transported to Dachau concentration camp in Bavaria.

During the Harvard conference, a provocative position was adopted by Horace Kallen, a Jewish-American academic from the New School for Social Research who was famous for advocating cultural pluralism and for opposing what he regarded as oversimplified answers to philosophical problems. He advanced the view that attempting to unify the sciences was a dangerous project, linked to fascist ideology. Neurath, a distant relative of Kallen, countered that, on the contrary, unification had a democratic motivation, and would facilitate criticism of any particular specialism. Neurath was one of several Circle members who believed that logical empiricism was integral to the struggle against fascism. Logical empiricism represented Enlightenment values of reason and progress, a buffer against dark and irrational emotions. Logical empiricism represented sense against nonsense, truth against fiction. The fight was more important than ever.

Vienna had until recently been a creative cauldron. An unusual combination of political, social, and economic forces had somehow combined to produce astonishing cultural and scholarly achievements, including those of the Circle. Then the political cauldron had bubbled over. The Vienna Circle had been forcibly dissolved in 1934. Later, its leader, Moritz Schlick, was murdered.

Schlick's killer, Johann Nelböck, a mentally unstable former student, claimed he was driven by political and ideological motives. Whether or not that was true—and it seems highly questionable—several Austrian newspapers took Nelböck at his word: logical empiricism was pernicious, antireligious, antimetaphysical. It was a Jewish philosophy, and Professor Schlick embodied all that was wrong with it. In this context, the argument ran, Nelböck's act was not unreasonable. Indeed, one article suggested, it was even possible that Schlick's death might facilitate the search for a solution to the "Jewish Question."

Following Schlick's murder the Vienna Circle continued to limp on informally. But the Anschluss and the outbreak of World War II marked points of no return. If its ideas were to survive, they would now have to take root in the Anglo-American world. That was a project for the future.

So what was the Vienna Circle, the "republic of scholars,"[4] as Otto Neurath once described it, and why did it matter? Why had it been crushed by the authorities? Why had its members been forced into exile? And had it succeeded in its ultimate ambition—to vanquish metaphysics and banish the multiple varieties of pseudo-knowledge?

2

◄O►

Little Rooster and the Elephant

The empiricist does not say to the metaphysician "what you say is false" but, "what you say asserts nothing at all!"

—MORITZ SCHLICK

IN 1905, Albert Einstein, then a doctoral student of physics working as a clerk in a Swiss patent office, published four papers as well as his dissertation. The year 1905 is known by scientists as Einstein's *annus mirabilis*—a miraculous year, for these papers gave the world $E = mc^2$, the special theory of relativity, and the claim that light must have particle-like as well as wave-like properties. The classical physics of Isaac Newton and James Clerk Maxwell was toppled. A new era of (at times) highly counterintuitive science had begun. In particular, time and space were not constants; they were relative, because they depended upon the observer who was measuring them.

Einstein would not become a household name for another decade and a half. But among those quick to grasp the magnitude of his break-throughs was a young, serious, articulate, bespectacled, mustachioed mathematician and philosopher named Hans Hahn, or Hänchen (Little Rooster) to his friends, an ironic nickname for a tall man.

Hahn was the originator of what would become known as the Vienna Circle. He was born in Vienna into a middle-class family in 1879 (his Jewish father was a journalist, then high-ranking in the civil service) and studied at the University of Vienna, initially law, before he turned to mathematics, receiving both a doctorate and the higher doctoral degree, the habilitation. He would become a figure of international standing after whom various complex theorems are now named, including the Hahn embedding theorem and the Hahn decomposition theorem. He would also become an important recruiting agent for the Vienna Circle: some of his students would surpass him in their impact on the world stage, most notably Kurt Gödel.

From 1907 Hahn began to hold regular meetings with a small set of other young, Jewish, postdoctoral, scientifically inclined, Vienna-based philosophers—usually in a coffeehouse—to mull over the philosophical foundations of science as well as "a great variety of political, historical, and religious problems."[1] Besides Hahn, there was Otto Neurath, who had been awarded his doctorate in Berlin, and Philipp Frank, the junior among them at twenty-three, a short man who walked with a limp after having been hit by a streetcar and who was already churning out academic papers, many on relativity. On occasion they were possibly joined too by scientist Richard von Mises, a close friend of both Hahn and Frank. These men discussed the French mathematicians/ physicists Pierre Duhem and Henri Poincaré as well as philosopher and scientist Ernst Mach. They were all fascinated and puzzled by the transformations under way in theoretical physics. They were interested in the methodology of science, the language of science, the claims and status of science, and the distinction between science and pseudo-science. They wished to demarcate the empirical sciences—involving experiments and evidence—from other forms of inquiry. They were interested in the foundations of geometry and mathematics. They wanted to understand how to make sense of probability. They shared the view that philosophy as traditionally practiced was needlessly esoteric and often nonsensical. They shared a belief that philosophy and science should be more collaborative, more closely linked. They wanted philosophy to be useful to science in clarifying the scientific enterprise. They had a broadly left-leaning political orientation. As we shall see, the politics and the philosophy were inextricably linked.

Their championing of progressive politics and the new science was hardly likely to appeal to supporters of the pre–World War I status quo. Vienna at the time was part of the Austro-Hungarian Empire, presided over by Franz Josef I, and Catholicism, the religion of the vast majority of the country, was a powerful cultural force, mostly hostile to social and political reform. The university too was resistant to change.

This informal discussion group met on and off until 1912. By the out-break of World War I, in 1914, they had scattered. Hahn had married a fellow mathematician, Eleanor (Lilly) Minor, and taken a chair at the University of Czernowitz, 1,000 kilometers to the east of Vienna at the furthest edge of the Austro-Hungarian Empire (in what is now Ukraine). Von Mises became professor of applied mathematics at Strasbourg. Frank occupied the chair of theoretical physics at the German University in Prague, where he was to remain until just before World War II. Frank would return to Vienna regularly; it was his place of birth and the city he thought of as home. Hahn, von Mises, and Neurath saw action in World War I, and Hahn was shot and wounded on the Italian front, the bullet that lodged in his back never to be removed.

Pre–World War I, these precocious scholars were not confident enough to accord their little group a title, but we may regard it as the Vienna Circle in embryonic form. They did not regard themselves as either entirely original nor, yet, as fermenters of philosophical revolt. They placed themselves in a tradition—an empiricist or positivist tradition. In particular, they felt themselves to be disciples of, and heirs to, Ernst Mach.

———

Mach should be most familiar as the name used when talking about the speed at which jet planes travel. A Mach number is a ratio of the speed of an object to the speed of sound (the latter will vary according to what the object is passing through, e.g., air or water). The Mach number is named in honor of Ernst Mach, a multitalented physicist who studied shock waves. He photographed many of his experiments and managed to capture bullets in mid-flight.

But as well as being a creative experimentalist, Mach was also a philosopher. There were many intellectual forerunners of the Vienna Circle, including eighteenth-century Scotsman David Hume and nineteenth-century Frenchman Auguste Comte, who first deployed the term *positivism*. But the most direct historical begetter of the Circle was Mach. Without Mach there would have been no Circle.

What marked him out was his combining philosophy and science to produce a philosophy of science. The elder Circle members were all brought up in "a Machian tradition," as Neurath put it.[2] "Few great men," wrote philosopher Karl Popper, "have had an intellectual impact upon the twentieth century comparable to that of Ernst Mach."[3] He made a similar impact on people who met him in the flesh. American philosopher and psychologist William James spent several hours talking to him in Prague, an "unforgettable conversation. I don't think anyone ever gave me so strong an impression of pure intellectual genius."[4]

Mach belonged to a post-Enlightenment era, in which a theistic worldview was coming under sustained attack: Nietzsche, in a book published in 1882, had proclaimed the death of God,[5] and there was an urge within certain circles to rebuild knowledge in purely secular, scientific terms. If knowledge was not guaranteed by God, what was its guarantor? And how did we distinguish truth from falsity? Even raising such questions was provocative for most Austrians.

Mach took his doctorate at the University of Vienna and ended his career as professor there, after spending three decades in the German University in Prague. He never regarded himself as a philosopher, but as a scientist reflecting on scientific practice. Philipp Frank and Mach met and corresponded, though Frank had not studied under him but under his successor, Ludwig Boltzmann, who also doubled as both a philosopher and physicist, though unlike Mach he was a theoretician rather than an experimentalist. From Boltzmann and Mach, Frank absorbed an important insight—that science was a social practice, used to solve interesting and usually practical problems, and, for most scientists at least, was not the search for Platonic and eternal truths.

Both Mach and Boltzmann maintained that ultimately all empirical claims had to withstand the test of experimental validation, and measurement essentially involved the senses; we could see, touch, smell, hear, and taste the world. Neither metaphysics nor mysticism had a place in science. To claim that there existed objects independent of our sensations of the object (the "thing in itself") was, for Mach at least, a kind of beguiling nonsense.

The origin of the term *metaphysics* goes back to a categorization of Aristotle's works in the first century CE, when some of his writings were placed under "physics," others in "after physics." Metaphysics became the study of the fundamental nature of reality beyond the subjective appearance of it. Mach's skepticism that one could talk meaningfully about a world beyond science then triggered an animated debate with Boltzmann about the existence of atoms. Several scientific theories posited their existence, but to Mach "atoms" were merely mental constructs, since they could not (at the time) be measured or perceived. Many well-known physicists of the day weighed into the Mach-Boltzmann atom quarrel, some on Mach's side, others on Boltzmann's. In fact, science was to prove Boltzmann right, though the deeper philosophical question, of what meaning, if any, can be given to statements about entities that cannot be observed, lay unresolved.

In the late nineteenth and early twentieth centuries Mach developed a considerable following. He even influenced Einstein's intellectual trajectory. Mach had criticized Newton's conceptions of space and time before Einstein published his bold new theories. What did it mean to talk about "absolute time" if this was not something you could detect, Mach wondered. In his autobiographical notes, Einstein mentions Mach several times and in admiring terms; he goes so far as to credit him as a vital precursor to his general theory of relativity. Of Mach's book *The Science of Mechanics*, Einstein wrote that it "exercised a profound influence upon me. . . . I see Mach's greatness in his incorruptible scepticism and independence."[6] In fact, at first Mach could not understand relativity theory and Philipp Frank was dispatched to explain it to him. Frank later described Mach as "a man with a gray, somewhat wild beard, who looked like a Slovak physician or lawyer."[7]

The dominant leftist force in Austria, the Austro-Marxists, were also admirers of Mach and his empiricism, especially when both philosophy and developments in science came under increasing attack in the 1920s and 1930s from the political right. Mach had a close friendship with Victor Adler, the leader of the Social Democratic Workers' Party (Sozialdemokratische Arbeiterpartei, or SDAP). Some future members of the Circle would canvass the notion that, although politicians might manipulate science for their own ends, science itself was essentially apolitical. But that position, even if tenable in some parts of the world, could hardly be upheld in Austria, where nearly everything was politicized.

Not that Mach was universally esteemed on the Left. One fierce critic, Vladimir Ilich Ulanov, published a book in 1909 in which Mach is linked to solipsism, relativism, and antirealism. Mach's claim that all knowledge came through the senses, Ulanov argued, led inexorably to the absurd conclusion that you could not be sure of a reality beyond your mind. The title of his anti-Mach diatribe, *Materialism and Empirio-criticism*, was hardly catchy. Eight years later, now operating under an alias, V. I. Lenin, his slogan *Peace, Land and Bread* would carry more populist appeal.

Materialism and Empirio-criticism was written as part of Lenin's power struggle with his Bolshevik rival Alexander Bogdanov, who maintained that ideas of an "absolute truth" and the reality of the external world were bourgeois and old-fashioned. "In our time a philosopher has to declare himself a 'realist' and an 'enemy of idealism,'" Lenin responded, "It is about time you Machist gentlemen understood this."[8] A list of Lenin's opponents would typically include Mensheviks, the Romanov dynasty, capitalists, and imperialists. The special contempt he held for Mach is less well known. Yet a biographer of Lenin says that after the 1917 revolution *Materialism and Empirio-criticism* "became a philosophical bible for official Soviet intellectuals."[9]

———

Otto Neurath has been briefly mentioned already. From the Circle's birth to its death throes, he was a constant presence, and he was no ordinary member of the Circle. There was nothing ordinary about Neurath.

All who met him were struck by his physical bearing, well built and tall, a huge bald head, and, until he shaved it off, an unrestrained red beard. Today, few nonphilosophers have heard of Otto Neurath. But he was an outsize character in interwar Viennese society, a Viennese dervish, the Circle's "big locomotive."[10] He would become the driving force behind the Circle's various manifestos, conferences, exhibitions, and publications. He was helped by preternatural levels of self-confidence. Popper delivered a backhanded compliment, when he said of Neurath that he was "a man who believed passionately in his social, political and philosophical theories, but who believed even more in himself . . . [a man] who would not look behind him or, when rushing ahead care very much about whom his big stride might knock down."[11]

Alongside his life of organizing and lecturing was his capacity for writing and reading: he got through two books a day, scribbling notes and references in the margins. He would sometimes read as he walked. But he was also the antithesis of the remote professor—ebullient and loud and funny. The wittiest man in Vienna, he was once called. Bookish but not book-bound, he loved to socialize and would talk volubly in coffeehouses. His volume and inexhaustibility left those who attempted to keep up with him drained: Carnap's second wife, Ina, told Neurath how "time and again I have observed Carnap trying to outshout you and ending up with a sore throat."[12]

Something of Neurath's idiosyncrasy is captured in the way he used to sign his letters—with a sketch of an elephant. But he did not always draw the same image; it changed according to his mood, and sometimes he went to the trouble to color it in. In one letter the trunk is facing down and the elephant is walking backward, his broad backside about to make painful contact with a cactus. That meant Neurath was in an awkward situation. Sagging ears and a tear in the elephant's eye would convey a depressed mood. A more typical image was the elephant with the trunk at full stretch, holding a flower. That was default Neurath, happy Neurath.

———

Otto Neurath was born on 10 December 1882. His mother, Gertrud, was a Protestant. His father, Wilhelm Neurath, was an economist who began his life in a poor, Orthodox Jewish family in Bratislava and took a well-traveled path into comfortable, secular, middle-class Vienna. Wilhelm married a German Protestant and converted. He built up an enormous library, the contents of which Otto would absorb into his oversize head, and part of which he would later sell to finance his studies. His third wife, Marie, later wrote, "Otto had read most of Kant and other philosophers when he still enjoyed playing with tin soldiers."[13]

Neurath's life was beset by tragedy and menace, although by nature he was irrepressibly optimistic, bouncing back from each of his many setbacks. His first wife, Anna, an accomplished scholar in her own right, whom he met at the University of Vienna, died of complications from the birth of their son, Paul, in 1911. He was suicidal for a short period but then, and to the disapproval of some of his friends, he quickly remarried, this time to Olga Hahn, a mathematician and philosopher, and sister of Hans. At the age of twenty-two Olga had gone blind due to typhus, after which Otto had organized a rota for friends to read books and articles to her so she could complete her studies. Following their marriage, Olga was unable to cope with a baby, and they dispatched Paul to a Protestant children's home near Linz in Upper Austria, close to Neurath's mother. The boy did not return until he was nine.

One Circle member said it was impossible to sum Neurath up in a few words: his "manifold activities and encyclopedic . . . interests defy classification."[14] His doctorate was on the ancient world and barter societies, but his expertise ranged from Goethe to Marx to the history of optics. Most members of the later Circle were primarily focused on what is sometimes called the hard sciences—particularly physics. Neurath was essentially a social scientist, though he began his studies in mathematics and physics in Vienna, moving to Berlin for his PhD and to absorb himself in politics, history, and economics. He returned to Vienna to teach political economy at the New Academy of Commerce. That came to an end in 1914 when war broke out, and he became an officer of the Army Service Corps, responsible for various logistical functions. Once, as he passed through Linz, Paul was brought to the station to meet his father for a brief reunion. But for much of the time Neurath was based in the eastern outreaches of the Austro-Hungarian Empire, in Galicia. For a period, he was commander of a small occupied town, Radziwillow, in what is now Ukraine.

Before the war, Neurath had become interested in how economies function during conflict. Somehow he now managed to convince his military superiors that his talents were wasted on the field and that he would be of more use setting up a department within the war ministry to analyze what did and did not work under conditions of warfare. That led to an overlapping job running the German Museum of War Economy in Leipzig, which in turn resulted in a job overseeing an office for central economic planning in Munich, the capital of Bavaria. In the midst of all this, he carved out time to achieve his habilitation at Heidelberg University.

Later, politics within the Vienna Circle would become contested, but by the war's end Neurath had become a committed socialist, convinced that the planned economy was both efficient and could deliver social justice. Bavaria brought the opportunity to put theory into practice. In March 1919, his proposal for the socialization of the economy was fiercely debated in the Bavarian council. Neurath was present and threatened to take his ideas directly to the people if they were rejected by the politicians. In the event, a Bavarian Office for Central European Planning was established, with Neurath in charge. While he was in Bavaria a group of communists, socialists, and anarchists announced the formation of a "Soviet Republic." It did not survive long, brought to an end in May 1919 by government troops and right-wing nationalists. Neurath was accused and found guilty of "aiding and abetting high treason." Some of his colleagues were executed, but his sentence, considered lenient, was a year-and-a-half's detention. In fact, he served only six weeks in jail before the trial following an intervention from Otto Bauer, the Austrian foreign secretary; the deal was that he should go back to Austria and stay out of Germany.

The misery of postwar Vienna to which Neurath returned could have been oppressive and paralyzing, but to Neurath it was pregnant with opportunity and energizing. Two decades on he would reminisce about his early days back home. "After the lost war there were more difficulties in the world, but more chances that things could change."[15] There is an amusing entry about Neurath in Robert Musil's diary, attesting to his vivacity. The novelist describes how Neurath made "energetic entries" in his notebook, striking them off as they were dealt with; he would also pull "some kind remark out of his pocket: 'Please give my regards to your esteemed wife' even though we were together with her only a quarter of an hour ago."[16]

One opportunity the end of war afforded was a chance to revive the discussion group of which Neurath had once been a part; but this time with a leader.

3

The Expanding Circle

Philosophy is the activity by means of which the meaning of statements is clarified and defined.

—MORITZ SCHLICK

HE WAS NOT AUSTRIAN, Jewish, or poor. To put it another way, Moritz Schlick did not suffer from the cultural, social, and political insecurities of so many of those with whom, in Vienna, he would spend his time. It was perhaps because he felt sufficiently sheltered from the personal circumstances that threatened his colleagues that he was able to exert a calming influence on those around him, moderating disagreement, keeping egos in check. He was a consensus builder: soft-spoken, often hesitant, exuding more charm than charisma. With poor performers he was impatient, and found marking and grading a tedious burden. But by his smartest students he was loved and admired. Author Hilde Spiel, a former student, called him "a truly wise, truly good man," a gentle mentor who "convinced us of the clarity and sincerity of his thinking through the force of his own clear, sincere personality."[1]

He was, in other words, the perfect man to lead the Circle.

Moritz Schlick was born into wealth in Berlin on 14 April 1882. His father was a factory manager, producing combs, among other products, and he was also moneyed and socially well connected on his mother's side. In Vienna he had a capacious apartment in the select *Prinz Eugen Strasse*, where the Rothschilds owned a mansion. His rooms looked out over the Belvedere park, but in the mornings he liked to go riding in another park, the Prater. In 1907, Schlick married an American—Blanche Guy Hardy—the daughter of a pastor, who had been sent to boarding school in Germany. They had two children. Schlick spoke fluent English and was cosmopolitan in outlook; family holidays were spent in Italy. Vienna became his home, but he had options. Austria was a choice.

His first passion had been physics, and he completed a doctorate on the nature of light (passing summa cum laude) under the future Nobel Prize winner Max Planck. Soon after, his interest shifted to the philosophy of science, and he got a job lecturing at the University of Rostock on the Baltic Sea. The long-term effects of a childhood illness (scarlet fever and diphtheria) saved him from the front line in World War I; instead he was dispatched to a military airfield near Berlin, where he worked in a physics department. A book published toward the end of the war, *Space and Time in Contemporary Physics* (*Raum und Zeit in der gegenwärtigen Physik*), was well received, and even reviewed in newspapers abroad. It attempted to grapple with the philosophical implications of the new physics, represented by Einstein and Planck. Another work, *General Theory of Knowledge* (*Allgemeine Erkenntnislehre*), appeared not long after.

A turning point in the history of twentieth-century philosophy came in 1922 when, age forty, Schlick was offered, and accepted, the chair for natural philosophy at the University of Vienna—a position once held by Mach. According to Friedrich Stadler, the historian of the Vienna Circle, Hans Hahn had been Schlick's principal backer for the post. Hahn had himself been appointed to a full professorship at the university only a year earlier, after teaching in Bonn, and had quickly developed a fan base. He was neither a magnetic presence nor indeed especially approachable, but he had a loud voice and his lectures were beautifully clear and concise: they were "a work of art,"[2] according to one of those (Karl Popper) who attended them.

Hahn admired Schlick's work and inferred, correctly, that he would prove a useful ally in the battle against what Hahn regarded as the university's reactionary elements. Schlick came with a strong recommendation from somebody whose opinions demanded respect—Albert Einstein. Hahn nonetheless had to lobby intensely for the appointment and override several objections, including the accusation that the German was too ready to embrace the latest scientific advances, which many regarded as mysterious and subversive. There was also the worry that Schlick was Jewish. On this point at least, Hahn could reassure his detractors: unlike Hahn, Schlick was pure Aryan.

———

Soon after Schlick took up his chair, he, Neurath, Hahn, and some other scientifically literate scholars began to meet casually for philosophical discussions. This core group would expand over the next few years, gathering around them a truly remarkable collection of brilliant minds.

Viktor Kraft had a job in the University of Vienna library and only secured an official academic role in 1924, at the age of forty-four; Kurt Reidemeister, a German mathematician, was working on how to mathematically understand knots; Edgar Zilsel had received his math PhD during World War I; Felix Kaufmann was a witty legal scholar interested in phenomenology (the study of conscious phenomena—how things appear to us). Josef Schächter was concurrently studying philosophy and training to be a rabbi; Marcel Natkin was a Polish-born student who wrote a highly regarded dissertation on the merits of simplicity in scientific theory; Béla Juhos was an aristocratic Hungarian studying under Schlick.

Then there was Karl Menger, who had studied mathematics under Hahn before moving to Amsterdam on a fellowship. Hahn was pleased to welcome him back. Hahn was also the supervisor of Kurt Gödel, a small, thin, strange, inquisitive introvert. Born in Moravia into a German-speaking Lutheran family, Gödel too was of middle-class background—his father ran a factory. He was a nervous, anxious boy who at school excelled in every subject. He then entered the University of Vienna to study physics before gravitating to mathematics. Hahn was quick to mention him to Schlick—and thus another member was recruited into the group.

Herbert Feigl and Friedrich Waismann were also recruited, students of Hahn and Schlick, respectively. Feigl had been raised in comfortable circumstances—his father was in the textile business—in what is now the Czech Republic, and so fitted the typical Circle background. Waismann, on the other hand, of Russian origin, had no money to fall back upon. Financial problems would darken much of his life.

It was Feigl's and Waismann's suggestion that the coffeehouse proceedings be placed on a more official footing, as it had become impractical for the enlarged group to hold a sensible dialogue amid the hubbub of the coffeehouse. Schlick was prevailed upon to be the leader of this group, as well as gatekeeper. He would determine who was worthy of inclusion and who was not. It still did not officially have a name.

As time and meetings passed, some thinkers moved on, and others joined in. The majority of the Circle were almost a generation younger than its old guard, Frank, Hahn, Neurath, and Schlick. The younger members included mathematicians Gustav Bergmann and Olga Taussky, rabbinical scholar Josef Schächter, Rose Rand, Walter Hollitscher, and Heinrich Neider; the latter shocked a friend, before he joined the Circle, by confessing that he had never heard of the Viennese dervish Otto Neurath.

Rose Rand was an intriguing case. Born in Lemberg (then in Poland, now Lviv in Ukraine), her family moved to Austria and in 1924 she began her studies in philosophy in Vienna, taught by Schlick and Rudolf Carnap. Her specialty was logic. A man of her aptitude would not have faced the same career ordeals; behind her back, some of her male peers disdainfully dismissed her as not being of the first rank. Still, she was sufficiently respected to be invited into the Circle and—one guesses because she was a woman—asked to take the minutes, which she did from 1930 to 1933. Later, she refused to sell the original minutes to Neurath, when he offered to buy them from her. Throughout her life, she struggled financially. She paid for her doctorate fees by giving private lessons to students, by teaching in adult education, and by translating articles on logic from Polish into German. For several years she treated and researched female psychiatric patients at the Pötzl Klinik. Schlick had helped her find work at the clinic, about which we will hear more.

Philosopher and logician Rudolf Carnap was undoubtedly the most crucial addition to the original group. He would turn out to be the most technically gifted of them all. He came from a solid middle-class and deeply pious German background. His father (like Schlick's, Feigl's, and Gödel's) ran a factory (making ribbons). Carnap had studied at Freiburg and Jena, taking courses with logician Gottlob Frege, whose importance was so underrecognized even at his own university that for one course Carnap was one of only three students. Carnap was influenced by Neo-Kantianism, a German philosophical movement that took a renewed interest in the philosophy of Immanuel Kant, and for a time Carnap was convinced that a priori reflection could provide us with knowledge about space.

Carnap gradually shed the religious beliefs inherited from his parents, but later wrote that this had no impact on his ethical outlook on life: "My moral valuations were afterwards essentially the same as before."[3] Always with leftist instincts, Carnap (like Neurath) was radicalized by the war in which he served for three years. He had not enlisted enthusiastically but out of a sense of obligation. "The outbreak of the war in 1914 was for me an incomprehensible catastrophe. Military service was contrary to my whole attitude, but I accepted it now as a duty, believed to be necessary in order to save the fatherland."[4] He later witnessed traumatic military engagements on the Western Front, and came to despise the incompetence and insouciance of the officer class. It was in the trenches in 1917 that he first read about Einstein's theory of relativity, which he would try to explain to his fellow soldiers.

After the war, he studied physics in Berlin, but his interests were already turning to philosophy. He was introduced to Schlick by the German philosopher of science Hans Reichenbach, and Schlick offered him a job in Vienna. Carnap was the antithesis of flamboyance: he worked steadily and methodically, building up his philosophical structure brick by brick by brick. To others he gave off an "aura of integrity and seriousness which was almost overwhelming."[5] Tolerant of the views of others, when confronted with new and interesting ideas he would jot them down in a little notebook. But beyond a certain time, in the early evening, he refused to discuss science—for fear of a sleepless night.

He first visited Vienna in 1924 for a conference on Esperanto and during this trip met Neurath. He was in Vienna again for a period in 1925, where as well as holding talks with Circle members he took full advantage of Vienna's cultural life, enjoying the cinema, theater, concerts, mountain hikes, and the companionship of Maja, a student of Schlick's. He arrived from Germany permanently in May 1926, leaving behind his soon-to-be divorced wife, Elisabeth, and their three children. It had been an unhappy marriage, and Carnap had been unfaithful to her with numerous partners, which, in his typically methodical fashion, he documented in detail, just as he did with the books he read. He had one more or less steady girlfriend, a married woman named Maue Gramm (whose husband, an art historian, lectured in Munich), and this relationship produced two more children. Maue would visit Vienna from time to time. Carnap, meanwhile, had several other dalliances—but apparently not with Maja, who was able to resist his charms. She helped persuade Carnap that a nonsexual friendship with a woman was workable.

Even before arriving in Vienna he had been working on *The Logical Structure of the World* (*Der logische Aufbau der Welt*), which eventually appeared in 1928 and is still regarded by many philosophers as his masterpiece. It melded logic with empiricism. Elementary, subjective experiences—seeing or feeling a table, smelling a rose—were the units from which complex and meaningful scientific language could be constructed, using the tools of modern logic. Many in the Circle attended Carnap's university lectures, and several members, most especially Feigl and Waismann, came to regard Carnap as a philosophical father figure.

———

The fall of 1924 saw a fresh beginning. From the noise and bustle of the coffeehouse, the Circle moved to a small, nondescript room at the Mathematics Institute in Boltzmanngasse, just north of the inner city, which had been built shortly before World War I and which was otherwise used for lectures and as a place to read. We have the minutes and several firsthand reports of how proceedings were conducted, though on some details they are contradictory.

Schlick would bring the meeting to order at 6:00 p.m. by clapping his hands. Up to twenty people might be there. Menger recalled that each session would begin with Schlick making announcements, drawing attention to a new publication, or reading out correspondence he or others had had with such luminaries as Albert Einstein. If a foreign guest was in town, Schlick would introduce him. Then the serious business of the evening would kick off—discussion about an agreed topic or a specific paper.

The Vienna Circle might have been more accurately labeled the Vienna Rectangle, for such was the shape of the long table around which they sat, with Schlick occupying one end and Neurath the other. Regular attendees usually headed for their favorite seats; Menger, for example, often sat on Schlick's right, Waismann to his left. Some seats were arranged at the front in a semicircle around the blackboard, which was put to constant use. There were always smokers. Kaufmann took up smoking after the publication of his first book, and adopted a strict rule of smoking neither more nor less than three cigarettes a day—until the publication of his next book, when the quota was raised to four.

Some in the Circle, like Neurath, were voluble; others, like Viktor Kraft, barely said a word. The timid Gödel was in the quiet camp, although there was much that he disagreed with. Menger said that you only knew when Gödel was interested in a topic by slight motions of the head, indicating assent or disagreement. Schlick was the acknowledged leader of the group, but it was far from a dictatorship. Driving the agenda were several influential members, including Hahn and, of course, by the sheer force of his personality, Neurath. If the topic was technical, Carnap or Hahn would take the lead. Later, Carnap would develop a reputation for patience and humility, but as a younger man he was driven and forthright, not timid to take on opponents. Discussion was often heated but mostly civil, although Neurath and Schlick rubbed each other the wrong way.

What was demanded in any discussion was clarity. Their antennae were highly sensitive to ambiguity and possible misinterpretation. There was suspicion of terms that were commonplace in philosophy but for which there was no agreed understanding or definition—words like *essential*, *reality*, *entity*. Neurath, apparently only half in jest, proposed an index of forbidden terminology. Proposals and statements were subjected to some key checks: what did they mean?; how were they known?

Over the next decade the Vienna Circle would gain in confidence, expand in ambition, and extend its influence beyond Austria. A few philosophers, not officially members of the Circle, became linked to it, though Karl Popper was never asked to join and Ludwig Wittgenstein refused many pleas to appear. On the whole, Schlick's instinct for identifying talent was unerring and to him talent was what really mattered. But Popper was a special case. As we shall see, Schlick thought him far too rude to receive an invitation. Nonetheless, the Circle would grapple with some of his ideas, though they had nowhere near the influence of Wittgenstein's.

Finally, there were the connections with like-minded groups abroad. The most important of these was the Society for Empirical Philosophy, founded in Berlin in February 1927 and led by Hans Reichenbach. It included important thinkers such as Carl Hempel and logician Kurt Grelling. Several members of the Circle lectured in Berlin, and several members of the Berlin Society visited Vienna. There were also links with philosophers in Prague, where Circle member Philipp Frank, a regular visitor to Vienna, was based, and with Warsaw, home to logician Alfred Tarski. From around 1930, they had visits from philosophers from Scandinavia, England, the US, China, and elsewhere—who then imported Circle debates back to their national homes.

———

So, what did the Circle believe? Philosophically, what bound its members together?

In answering this question, I must note one crucial caveat: almost every statement of the form "The Vienna Circle believed X . . ." can be refuted by pointing to at least one person linked to the Circle who rejected X. Nonetheless, some generalizations are possible.

To start with, Circle members and associates were impatient of, and certainly not scholars in, the past two millennia or more of rich philosophical history. They would draw on previous thinkers, but a careful exegesis of an ancient historical text, line by line, paragraph by paragraph, was not their style. They were engaged with the present and the future rather than the past, and with developments in science more than trends in philosophy. They had a passion for science, a belief in its transformative possibilities, and a fervor about the power of philosophy to assist. Philosophy should be the handmaiden of science—it could clarify the methods and reasoning of science. Above all, they detested metaphysics—claims about the nature of reality that rely on intuition and that go beyond what can be established by math/logic and by empirical science. The objective was to distinguish genuine knowledge from pseudo-knowledge and in the process destroy metaphysics. In the 1920s, they were confident that their project was achievable. But this was a dangerous and provocative project. It ran counter to the German philosophical tradition and destablized the foundations of far-right political ideology.

The Circle was largely unfamiliar with the tremendous advances in biology that had begun to take place at the turn of the twentieth century—and paid little attention to what became known as genetics and the science of inheritance.[6] What they were engaged with was physics. The Circle was formed and evolved during what was the most extraordinary era of scientific advance since the days of Newton in the second half of the seventeenth century. Alongside Einstein, physicists such as Max Planck, Niels Bohr, and Werner Heisenberg were reimagining and redescribing the way the world was constructed. Apparently preposterous theories were being embraced by science that made a mockery of common sense.

These theories had concomitant descriptions, complementarity and uncertainty. Is light a particle or a wave? It could not be both, yet complementarity claimed that treating it as both was necessary to understanding it. Bohr was developing this principle of complementarity as Werner Heisenberg worked on his *Uncertainty Principle*, published in 1927, which stated that it was impossible to measure the velocity and position of a particle simultaneously, since measuring the one will necessarily distort the other. Complementarity and uncertainty seemed to undermine the notion that science, at least in theory, could give a complete, and completely objective, picture of the world. That was too much even for Albert Einstein.

The Circle revered these great contemporary scientists and Einstein above all. Three years before Moritz Schlick arrived in Vienna, and virtually overnight, Einstein had become an international celebrity—not a status, then or now, common among physicists. For ordinary members of the public it was impossible to grasp his achievements. But many of the empiricists were trained in physics and were swift to acknowledge both that Einstein had turned physics upside down and that in so doing he had raised hitherto unimaginable philosophical problems.

This was only one of several reasons the Circle held Einstein in such esteem. Another was that he encapsulated their empiricist approach. He had offered up bold hypotheses, and crucially, these hypotheses were testable. Physics was not, for him, dogma. He was open to amending or abandoning theories if they were found empirically wanting. His wildly improbable claim that gravity affected light, space, and time was tested by the solar eclipse on 29 May 1919. After the results were announced on 8 November 1919, and his predictions were validated, newspapers across the globe hailed his triumph. By 9 November everyone had heard of Professor Einstein.

As well as being sympathetic to his empiricism, the Circle venerated Einstein because they believed he had dealt a hammer blow to a leading bogeyman, the eighteenth-century citizen of Königsberg, Immanuel Kant. Some philosophical context is required to understand the depth of the wound Einstein was believed to have inflicted upon Kant. Philosophers had drawn a distinction between analytic and synthetic truths, and a separate distinction between the a priori and the a posteriori. The analytic/synthetic distinction pertains to the way in which statements can be true or false, whereas the a priori/a posteriori distinction pertains to how we can know whether a statement is true or false.

An analytic truth is a truth in virtue of the meaning of the terms used. Thus, *All bachelors are unmarried* is a true statement by definition. It tells you nothing about the world. By contrast, synthetic statements are substantial descriptions of the world. *There is a cathedral in Vienna called St. Stephen's*; *It is raining*; *Hot air rises*; *Albert Einstein's first wife was*

Mileva Marić; Otto Neurath had a wild red beard—all these tell you something about the world, which may or may not be true (some statements—*Otto Neurath had a wild red beard*—are true when referring to one moment in history and false when referring to another).

As for the a priori/a posteriori distinction, a priori knowledge can be justified independently of experience of the world, whereas a posteriori knowledge relies on empirical evidence. We do not need to know anything about the world to deduce that *a square has four sides of identical length*—this is an example of something that we can know a priori. The truth of the claim that *ice melts if heated*, on the other hand, cannot be established without observing what happens when ice is exposed to a Bunsen burner or left in the sun. Hence this is something that we can only know a posteriori.

It seems obvious that analytic truths can be deduced in an a priori way. I do not need experience to know that ice is frozen water, I just need to understand the meaning of the terms *ice* and *frozen water*. It seems equally clear that synthetic propositions can only be known a posteriori. I can only assess the veracity of the claim that *Neurath has a wild red beard* by seeing him, or a photo of him, or by being told what he looks like by someone with reliable evidence. I could not work out from the meaning of the sentence alone what Neurath's policy was on chin hair.

So there are analytic a priori propositions and synthetic a posteriori ones. But Kant also believed there was a third category, the synthetic a priori: truths about the world that could be deduced without any experience of the world. Kant thought there were a number of such propositions, including truths about space and time and about geometry (e.g., *the angles in a triangle add up to 180 degrees*).

For Kant, the synthetic a priori truths are vital: they provide the framework through which we understand the physical world. The shortest distance between two points is a straight line, is one example. All experiences must have the form of enduring in time, is another. That all events have a cause is also a synthetic a priori truth, and one that frames our understanding of the inner workings of nature. This principle of causality is a basic assumption. It is not one of the things that we have learned about the world; it is a part of the scaffolding needed to learn about the world. The synthetic a priori truths make scientific knowledge possible.

The claim that there existed synthetic a priori truths naturally posed a head-on threat to the empiricist project, to positivism. If Kant was right about the synthetic a priori, there were things about the empirical world that could be deduced without recourse to experimentation, or measurement, or observation. But Einstein showed how some principles that Kant insisted were synthetic a priori were not even true, let alone knowable to be true through reflection alone. So-called laws about time and about space, the "self-evident" certainties of Euclidean geometry, were among the things debunked by this German physicist—the shortest distance between two points in space was a curved not a straight line. In this way, it seemed that Einstein had clarified empiricism. He had shown how his spatio-temporal framework requires prima facie counterintuitive premises that nevertheless allowed us to make better sense of our experience overall.

———

Einstein was a near contemporary of the eldest Circle members—born, like Hans Hahn, in 1879. As it happened, several of the Circle knew Einstein personally, and he was sympathetic to their mission. He had read and admired David Hume. In *An Enquiry Concerning Human Understanding*, a proto-positivist work that built on Hume's earlier *A Treatise of Human Nature*, the Scot rejected the notion that there could be any knowledge that did not come through the senses. If statements or claims were not about what he called "relations of ideas"—akin to the empiricists' use of the term *analytic*—then, to be valuable, they had to be about the real world, the empirical world. His *Enquiry* contains this famous dismissal of statements that fail to fall into either category: "If we take in our hand any volume; of divinity or school metaphysics, for instance, let us ask, Does it contain any abstract reasoning concerning quantity or number? Does it contain any experimental reasoning concerning matters of fact and existence? No. Commit it then to the flames: for it can contain nothing but sophistry and illusion."[7]

In a letter of 14 December 1915, Einstein explains how in Switzerland, where he had written his first pioneering papers, he had read and discussed the ideas of both Hume and Mach with fellow scientists. "Your exposition is also quite right that positivism suggested [relativity] theory, without requiring it. Also you have correctly seen that this line of thought was of great influence on my efforts and specifically E. Mach and still much more Hume, whose *Treatise on Understanding* I studied with eagerness and admiration shortly before finding relativity theory."[8] This was not especially remarkable; several times he acknowledged his debt to Hume and Mach. But this particular letter was to Moritz Schlick. Einstein had read Schlick's book about relativity and had written to Schlick with a number of suggestions that were incorporated in the book's later editions. Einstein thought that "from the philosophical side nothing has been written about the subject with anything like the same degree of clarity."[9] Post World War I Einstein wrote to fellow physicist and future Nobel Prize winner Max Born, "Schlick is a fine thinker, we must see to it to get him a post as professor. Given the current inflation, he will need it badly. It will be hard to get this through, though, as he is no member of the indigenous 'church' of Kantians."[10]

Schlick and Einstein remained in regular contact, and Schlick put him up when Einstein visited Vienna. Another Circle member, Philipp Frank, knew the physicist even better. Frank had published an article in 1907, *Causality and Experience*. It was read by two men who were revolutionaries in their different fields. Lenin, the antipositivist, hated it. Einstein loved it, and he and Frank became friends for life, with Frank eventually becoming his first biographer.

When in 1912 Einstein moved on from his post as chair of theoretical physics at the German University in Prague, he recommended Frank to be his successor. The new job required an imperial uniform. Until the Austro-Hungarian Empire collapsed, all professors had to swear an oath of allegiance to the emperor, and for this ceremony academics were expected to wear trousers with gold bands and a three-cornered hat with feathers. Einstein sold his to Frank for a knock-down price. Frank later gave it away, during a cold Prague winter, to a hard-up former Cossack commander who showed no interest in its distinguished provenance.[11]

Their intimacy is conveyed in many anecdotes. They saw each other again when, two years after becoming famous, Einstein went on a rock-star tour in 1921, speaking to packed houses in Europe, including Prague. To protect Einstein from unwanted attention, Frank proposed that the visitor stay in his apartment and sleep on the sofa. Frank would later recall their meal together. His wife, not an experienced cook, was heating calf's liver on a Bunsen burner. Einstein suddenly jumped up. "What are you doing? Are you boiling the liver in water?" Frau Frank responded in the affirmative. "The boiling-point of water is too low," admonished the physicist. "You must use a substance with a higher boiling-point such as butter or fat." Frank later wrote, "Einstein's advice saved the lunch."[12] Frank also describes how, at a Prague gathering, when people were waiting to hear the thoughts of the great man, he instead took out his violin: "It will perhaps be pleasanter and more understandable if instead of making a speech I play a piece for you."[13] They were treated to a Mozart sonata.

All these stories made it into Frank's biography of his friend. Besides Frank and Schlick, others of the Circle who knew Einstein included Gustav Bergmann and Herbert Feigl, the latter having first read relativity theory as a teenager. "Einstein became my number one political hero."[14] Feigl wrote a prize-winning essay on Einstein and relativity theory in 1922 and the following year went on a pilgrimage to visit him: "He advised me on further studies in theoretical physics."[15] In 1929 Feigl published a book, *Theory and Experience in Physics* (*Theorie und Erfahrung in der Physik*), and received Einstein's commendation. A year later, Bergmann joined Einstein for a spell as his assistant in Berlin. In Berlin, Reichenbach had been one of Einstein's first students in his general relativity seminar, and Einstein had then helped him get an appointment at the university in Berlin in the foundations of physics.

The veneration in which Einstein was held is captured in Karl Popper's account of a lecture the Nobel Prize winner delivered in the

Austrian capital during his 1921 speaking tour. Einstein gave two academic lectures there and then addressed a concert-hall audience of three thousand. Popper, however, could not describe it: "I remember only that I was dazed."[16] Popper also says that Einstein was "the dominant influence on my thinking—in the long run perhaps the most important influence of all."[17] After Popper published *The Logic of Scientific Discovery* (*Logik der Forschung*), in 1934, he sent a copy to his hero. Einstein loved it and offered to promote it.

The theory of relativity was, in theory, politically neutral—it was, after all, a depiction of how the physical world operated, and there was nothing inherently socialist, or liberal, or conservative, about that. In practice, however, the new physics aroused intense hostility, which rapidly became politicized. Einstein himself had astutely foreseen the danger. In 1922, he said, "If my theory of relativity is proven successful, Germany will claim me as a German and France will declare that I am a citizen of the world. Should my theory prove untrue, France will say that I am a German and Germany will declare that I am a Jew."[18]

An idea was germinating that Einsteinian physics was alien physics—alien being shorthand for Jewish. A Working Group for German Scientists for the Preservation of Pure Science was established, financing lectures to counter the popularity of relativity theory. The allegation was that Jewish science, unlike Aryan science, was overrefined, appealed to formalism and symbols rather than the world, and somehow (this charge was difficult to comprehend let alone substantiate) lacked the Aryan commitment to truth. It also, and again the Circle should have paid closer note, had no respect for the mystical, failing to acknowledge that the world was ultimately mysterious and inaccessible to human reason.

This nonsense mostly bypassed the Circle. Einstein for them was always on the highest pedestal. Meanwhile they reserved the next pedestal down for a patrician Englishman.

4

◄○►

The Bald French King

We are your intellectual grandsons.

—HERBERT FEIGL TO BERTRAND RUSSELL, 1935

WHAT MADE the Vienna Circle new was its fusion of two different approaches. The members became known as "logical positivists" for a reason. While the second half of their nomenclature owed much to their forerunners Hume and Mach, the first was inspired by Bertrand Russell.

———

Russell was born in 1872 into a wealthy, aristocratic family that had long been at the heart of the British establishment. Russell's grandfather Lord John Russell had been prime minister under Queen Victoria; his secular godfather was John Stuart Mill, philosopher, campaigner, and politician.

Although he emerged into the world with a silver spoon in his mouth, it left a bitter taste. He had a lonely, miserable, repressed childhood. His sister, mother, and father all died before he was four and he was raised, together with his elder brother, in an austere household run by his grandmother, who encouraged her grandchildren to believe that they were sinful. They took this to heart. Salvation, Russell later wrote, came in the unlikely form of mathematics, with which, aged eleven, he fell immediately and deeply in love. "The world of mathematics . . . is really a beautiful world; it has nothing to do with life and death and human sordidness, but is eternal, cold and passionless."[1]

At Cambridge, his main interest switched from mathematics to philosophy and then to the foundations of mathematics in particular. On what is mathematics built? What are its fundamental ideas and axioms? What is a number? What is a whole, what is a part? How can we make sense of infinity? Russell was what would now be labeled a "logicist": he thought, and attempted to demonstrate, that mathematics was reducible to logic. In 1902, while working on a book on the topic, *The Principles of Mathematics*, he discovered the writings of Gottlob Frege, who taught in Germany at the University of Jena. Frege was another mathematician with philosophical leanings and coincidentally was engaged in a similar project. Both Frege's and Russell's theories had drawn on the idea of a "class" or "set," such that the number 5 was to be understood as the set of all things containing five members.

Russell identified a paradox about classes that threatened to derail his own enterprise and which posed a fundamental problem for Frege too. Here's a helpful illustration of this paradox. Imagine a village with a barber. Suppose the barber shaves everyone in the village who does not shave himself—who, then, shaves the barber? If he does, then he does not. If he does not, then he does. A parallel example might be a library book that lists the names of all books in the library that do not mention their own names.

Russell informed the German of the analogous paradox in set theory; Frege wrote back that the contradiction had left him "thunderstruck."[2] Nonetheless, it was thanks to Russell that the significance of Frege's work was first acknowledged—although it took several more decades before it achieved the international prominence it deserved.

After completing *The Principles of Mathematics*, Russell cooperated with English philosopher and mathematician A. N. Whitehead on the mammoth three-volume *Principia Mathematica*, completed in 1911. The project was a defense of logicism and aimed to lay out the axioms, and the rules of inference from these axioms, that could prove all the truths of mathematics. It took several hundred pages to secure the result 2 from the addition of 1 + 1. The tome was so unappealing a publishing prospect that both authors were made to contribute to the printing cost.

Absorbing math into logic was not the only ambition. There was also the deployment of a new type of logic as a weapon to dissect language. Scholars now regard the Frege-Russell breakthroughs in logic as representing the biggest leap forward since Aristotle, two and a half millennia earlier. In particular, they offered fresh insight into the operation of "logical constants." Logical constants are words or phrases whose meaning remains fixed (e.g., *and, not, or*). Frege's work was vital for a branch of logical constants known as quantifiers—examples of quantifiers are *all, some, none*. The word *some*—as in *Some Austrians live in Vienna* and *Some books have more than 400 pages*—essentially performs the same function and these two sentences, making different claims, nonetheless possess the same logical form. *All philosophers are wise* and *All cats are furry* both have the same form; namely, for all things x, if F is an x, then it is also a G.

There were valuable consequences from transposing language into logical notation. For one thing, the hidden structure of sentences was exposed. Sentences with a surface simplicity were often revealed to be far more complex than they appeared. For another, ambiguity could be identified and eliminated. This heralded a revolutionary turn in philosophy; old problems could be tackled afresh. Language, of course, had always been the necessary apparatus with which to examine philosophical problems. But now language itself became the object of analysis. And whereas language had once been seen as a window between us and the world—clean, flat, and transparent—now it was treated with suspicion as grimy, warped, and opaque, requiring attention precisely because of the way it was capable of distorting or masking reality.

One example concerned so-called denoting phrases. Both Frege and Russell were interested in the analysis of such phrases—those that seem to refer to, or pick out, something in the world. They come in many forms. Some phrases, like *A train chuffed to Vienna*, are ambiguous: they do not identify any specific train. Others, such as *The present coach of Rapid Vienna FC*, have a very particular denotation: they pick out one individual or thing.

So far so good, but what of denoting phrases that somehow fail to denote anything—empty denoting phrases. These might be phrases denoting fictional creatures such as mermaids or unicorns. *Mermaids have the head of a female human and the tail of a fish*, or *Unicorns do not exist*. What sense can be made of these sentences if there are no mermaids or unicorns?

Initially, Russell took the position, proposed by the Austrian philosopher Alexius Meinong, that every denoting phrase refers, in some way, to an existing object. There was a way in which even imaginary people or things had to be real. We can only make sense of sentences such as *Sherlock Holmes smoked a pipe* or *A centaur is half-man, half-horse* by positing the actual existence of the fictional detective or the mythological horse/human.

But later Russell changed his mind. Russell's most important contribution to the logic of language was his Theory of Descriptions, which first appeared in an article published in 1905. He used as an example the phrase *The present King of France is bald*. This does not seem to be a meaningless statement, and one could even imagine someone believing it to be true. To assess the veracity of this claim, one might assume we would have to check the hairline of the current French king (a task made more challenging by the fact that France is a republic). If we then determined that the proposition *The present King of France is bald* is false, must we conclude that *The present King of France has hair* is true?

Russell came to reject this way of looking at the proposition. Instead, he broke down the statement about the nonexistent French monarch into three separate assertions. *The present King of France is bald* states:

> *There is a King of France*
> *There is only one King of France*
> *Whatever is King of France is bald.*

In logical notation—and using the logician Gottlob Frege's breakthrough analysis of quantifiers—this is expressed as follows: $\exists x[(Kx \,\&\, \forall y(Ky \to y = x)) \,\&\, Bx]$. Similarly, *The present King of France has hair* can be deconstructed as: *There is a King of France; there is only one King of*

France; whatever/whoever is King of France has hair. Although the statements seemed to contradict each other, they are both false, since the first proposition, *There is a King of France*, is untrue.

———

The Theory of Descriptions has withstood more than a century of analysis, and Russell has become recognized as one of founding fathers of analytic philosophy, the tradition within which Russell's 1905 paper is a paradigm of philosophical work. Hans Hahn thought that Bertrand Russell would come to be seen "as the most important philosopher of our time,"[3] a judgment that seemed hyperbolic in the 1920s but which, a century on, has been vindicated. Hahn ran a seminar for advanced students on *Principia Mathematica*. Others in the Circle shared Hahn's assessment. Carnap never forgot an amazing act of kindness from the great man when he, Carnap, had yet to establish his reputation. In the early 1920s, when hyperinflation had eroded almost all savings, Carnap wrote to Russell to say that neither he nor his university could afford a copy of *Principia Mathematica*. Russell replied with a thirty-five-page letter summarizing his findings. Carnap treasured that letter for the rest of his life. When Russell was about to turn ninety in 1962, Carnap wrote to him. Russell's books, he told him, "had indeed a stronger influence on my philosophical thinking than those of any other philosopher."[4] American philosopher W.V.O. Quine also regarded Russell as the dominant figure in philosophy in the first three decades of the twentieth century: "many of us were drawn to our profession by Russell's books. . . . We were beguiled by the wit and a sense of new-found clarity with respect to central traits of reality."[5] Popper worshipped Russell, admiring not just his raw intellectual power but the unforced elegance of his prose.

There was another vital lesson to be learned from Russell. Although he drew no direct connection between politics and his work in logic, Russell was politically active for decades. He stood for parliament as the Suffragist candidate in 1907. His opposition to World War I resulted in his dismissal from Trinity College, Cambridge, and later, when he campaigned for the US not to enter the war, a six-month spell in jail. He found his incarceration "quite agreeable,"[6] using it to write one philosophy book and start another. He had views on everything, including religion, education, war, and marriage. His abiding sense that philosophers had a duty to be publicly engaged with politics—and to bring the intellectual rigor of philosophy into the political domain—would be taken to heart, by Popper at least.

The respect in which Russell was held by Popper and the Circle was reciprocated. In *An Inquiry into Meaning and Truth* (based on his 1940 William James Lectures), he writes in the preface, "I am, as regards method, more in sympathy with the Logical Positivists than with any other existing school."[7]

But it is now time to introduce one other character, a man who would exert a huge influence on both Russell and the Circle.

5

Wittgenstein Casts His Spell

Mr Wittgenstein is a philosophic genius of a different order from
anyone else I know.

—FRANK RAMSEY

THERE ARE SOME writers whose personality is at odds with their style
of writing and others with whom it corresponds. Ludwig Wittgenstein
fell into the latter category. The only philosophy book he ever published
in his lifetime, the *Tractatus Logico-Philosophicus*, is intense, uncompromising, and categorical, much like the author. Wittgenstein had definite
opinions about how life should be led. He did not do indifference or
vacillation or give-and-take. The forceful certainty with which he expressed his views was frightening and unnerving.

He was born in 1889 into a supremely wealthy Viennese family. His
domineering father, Karl Wittgenstein, more or less controlled the iron
and steel industry in the Austro-Hungarian Empire. Ludwig was one of
eight children, five boys (his four elder brothers were Hans, Kurt, Rudolf, and Paul) and three girls (Hermine, Margaret, and Helene). All
eight were beset by anxiety, although pressure from their father was felt
most keenly by the boys. Emotionally overpowering, Karl wanted his
sons to follow him into business, but only one showed any interest. For
the rest, their preferences were artistic. Karl's intransigence was but one
factor in the children's misery. Three of his sons killed themselves, and
Ludwig himself was constantly troubled by thoughts of suicide. Hans,
exceptionally musically gifted, fled his father in 1901 and took his life a
year later. Rudolf poisoned himself in 1904 by dropping potassium cya-
nide into a glass of milk. Most likely he was ashamed of his homo-
sexuality and feared exposure. Kurt shot himself toward the end of

World War I, on the Italian front. The immediate cause has never been definitively established: it may have been because his soldiers had disobeyed him, or else because he preferred death to the dishonor of being taken prisoner. Paul, the last remaining brother, lost an arm in the war. A concert pianist, he used his riches and connections to commission a series of one-handed pieces from composers including Richard Strauss, Sergei Prokofiev, and Maurice Ravel, which enabled him to continue his successful performing career.

With more money than he needed or could spend, Karl became a benefactor of the arts. The Vienna Secession Building was funded by his generosity and completed just before the turn of the century. It was designed to exhibit works from an avant-garde generation of artists, led by Gustav Klimt. At home, an imposing Viennese mansion known as the Palais Wittgenstein, there were private music concerts. Leading musicians, such as Brahms, Strauss, Mahler, and Schoenberg, were invited along.

It was in this refined milieu that Ludwig (Luki or Lukerl, to his family) was raised. Initially he was schooled at home, but later he was packed off to secondary school, a *Realschule*, in Linz in north Austria. His potential was not yet apparent: he was a good but by no means outstanding student, though obviously smarter than another pupil with whom he overlapped, who before entering politics scraped a living as a competent if uninspiring artist. Adolf Hitler, though of the same age, was two school years behind Wittgenstein: he would later lambaste his former teachers for being messy, ignorant, and in some cases mentally deranged.

In 1906, Wittgenstein went to Berlin to attend the Technical High School. He lodged with a nice couple, Stanislaus and Adele Jolles. Stanislaus was a mathematician and had high hopes that Wittgenstein would follow an engineering career. He came to look on "Little Wittgenstein" almost as a surrogate son. Two years later, in 1908, at age nineteen, Little Wittgenstein moved to the University of Manchester, in the north of England. His interests at this stage remained principally in engineering. In Berlin he had researched hot air balloons; in Manchester he investigated propellers and kites.

This was the age of flight. In 1908 Wilbur and Orville Wright hit the front pages by demonstrating that machines could stay airborne. Their triumph raised thrilling possibilities and must have captured Wittgenstein's imagination. In 1910, he applied for and was granted a patent for a new aircraft engine: his design worked by gas driven to nozzles resting on the propeller blades.

The calculations required for this engine forced Wittgenstein to undertake some serious math, and this in turn nourished an already nascent interest in philosophy. He became preoccupied with the foundations of mathematics. What kinds of truths were mathematical truths? What was the status of a mathematical proof? He was introduced to and devoured *The Principles of Mathematics*. And that is how, on 18 October 1911, we find the young engineering student knocking on a door in Trinity College Cambridge to present himself to the book's famous author, Bertrand Russell.

The close and stormy relationship between Wittgenstein and Russell, who initially mistook the Austrian for a German, has been well documented and needs no repetition. But for our purposes one of the fascinating aspects of Wittgenstein's life is how he convinced Russell and other intellectual giants of his genius. In the following decade, most members of the Vienna Circle (not all) would be equally bewitched. Russell was a little slower than others to hit on the genius verdict. For weeks the irritating "German" would not leave him alone; he would argue incessantly even when Russell was preparing to go to dinner. Russell's judgment on him vacillated. A fortnight after they first met, Russell wrote to his lover, Lady Ottoline Morrell, "My German engineer, I think, is a fool. He thinks nothing empirical is knowable—I asked him to admit that there was not a rhinoceros in the room, but he wouldn't."[1]

Still not sure whether or not he should return to aeronautics, Wittgenstein asked Russell whether he was "an absolute idiot."[2] If he were an absolute idiot then he would become an aeronaut; if not, he would become a philosopher. In his autobiography Russell says he asked Wittgenstein to write an essay over the holiday so he could assess his ability. Wittgenstein did so and returned to Cambridge for the second term of that academic year. "As soon as I read the first sentence, I became persuaded that he was a man of genius, and assured him that he should on no account become an aeronaut."[3]

Indeed, by early 1912 Russell was convinced that he had found his intellectual heir. "I love him and feel he will solve the problems I am too old to solve. . . . He is the young man one hopes for."[4] In his autobiography he described Wittgenstein as "perhaps the most perfect example I have ever known of genius as traditionally conceived, passionate, profound, intense, and dominating."[5] By the end of the first year, when Wittgenstein's eldest sister, Hermine, came to visit, she was astounded to hear from Russell, "We expect the next big step in philosophy to be taken by your brother."[6]

That the Englishman was able to reassure Wittgenstein of his intellectual worth gave the miserable young Austrian a reason to live since, for Wittgenstein, life was genius or nothing (the cult of genius in fin de siècle Austria having been firmly established). However, if Russell salvaged Wittgenstein's life by persuading him of his merit, Wittgenstein clouded Russell's by convincing him of his inadequacy. By 1913 Russell was deferring meekly to Wittgenstein when they discussed matters of logic. Although it was not his intention, Wittgenstein made Russell believe that he, Russell, now in his forties, was past it, beyond breakthroughs and originality. There was no point in straining his intellectual powers; for even at his best he could no longer keep up. "I must make room for him when I can, or I shall become an incubus."[7]

Wittgenstein's combination of unquestioned brilliance, domineering aura, and manic charisma had the effect of mesmerizing many of those around him. His relationship with G. E. Moore is instructive in this regard. Moore soon came to acquiesce in Wittgenstein's philosophical judgment, even when he failed fully to grasp the nature of Wittgenstein's objections to his own position. He thought Wittgenstein much more profound than himself and told Russell that he "always feels W[ittgenstein] must be right"[8] whenever they disagreed.

In 1913, as was to prove a sporadic lifelong habit, Wittgenstein resolved to seek isolation in order to think. He set off for the fjords of Norway, a little to the north of the city of Bergen. From there, some months later, he sent for Moore. Norway was a long and choppy boat ride away. Moore was reluctant to make the trip but found Wittgenstein's entreaties impossible to resist. Once there, Moore served as amanuensis, with Wittgenstein dictating his thoughts about logic. The peculiarity of this arrangement needs emphasizing. Wittgenstein was only twenty-four, and without even an undergraduate degree in philosophy; Moore was a professor and internationally renowned.

———

When World War I broke out in 1914, Wittgenstein initially tried to leave Austria for Norway, but when that proved impossible, he volunteered to fight for his homeland—although he had a medical condition (a hernia) that would have spared him from conscription. He then agitated, much to his superior officers' confusion, for more rather than fewer dangerous deployments, earning commendations and a medal for exceptional courage. He saw action during the Kerensky Offensive (the final Russian assault) on the Eastern Front in July 1917, and was then transferred to the Southern Front in Italy, where he was captured on 3 November 1918 and spent the next nine months as a prisoner of war. The war radicalized both Neurath and Carnap politically, but that was not its effect on Wittgenstein. Instead, it served to make an already intense man more intense still. While serving on the *Goplana*, a Russian patrol ship that the Austrians had captured early in the war, he read Tolstoy's *The Gospel in Brief*, a synthesis of the New Testament gospels. It spoke to an evolving religious and mystical strain in his personality.

His family tried to sustain him with provisions and encouragement, especially his loyal, adoring, eldest sister, Hermine. "You are, for me," she wrote in one letter, "inseparably connected with everything that's good and great and beautiful in this world, more than and in a manner different from any other human being."[9] Throughout the war Ludwig somehow continued to work on the manuscript that became the *Tractatus Logico-Philosophicus*, which contained some of the thoughts he had discussed in Norway with Moore. The book was completed in 1918, and from prison he implored Bertrand Russell to visit him so that he could explain it. He stressed the book's importance. "I suppose it would be impossible for you to come and see me here? or perhaps you think it's colossal cheek of me even to think of such a thing. But if you were on the other end of the world and I *could* come to you I would do it."[10]

They did meet, but in The Hague, after Wittgenstein's release. The German version of the *Tractatus* did not appear until 1921 and then only after Russell had agreed to write the introduction (the famous Englishman's imprimatur was taken as a guarantee to the publisher of this impenetrable book's worth). As it was, Wittgenstein was dismissive of Russell's contribution. He delivered his assessment in typically unvarnished form: "All the refinement of your English style was, obviously, lost in the translation and what remained was superficiality and misunderstanding."[11] To his friend Paul Engelmann, he seemed more phlegmatic: "He has brewed up a mixture with which I don't agree, but as I have not written it, I don't mind much."[12] The English edition was published in 1922. Wittgenstein's up-front payment was zero. His royalty payments were no higher, although the book did eventually go on to sell. It would be the only work of philosophy Wittgenstein would publish in his lifetime.

In *The Philosophy of Logical Atomism*, first presented as a series of lectures toward the end of World War I, Russell explained that the thoughts therein were "very largely concerned with explaining certain ideas which I learnt from my friend and former pupil Ludwig Wittgenstein. I have had no opportunity of knowing his views since August 1914, and I do not even know whether he is alive or dead."[13] Crudely put, Russell's logical atomism was the theory that all propositions can be analyzed into simpler and simpler constituents until we reached the irreducible elements that correspond to atoms—things. These atoms/ things are known to the mind directly and are the most basic elements of reality.

Certainly, the *Tractatus* and logical atomism possessed elements in common. But Wittgenstein held that facts not things were the most basic level of reality. Language connected to reality at the level of the proposition (e.g., *The cat is on the mat*). Given Wittgenstein's fury at

Russell's failure to grasp the *Tractatus*, it is unsurprising that there has been scholarly debate about whether the book should be read as a rendering or variety of logical atomism.

———

The *Tractatus* is not easy to summarize. It proceeds in numbered propositions, in seven main sections, in what amounts to a hierarchy. The most important propositions are the whole numbers, 1, 2, 3, etc. Then there are commentaries on these propositions (3.1, 3.2, etc.) and commentaries on these commentaries (3.11, 3.12 . . .), and so on, sometimes to several decimal places. It has a well-known opening salvo, "1. The world is everything that is the case," and an even better-known ending, "7. Whereof one cannot speak, thereof one must be silent." The *Tractatus* gives its arguments in highly condensed form, often leaving many of the steps for the reader to fill in. Wittgenstein once told Russell that argument risked spoiling a claim's beauty and, as Russell recounted it, would make him "feel as if he was dirtying a flower with muddy hands."[14] At fewer than eighty pages, the *Tractatus* has an economy that has rarely been matched in the history of philosophy.

According to the *Tractatus*, language pictures reality—language and thoughts and the world share a logical form. Certain words—names—stand for objects. Words in the appropriate order—propositions—mirror the world; they picture a possible state of affairs. The sentence *Wittgenstein holds a flower in his muddy hands* somehow pictures a state of affairs in which Wittgenstein does this very thing. Of course, it may not be a true proposition—he may not be holding a flower, or not in the way described.

A crucial distinction is drawn in the book between what can be *said* and what merely *shown*. This is not easy to explain, but we might think of it this way. If we can say something with a proposition, it must relate to facts about the world. *Wittgenstein holds a flower in his muddy hands* is a proposition that may or may not picture a true state of affairs; it *says* something that is either true or false. According to the *Tractatus*, propositions about what is good or valuable, or about the mystical or the sublime, do not picture possible situations; they do not relate to facts about the world. As he put it, "If there is any value that does have value, it must lie outside the whole sphere of what happens and is the case."[15] Putative propositions about God, or ethics, or aesthetics, are—at best—attempts to say what can only be *shown*.

What is more, although language can describe reality, there is a limit to what it can do to describe *how* it describes realty. For, just as ethics and aesthetics are in an important sense undiscussable, so is the skeleton of language itself. Attempting to discuss linguistic limits inevitably leads us over the horizon of sense and into the realm of nonsense. This creates an infamously paradoxical problem for the *Tractatus* itself. After all, had Wittgenstein not been addressing these very matters in his text? He offered an answer in his penultimate paragraph. "My propositions serve as elucidations in the following way: anyone who understands me eventually recognizes them as nonsensical, when he has used them—as steps—to climb beyond them. (He must, so to speak, throw away the ladder after he has climbed it.)"[16]

———

However anguished Wittgenstein was, he never suffered from false modesty. Believing that he had solved all the fundamental problems of philosophy and that there was no substantial work still to be done in the field, he retrained as a schoolteacher and disappeared to practice his new profession in remote and impoverished villages in Lower Austria. Karl Wittgenstein's death in January 1913 had left his children immensely rich—but Ludwig now gave away his fortune to his remaining siblings (except Gretl, married to a rich American and whom he regarded as having more than enough). His wealth had become a heavy psychological burden, and shedding it felt like liberation.

The family name and fame were felt to be a burden too. Wittgenstein preferred the villagers not to know about his background and hurt the feelings of his sister Hermine by telling her to stay away. "You're not made for this world!"[17] wrote the wounded Hermine, warning him that "[O]ur facial features alone betray a good family."[18] She was right to this extent: inevitably the truth emerged. Ludwig's brother Paul mocked him. "Given the unbelievable degree to which our name is known . . . the properties we own spread across the whole of Austria, the various charitable causes we're involved in, etc., etc., it is impossible, truly perfectly impossible, that any person bearing our name, and whose distinguished and refined upbringing anyone can see from a thousand feet off, will not be recognised as a member of our family."[19]

Meanwhile, although publishers had regarded the *Tractatus* as unfathomable and as an inevitable financial loss-maker, it slowly began to find an influential readership. It was discussed at the Cambridge philosophy society, the Moral Sciences Club. The book had been translated by Frank Ramsey while he was still a Cambridge undergraduate. Ramsey had been chosen because he understood some German and because he too, by any reasonable definition, was a genius.

Some sense of Ramsey's brilliance is captured in his reminiscence after meeting economist John Maynard Keynes for the first time. "He [Keynes] is very pleasant. After lunch we went for a walk, getting back at 4:30pm. Talked of difficulty of writing, philosophy (epistemology, Occam's Razor), history of mathematics, probability in mathematics, objective interest, puzzles, games, history of economics, Marshall, books to appear shortly, Keynes on probability."[20] That might not sound so remarkable, until one realizes that at the time Ramsey was seventeen. Ramsey would die at the peak of his powers, only twenty-six, when he was misdiagnosed (the cause of death is unclear but it is most likely to have been an infected liver).[21] By then he had already made pioneering contributions to philosophy, economics, mathematics, probability, and decision theory.

In 1923, Ramsey traveled to see Wittgenstein in the village of Puchberg. Before his first Austrian trip, Ramsey knew nothing of the spectacular riches of the Wittgenstein family. Nonetheless he was taken aback by the spartan conditions in which he found the philosopher. "He has one TINY room, containing a bed, washstand, small table and one hard chair and that is all there is room for. His evening meal which I shared last night is rather unpleasant coarse bread and butter and cocoa."[22] After Wittgenstein had finished his morning teaching, they spent several hours each day working their way through the *Tractatus*, leaving them both exhausted. Wittgenstein cast his usual spell. "He is great. I used to think Moore a great man, but beside W! . . . It's terrible when he says, 'Is that clear?' and I say no and he says, 'Damn! It's horrid to go through all that again.'"[23] When Ramsey left, Wittgenstein was unable to talk for a few days. Ramsey was to return to Austria in 1924, of which more soon.

In the usual account of how the Circle was introduced to the *Tractatus*, mathematician Kurt Reidemeister is accorded the starring role. He is said to have somehow stumbled upon the *Tractatus* and to have spoken to the Circle about it one evening. In fact, a new biography of Ramsey provides compelling evidence that it was a conversation between Ramsey and Schlick that really awakened Schlick to the originality of the *Tractatus*. Schlick wrote to the German philosopher Hans Reichenbach on 5 August 1924:

> Do you know the *Tractatus-logico-philosophicus* from L. Wittgenstein, which appeared in the *Annals of Natural Philosophy* and which has been edited by Russell in a book version in German and English? The author lives close to Vienna, and is highly original, also as a human being; the more one studies his treatise, the more one is impressed by it. The English translator, a mathematician from Cambridge, whom I met in the summer, is also a very intelligent and sophisticated mind.[24]

What they talked about before the *Tractatus* is unclear and not well documented. It's very likely that under the influence of Hahn, they discussed Frege and Bertrand Russell's mathematical philosophy. In any case, what had now become the Circle abruptly changed direction. Within the Circle the *Tractatus* acquired a status of almost biblical significance. Hahn as well as Schlick was immediately taken by its depth and ingenuity. A young member of the Circle, Olga Taussky, reported that the text was "used to settle all disputes, as the last authority."[25]

This was really the Vienna Circle's first major project. Between 1925 and 1927, the Circle dissected the *Tractatus* sentence by sentence, like yeshiva students trying to unlock the mysteries of the Talmud. There was one vocal skeptic among them, Otto Neurath, who detected nonsense behind many of Wittgenstein's oracular pronouncements.

Nonetheless, even when they disagreed on the interpretation of individual *Tractatus* propositions, most members of the Circle were broadly sympathetic to what they took to be its philosophical project. Wittgenstein, in the tradition of Frege and Russell, held that the tools of modern logic could be used to dissect the nature of language. He thought that philosophy should be limited in its ambition: the task of philosophy was the clarification of propositions.

The Circle also embraced Wittgenstein's discussion of logical truths. Wittgenstein held that logical truths were tautologies; they are true, but not in the way that empirical propositions can be true. Logical truths—e.g., it is either raining or not raining—do not picture the world. No state of affairs could clash with or contradict such a truth. And, in that way, they have no sense. But neither are they nonsense. They are the essential frame to permit propositions to picture the world. They are the limits of sense.

The Circle extended this proposal to mathematics—possibly after reading an article by Ramsey, "The Foundations of Mathematics," which makes a similar move.[26] Mathematics posed a conundrum for the Circle. Did truths of mathematics really require empirical corroboration? Nineteenth-century philosopher John Stuart Mill had proposed this sort of account: arithmetic "truths," he claimed, were generalizations reached by conducting repeated counts. But this never seemed compelling. Frege was contemptuous, dismissing it as "pebble arithmetic."[27] Surely we could work out the answer to 2 + 2 without reference to the real world. "It really does seem on first sight as if the very existence of mathematics must mean the failure of pure empiricism," Hans Hahn wrote, "as if we had in mathematics a knowledge about the world that doesn't come from experience, as if we had *a priori* knowledge."[28] Recall that Kant had his own analysis, less counterintuitive than the Millian strategy. Mathematical truths were synthetic a priori propositions. The snag for the logical empiricists was that this explanation was unavailable to them since it drew on an extra-empiricist account of knowledge—that is, Kant believed things could be known without reference to any particular experience. Einstein had chipped away at some of Kant's synthetic a priori pretensions. But math seemed a tougher conundrum to crack.

Of course, as we have already seen, Frege and Russell tried to reduce math to logic. But the Vienna Circle found what they regarded as the ultimate solution (to the problem of how mathematical knowledge is compatible with a strict empiricism) in their interpretation of the *Tractatus*. In fact, Wittgenstein's position on mathematics was subtly different from his stance on logic. Nonetheless, the Circle believed the same line should be applied to mathematical truths: they too also served as tautologies.[29] The truth of $2 + 2 = 4$ was like the truth of *All triangles have three sides* or indeed like the truth of the phrases *All nephews have at least one aunt or uncle* and *It is either raining or not raining*. The reason we do not need to refer to the world to establish their veracity is because the meaning is built into the terms themselves (although in high-level mathematics these meanings required some complex unfolding). The mathematician was not trying to discover the structure of reality, like the physicist, biologist, and chemist. Mathematical breakthroughs were made by people with rare talent, but these breakthroughs were not bringing insights about the outside world in the same way as the astrophysicist's revelations of planetary movement, or the chemist's discovery about a compound.

In a stroke, the problem had been resolved. It seemed to the Circle like a turning point, a release from the most troubling challenge to their worldview.

———

With Wittgenstein's self-imposed disappearance from the world of philosophy, he was only dimly aware of the *Tractatus*'s growing reputation. He initially found fulfilment in his teaching but soon became disenchanted. Several times he landed himself in trouble for his overly liberal use of corporal punishment: he was known to pull the hair of recalcitrant children and box them on the ears. After that, he tried his hand as a gardener in a monastery and briefly considered becoming a monk.

Then, from 1926 until 1928, he worked on the design and construction of his sister Margaret's (Gretl's) mansion in Vienna.

Schlick had written to Wittgenstein at the end of 1924, expressing his admiration for the *Tractatus* and a desire to call on him in Puchberg. He believed, along with a number of others, in the "importance and correctness"[30] of Wittgenstein's fundamental ideas. He mentioned having met Ramsey. Wittgenstein was between teaching posts, and the letter took some while to reach him. When it did, he wrote back to sanction a visit. There must have been various delays, because it was only in April 1926 that Schlick headed south. Blanche Schlick described her husband's state of mind. "It was as if he were preparing to go on holy pilgrimage, while he explained to me, almost with awesome reverence, that W. was one of the greatest geniuses on earth."[31] It turned out to be a futile journey: Wittgenstein had just quit his teaching post and moved on.

It took another year for Schlick and Wittgenstein finally to meet, an occasion orchestrated by Gretl, the youngest and most sociable of Wittgenstein's sisters. In February 1927 she invited Schlick to supper. Her brother felt unable to meet with a group to talk over the topics Schlick had suggested, she wrote, but he thought that "if it were you alone . . . he might be able to discuss such matters. It would then become apparent, he thinks, whether he is at present at all capable of being of use to you in this connexion."[32]

Schlick's wife reported that he once again had the "reverential attitude of the pilgrim." He returned from that meal "in an ecstatic state, saying little."[33] Blanche sensed that she "should not ask questions," while Wittgenstein told a friend that "Each of us thought the other must be mad."[34] Within a few months, and after several more appointments with Schlick alone, Wittgenstein had been persuaded to get together with a select group from the Circle, though he never once attended an official Circle gathering.

Carnap had now moved to Vienna. Apart from the *Tractatus*, the other text to receive close scrutiny from the Circle was Carnap's *Aufbau*, a book written in a very different style. Many of the ideas that would eventually appear in Carnap's *The Logical Syntax of Language* (1934) would first be presented to the Circle. Besides Schlick, Carnap attended the earlier discussions with Wittgenstein, along with Feigl. As usual, Wittgenstein sprinkled these encounters with his magic dust. "As a person of great seriousness and ruthless intellectual honesty and self-criticism he remains, next to Einstein, certainly the most fascinating thinker I ever encountered,"[35] wrote Feigl. Before his first encounter with Wittgenstein, Carnap recalled that Schlick had warned them that this unusual character was sensitive and fragile and it would be best just "to let Wittgenstein talk."[36]

Over the next two years, there were various gatherings in a variety of locations: coffeehouses, Schlick's home, once at the house of student Maria Kasper, who would become the future Mrs. Feigl. They were usually on a Monday, and the deal was that discussion not be restricted to philosophy: sometimes Wittgenstein would insist on reading poetry by Rabindranath Tagore, the Bengali Nobel Prize winner. He recited the lines with his back to them, not wanting to see their expressions.

When he was on philosophical fire, however, "we witnessed his most impressive and highly intuitive approach to various philosophical problems."[37] Not that everyone was entirely overwhelmed. Carnap and Feigl, in particular, retained some critical distance. Carnap's relationship with Wittgenstein had not begun auspiciously. Carnap met him for the first time in June 1927, and his diary records how original he found Wittgenstein as a thinker. But Schlick told Wittgenstein, perhaps assuming he would find it charming, that Carnap was an aficionado of Esperanto, the artificial language developed in the late nineteenth century. Wittgenstein was outraged: "A language which had not 'grown organically' seemed to him not only useless but despicable."[38] Carnap's interest in the claims of parapsychology further disgusted him.

The main cause of tension between the two men, however, ran deeper. Carnap and Wittgenstein approached philosophy in entirely different ways. Carnap, the logician, proceeded systematically, slowly, and technically, step by careful step; premises stated, argument laid out as transparently as possible. Wittgenstein came at philosophy from the other direction, and even more so as he aged. He tackled the most fundamental questions but, at least in his later philosophy, was not inclined to do so using logical notation or by advancing inch by inch from the bottom up. Whereas Carnap was a theoretician, with the mentality of a scientist and with a scientifically inclined philosophy, Wittgenstein was a highly instinctive thinker with the temperament of an artist, a personal grasp of problems, an aphoristic style, and—again, in his later work especially—a tendency to deal with a problem from multiple angles. Once, after Carnap had politely asked Wittgenstein to explain something in greater depth, Wittgenstein complained to Feigl: "If he doesn't smell it, I can't help him. He just has got no nose!"[39] Carnap himself came to recognize the gulf between them. He was shocked to discover how badly he had misinterpreted Wittgenstein's philosophical sensibility. His attitude was closer to a creative artist than a scientist, wrote Carnap, "similar to . . . a religious prophet or a seer."[40] As they talked philosophy, he and the others observed Wittgenstein's agony and struggle as he sought illumination. "When finally . . . his answer came forth, his statement stood before us like a newly created piece of art or a divine revelation. . . . [T]he impression he made on us was as if insight came to him as through a divine inspiration."[41]

And this was not merely a matter of philosophical style. The Circle was engaged in a heroic struggle to conquer metaphysics. This was, in part at least, why it would subsequently fall foul of the authorities, its members forced to emigrate or flee. Metaphysical statements could be dismissed as unempirical. But Wittgenstein's position was subtly, but vitally, distinct. There were claims that, he would say, were inexpressible. The Circle did not initially appreciate the difference. As we shall see, logical empiricism was much more evidently and full frontally at odds with fascist ideology than was the underlying message of the *Tractatus*.

For the time being, however, Wittgenstein and the Circle representatives were engaged in technical discussions. Among the topics for discussion was that of identity. How do we make sense of the proposition $A = B$. "Identity is the very devil,"[42] Wittgenstein had written to Russell in 1913. What made it so devilish was a puzzle of Frege's that goes like this. In the morning, I notice the last star visible, the morning star. In the evening I look up at the sky and see the evening star, the first star visible. Suppose someone makes the claim that *The morning star is the evening star* (actually the planet Venus)? On the face of it, that is a statement that provides real information: I may not have known that the morning star and the evening star were one and the same. But if *The morning star is the evening star* expresses a relationship between the morning star and the evening star, namely, that they are identical objects, is it equivalent to stating that *the morning star is the morning star*? That does not feel right, for this latter statement is uninteresting and uninformative—it tells us nothing useful at all.

Frege resolved the puzzle by drawing a distinction between what he called the "reference" and the "sense." The *morning star* and the *evening star* have the same reference—they refer to the same object. But they have a different sense: they are presented in a different way. Russell had an alternative analysis. According to Russell, names are shorthand for definite descriptions. That is, *Margaret Stonborough* is an abbreviation of, say, *the youngest of Wittgenstein's three sisters*; that is whom we mean when we use the name *Margaret Stonborough*. In the same way, *the morning star* is a truncated form of something like *the planet visible in the morning*. So Russell proposed a threefold deconstruction of the statement *The morning star is the evening star*:

1. There is one and only one planet visible in the morning sky
2. There is one and only one planet visible in the evening sky
3. Whatever planet is visible in the morning sky is also visible in the evening sky.

What about the apparently empty statement, *The morning star is the morning star*? In an exchange between Ramsey and Wittgenstein, with Schlick serving as messenger,[43] Ramsey and Wittgenstein discussed the status of *the morning star*: was it a name or was it a description? The details of this argument between them continue to baffle philosophers to this day. At the root of the dispute was Ramsey's attempt to improve on Russell's project of transforming mathematics into logic—with

Ramsey believing that to make his effort work, he had to come up with an alternative notion of identity.

————

Within the Circle subgroup granted a regular audience with Wittgenstein, it was Schlick and Waismann who remained most in his thrall. They deferred to him on all tricky questions. For Schlick and Waismann, Wittgenstein's position and the correct position were like the morning star and the evening star, one and the same. Waismann began, subconsciously, to imitate Wittgenstein's speaking patterns. Schlick began to attribute some original ideas of his own to Wittgenstein, although they had been expressed before he had even read the *Tractatus*. Wittgenstein must have approved of this submissive attitude: by the fall of 1929 he was choosing to restrict his discussions to Schlick and Waismann alone, usually at Schlick's home.

Still, it was Feigl who claimed the credit for resuscitating Wittgenstein's interest in philosophical matters, mentioning a lecture to be delivered on 10 March 1928 by L.E.J. Brouwer, a Dutch mathematician (with whom Menger had collaborated), and persuading the initially reluctant Wittgenstein to attend.[44] Brouwer had been invited by Hahn to give two lectures. A mathematical intuitionist, Brouwer was convinced that mathematics was a creation of the mind, not a discovery and description of eternal truths. We might typically assume that if a theory is disproved after the identification of an error, it must always have been false, whether or not its falsity had been yet acknowledged by mathematicians. Likewise, we might believe that if a mathematical theory has yet to be proved or disproved, it must nonetheless either be true or false. Both these beliefs are tempting but, the intuitionist claims, should be resisted. It follows that the intuitionist rejects a basic principle assumed by Russell and Whitehead in *Principia Mathematica*, namely the principle of the excluded middle—that every proposition is either true or false. Propositions that could not be proved or disproved were neither determinately true nor false, pro tem.

In the audience were all the members of the Circle who were in town. Before the lecture, entitled "Mathematics, Science and Language," Menger watched Hahn go to introduce himself to Wittgenstein, who, according to Menger, had "his eyes focused at infinity"[45] and basically ignored him. After the lecture, several people from the audience, including Feigl and Wittgenstein, retired to a café. "Suddenly and very volubly Wittgenstein began talking philosophy—at great length. Perhaps this was the turning point. . . . Wittgenstein was a philosopher again,"[46] Feigl wrote. This is a touch self-aggrandizing. Wittgenstein had already begun to wrestle with new philosophical ideas, as his exchange with Ramsey on identity attests. Nonetheless, it was an important moment and Wittgenstein now took a crucial decision. When he left for Cambridge in January 1929 it was theoretically just for a holiday. But he decided to stay, readmitted to the university on 18 January.

————

John Maynard Keynes was there to greet him upon his arrival. The economist wrote to his wife, "Well, God has arrived. I met him on the 5.15 train."

In support of a grant application for Wittgenstein, Ramsey wrote to G. E. Moore, the head of the philosophy department. "In my opinion, Mr Wittgenstein is a philosophic genius of a different order from anyone else I know."[47] It turned out that if he had lived in Cambridge for a certain length of time (including the period he had been in the university before World War I), he could submit the *Tractatus* as a PhD. The regulations required him to have a supervisor, and Ramsey, despite being two decades his junior, was the obvious choice for the job—being as familiar with the *Tractatus* as anyone in the country. There was one hitch, when Wittgenstein obstinately refused to write the requisite summary of three hundred words—but the ever-obliging Ramsey did it for him.

There is an amusing account of the *viva* process, which took place in June. Russell and Moore were the two examiners; Russell feared that since Wittgenstein bore him so much ill will, the Austrian might storm out of the room halfway through. Moore and Russell went through the surreal charade of interrogating Wittgenstein. The *Tractatus* had already achieved cult status, and it was inconceivable that it would be failed. Russell raised some problems, which Wittgenstein dismissed, before he summarily ended the farce by telling the two older men, "Don't worry, I know you'll *never* understand it."[48] Procedure required Moore to produce a report with a verdict on whether the "thesis" had passed the PhD quality threshold. "I am inclined to think that the dissertation as a whole is a work of genius, comparable with acknowledged philosophical masterpieces; but, even if that is not so, I feel quite sure that its quality is such that it would be a sheer absurdity not to grant the PhD degree to Mr. Wittgenstein."[49]

The following day, Wittgenstein was awarded a research grant. He wrote to Schlick on 18 February. "I have decided to remain here in Cambridge for a few terms and work on visual space and other things. . . . Please give my regards to the Round Table and to Mr. Waismann in particular."[50]

For the rest of his life, the UK would be his main base. But his home, his *Heimat*, was always Vienna. And often, in the Christmas, Easter, and summer breaks, he would return. He did so in the summer of 1929 but saw neither Schlick nor Waismann on this trip. Waismann married that year, while Schlick had taken a sabbatical in Stanford. Schlick was considering an appointment to the University of Bonn. His decision would change the nature of the Circle—which would become more public, more political, and more exposed.

6

⤙◦⤚

Neurath in Red Vienna

Austria, a "smallish provincial republic of great beauty, which did not believe it ought to exist."

— ERIC HOBSBAWM

PRAGUE IN THE NORTH; Innsbruck in the west; Sarajevo in the south; Bukovina (historically part of Moldova) in the east. Before World War I all these cities belonged to the Austro-Hungarian Empire. Spread across this vast space were some 55 million people; Croats and Serbs, Italians and Hungarians, Ukrainians and Romanians, Czechs and Moravians. Vienna was German-speaking, but it was not German. This is the depiction of the city in 1898 by an American diplomat: "A man who had been but a short time in Vienna, may himself be of pure German stock, but his wife will be Galician or Polish, his cook Bohemian, his children's nurse Dalmatian, his man a Serbian, his coachman a Slav, his barber a Magyar, and his son's tutor a Frenchman. A majority of the administration's employees are Czechs and the Hungarians have most influence in the affairs of the government."[1] *The melting pot* was a term popularized by a play of that name by Israel Zangwill in 1908. It was about America's absorption of immigrants. But it could equally have been about Austro-Hungary.

Per capita, Austro-Hungary had lost more soldiers in the Great War than any other country. With the Treaty of Versailles at the end of World War I, the map of Europe was redrawn. Austria now emerged as a shrunken state, a state which, in the words of one historian, "nobody wants."[2] The country had no access to the sea. It was now entirely German-speaking. It had a population of barely 7 million, who were half starved and battered by the Spanish influenza pandemic (which from

1918 to 1920 claimed the lives of tens of millions around the world). Historian Eric Hobsbawm would later describe the Austria he grew up in as a "smallish provincial republic of great beauty, which did not believe it ought to exist."[3]

To live in Vienna before World War I was to feel at the heart of one of Europe's most powerful political entities. To stay on in the city after the war required a psychological adjustment, the recognition of a downgrading of status, the adoption of a new *Weltanschauung*—worldview.

———

While Vienna had been the most glittering city within Austria-Hungary, there had been other centers of economy and culture, most notably Budapest and Prague. After the dissolution of the Empire, Budapest and Prague became capitals of newly formed states, Hungary and Czechoslovakia respectively. Within the now rump state of Austria, Vienna was unrivaled. It accounted for a third of the total population, and increasingly came to seem like a place apart, sharing a language but little else with the quaint, alpine villages and small towns beyond. Decades later, in the United States, an Austrian, hearing Karl Menger's accent, said, "You must be Austrian?" "Certainly not," shot back Menger, "I'm Viennese."[4]

Politically, at any rate, there was not one country but two. In 1919 the Social Democratic Workers' Party (SDAP) took control of the capital in municipal elections, marking the beginning of "Red Vienna," an era that was to last fifteen years. SDAP ideology was forged by several formidable intellectuals, such as Otto Bauer and Friedrich Adler. It became known as Austro-Marxism, though it bore little resemblance to the increasingly totalitarian communist regime that had seized power in Russia in 1917, and it rejected some of the main planks of Bolshevik ideology, including the notion that a vanguard of class-conscious activists was required to bring about revolutionary change. It did absorb some elements of Marxist theory, particularly with its emphasis on private ownership of the means of production as the cause of inequality. But the distinctiveness of Austro-Marxism had as much to do with practice as doctrine; it had a very concrete program of reform. Although war had emptied the state coffers, the SDAP was grandly ambitious, seeking modern, technocratic solutions to traditional problems such as unemployment and poor housing and working conditions. It embraced empiricism, facts, and figures, evidence of every kind. It advocated equality but was pragmatic about how this was to be achieved. The adherents of Austro-Marxism "showed a close affinity, in their general outlook and preoccupations, with the new positivist doctrines . . . in the Vienna Circle."[5] Carnap and Neurath sometimes went to Bauer's private discussion group.

From 1922, Vienna had the powers of a *Land* or province, granting it considerable scope to both tax and spend. It took full advantage: indeed, as an experiment in democratic socialism, Austro-Marxism produced some spectacular results. In came an eight-hour working day and unemployment benefits. In came an impressive housing program, 64,000 dwellings in vast blocks, accommodating 200,000 people (a tenth of the city's population). In came rent control. Major investment went into hospitals and public health, and money flowed to set up and support libraries, parks, and sports facilities. Education was given a high priority, and not just in schools. Over the years there developed an extensive network of adult evening classes. The aim was to improve the minds of the masses, both as an end in itself and also because an educated worker, as everyone knew (or thought they knew), is a socialist worker. While many leftist European parties without power were promoting policies to improve the lot of the least advantaged, in Vienna the policies were being put dramatically into effect. The rich had to pay: taxes were raised from luxury consumption and goods (including servants).

Another social revolution was under way. The need for women to work during World War I had shifted attitudes. Now, encouraged by the SDAP, women were entering the university in considerable numbers. They would include the cigar-puffing Olga Hahn as well as Olga Taussky and Rose Rand, all three of whom would join the Circle.

―――――

One should be wary of presenting too positive a picture of the socialist republic of Vienna. The city in the 1920s and '30s was some distance from becoming a proletariat's Shangri-La.[6] At the war's end, as an almost inevitable fallout from war, the economy went into free fall, bringing appalling food and fuel shortages. Unemployment rose and prices spiraled. In spite of the house-building achievements, the number of homeless living in shelters tripled between 1924 and 1934 to nearly 80,000. The old housing stock was in a parlous state. Menger was almost squashed when half a ton of stucco fell from a house just in front of him. Few homes had indoor toilets, most lacked running water. Neurath became the first occupant of his building in the Fifth District to install a lavatory, but not until the mid-1920s.

The bourgeoisie fared little better than the working class. Power shortages hit everyone, regardless of position: until 1920 electricity was cut off each evening at 8:00 p.m. The middle class suffered food shortages too. You would hunt in vain for butter and milk. In the postwar hyperinflation, many middle-class families had their savings wiped out. They included the Kaufmanns and the Poppers. The Kaufmanns had regarded themselves as affluent but lost everything. Karl Popper's father, Simon, had been a wealthy lawyer, and the family had acquired a large apartment in the center of Vienna, close to the cathedral that dominated the capital's skyline, St. Stephen's ("that abominable steeple," as Sigmund Freud called it[7]). Popper might have anticipated an ample inheritance and a comfortable middle-class life. That prospect, at least in the immediate future, was now gone. He could barely clothe himself: "most of us could afford only discarded army uniforms, adapted for civilian use."[8] Hans Hahn fared better, though he had to divest himself of his father's holiday home. In one month in June 1922, the year Schlick arrived in Vienna, the already pathetically depreciated krone collapsed from 52,000 to 125,000 to the pound. It then dive-bombed further, hitting a nadir of 350,000 to the pound in August.

Given the economic conditions, it was hardly surprising that the politics of Red Vienna were bitterly contested. The Christian Socials were the main right-wing party; they fed off the anti-Semitism of the Catholic Church and disenchantment with disruptive change in the modern economy. But there were also pan-German nationalists, who pushed for closer ties with Germany. The Right made its influence felt in many areas, not least, as the Vienna Circle was all too aware, in the university. There were regular right-wing marches and demonstrations, and a combative and venomous right-wing press. Both the Right and the Left ran paramilitary "self-defense" forces: the *Schutzbund* (Left) and the *Heimwehr* (Right).

A pivotal event occurred on 15 July 1927. On that day, three right-wing paramilitary men were acquitted of the murder, six months earlier, of a half-blind World War I veteran and his eight-year-old nephew, who had been on a Social Democratic march. Enraged protestors set the Justice Palace alight. The police opened fire, and in the ensuing pandemonium eighty-nine people were killed and hundreds more injured. The socialists called for a general strike and demanded that the chief of police step down. Austria was on the brink of civil war.

The fear of anarchy was probably what made the city government hesitate: they stood by and watched as the strike was crushed by the right-wing paramilitaries. Almost all members of the Circle had been in sympathy with the demonstrators. When the university rector asked for donations for police victims of the violence, Hans Hahn responded by appealing for donations to the Social Democratic Workers' Party. But as much as anything, the episode was a psychological victory for the Right; the Left never quite regained its confidence.

Popper claimed afterward that he recognized the unrest of 15 July as a harbinger of extremism. "I began to expect the worst: that the democratic bastions of Central Europe would fall, and that a totalitarian Germany would start another world war."[9] If true, he was preternaturally prophetic. But for most, this was still a time to fight one's political corner, not to concede and flee.

———

That was Otto Neurath's attitude. Red Vienna was the perfect laboratory for those, like Neurath, with the motivation and drive to experiment. Some enthusiasms of the SDAP—opposition to alcohol, promotion (for some reason) of bobbed hair—he regarded as merely frivolous. What he wanted was to overturn the whole social order.

After his release from jail in Germany and his return to Austria, he initially devoted his energies to an organization providing people with housing and garden plots. His vision was for simple terraced houses with connecting gardens, a communal gathering point, and no private kitchens. His next venture was a museum for housing and city planning. He had an ideological commitment to museums, which stemmed from his belief in the power of reason; he was convinced that if people had the means and were provided with the appropriate information, they would make sensible choices, whether about housing or any other aspect of life. He described how he had once been handed a puzzling report about pigs being kept in a tenant's bath. This seemed to defy explanation, but he paid a visit to the tenant, who provided a perfectly coherent rationale. "Well, Dr. Neurath, last year I kept my pigs in the sty provided by the Town Council but there was no heating and the sty was so cold that all my pigs died; so now I keep them in the bath."[10] A small heating unit in the pigsty allowed the pigs to be returned to their old quarters.

Neurath had a long-standing interest in housing, but he had an even greater passion for education. On 1 January 1925, he opened a museum based on an ingenious idea that would preoccupy him—and provide him an income—for the rest of his life. The Museum of Society and Economy (Gesellschafts- und Wirtschaftsmuseum), set up partly with money he had browbeaten out of municipal officials, was designed to instruct visitors through pictures. Statistics were creatively and beautifully translated into images with quantities represented by repeated "pictorials." Through these pictorials, visitors could learn about all manner of things from industry to emigration. The museum put on three dozen exhibitions.

Neurath coined a phrase (he was always coining phrases), "Words divide, pictures unite" (*Worte trennen, Bilder verbinden*). The slogan was placed on his museum office wall. Not everyone spoke the same language, a fact taken for granted by those raised in the Austro-Hungarian Empire, but almost everyone could grasp the meaning of images, even if images had limitations (they were not ideal for expressing emotion, for example).

There were no other Circle members directly involved in the museum. However, there were clear parallels between pictorials and logical empiricism, even in the sloganeering. Another Neurathian phrase was "Metaphysical terms divide, scientific terms unite." Certainly, Neurath saw communication as central to both movements. He was permanently at war against waffling. He wanted the images to be simple, free of ornament, and to strip away anything surplus to the transmission of meaning. That was tough to achieve: simplicity was rarely simple.

The museum was strongly socialist in orientation: in educating working-class people, it also aimed to politicize them at a time when there was a serious problem of illiteracy. The numbers themselves were as accurate as the museum could establish, but the choice of which numbers to display was inevitably political, some might say even propagandistic. There were figures, for example, on illness and worker conditions (as reflected in changing infant mortality rates), contrasted with the mortality rates for the rich. And Neurath believed that pictorials could assist in combating racism—by exposing such falsehoods as that "yellow peoples" were outbreeding "white peoples."[11] He dismissed critics charging him with what might now be called "dumbing-down." There was nothing condescending about pictorials, he insisted. Information was liberating. And sometimes it was more effectively processed through picture than word. Behind most of his ideas, including the museum, was the conviction that the lives of the poor could and should be improved.

Although the museum was Neurath's brainchild, he himself had no training in art or graphic design. The museum would never have functioned without his two main collaborators. One was a talented German illustrator, Gerd Arntz, the other a recent graduate, Marie Reidemeister, who had come to Vienna in 1924 to visit her brother Kurt. She attracted Neurath immediately because she confessed to not understanding Hegel. She soon became his mistress—an arrangement that he never attempted to conceal from his wife, Olga.

From the beginning, their enterprise proved popular; it was a favorite haunt of a British woman, Esther Simpson, who lived in Vienna for several years from the late 1920s, and whose help Neurath would later need to call on. There was a delegation too, from the Russian embassy.

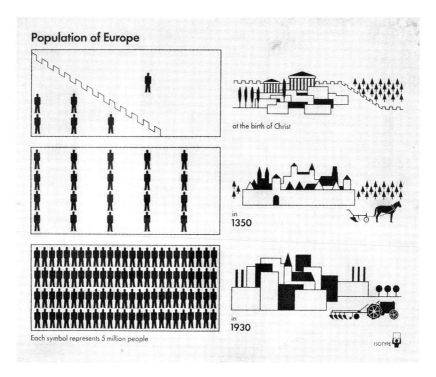

FIGURE 1. An example of Neurath's Isotypes. *Source*: Christoph Limbeck-Lilienau and Friedrich Stadler, *Der Wiener Kreis* (LIT Verlag, 2015). Reprinted courtesy of the Vienna Circle Society / Wiener Kreis Gesellschaft.

So impressed were they with what they had seen that they asked Neurath and Reidemeister to assist with setting up their own institute, the All-Union Institute of Pictorial Statistics of Soviet Construction and Economy—Izostat for short.

That Neurath readily agreed to do this, committing himself to be in Russia for sixty days a year, reveals either a political naïveté or a willful blindness. Of course, he was a socialist and sympathetic to some of the aims of the Russian revolution. And there were other Western intellectuals who traveled to the Soviet Union and returned with gushing enthusiasm. But that country's dictatorial turn had already been transparent to more perspicacious visitors.

Neurath got paid, of course. And no doubt he took some pleasure in being feted by a foreign government. A decree from the Council of

Peoples' Commissars in September 1931 stated that "all public and co-operative organizations, unions and schools are obliged to apply picto-rial statistics according to the method of Dr Neurath."[12] He and Marie received lavish hospitality, at least initially, put up in the Grand Hotel, which was indeed grand. But as time wore on, the reception cooled, the accommodation on offer became less grand, and the work, which was beyond Neurath's control, became more blatantly propagandistic.

Izostat grew to more than seventy people. Its main purpose was to illustrate the successes of the first Five-Year Plan (1928–32) in the devel-opment of coal and iron and steel and electricity, and also to predict the achievements of the second Five-Year Plan (1933–38) in road and rail and water. Neurath became increasingly disillusioned with Izostat and in one letter confessed to having to overlook certain ideological differ-ences with his hosts. Still, this lover of facts and despiser of flimflam had for a period to reconcile his advisory role in the Soviet Union with his empiricism. It must have required some agile mental gymnastics.

Neurath's pictorials seem less radical today, since we have become accustomed to visual pointers on signage, but it seemed revolutionary in the 1920s. Even so, his museum is best understood as part of a wider movement—modernism—as is the Circle as a whole.

But, before we go there, time for coffee?

7

Coffee and Circles

Any city that could produce Freud, Wittgenstein, Mahler, Schoenberg, Herzl, Kelsen, Popper, Hayek, Klimt, Schnitzler, Musil, Loos, Kraus—and Hitler—clearly had something important going on in it.[1]

WHY DO SUCH constellations occur?

It is a natural human instinct to want to draw patterns, to proffer causes, to seek explanations. How can we account for the gathering of so many first-rate thinkers—not just philosophers—in one European city? Why Vienna? Why then, in the first three decades of the twentieth century?[2]

The role of coincidence and fluke should not be dismissed. In the Circle, for example, a multiplicity of personal reasons brought about the convergence of so much talent: Neurath might have stayed in Germany had the Bavarian revolution not been suppressed. Menger might have stayed in Amsterdam, had he not had a stormy relationship with his supervisor. We can speculate on what-iffery.

But all that aside, it is implausible to claim that there was nothing deeper going on, nothing in the local soil to nurture the Circle: it did not emerge from a barren field. For several decades Vienna was the stage for remarkable developments in literature, journalism, the visual arts, music, and architecture, as well as philosophy. There have been other clusters of genius in history: Athens in the fifth century BC, Florence in the fourteenth century, and Edinburgh in the eighteenth. Vienna merits a place in that company.

One pattern to such clusters is the role of money. Culture sometimes represents itself as the antithesis of material motivation, driven by loftier concerns. But it is as dependent on financial support as any other sector, probably more so. Throughout history artists have relied on patronage. And fin-de-siècle Vienna was the glittering capital of a great empire. There was serious money, some of it on display at number 4, Alleegasse—the street address of the Palais Wittgenstein. Ludwig's father, Karl, the mansion's owner, funneled huge funds into the Viennese art world.

On the other hand, the heyday of the Circle coincided with a period of severe economic contraction. In the 1920s and '30s only a minority felt confident, safe, and wealthy. The more prevalent feelings were of insecurity and fear of impending doom. Could menace and fear have been the spur to the creative achievements of post–World War I Vienna? Perhaps this is mere rationalization, a post hoc explanation. Less easy to dismiss is the theory that intellectual life burgeoned as a by-product of a cross-fertilization of cultures. Recent research suggests that what best predicts the spread and flourishing of good ideas is the intermingling of communities.[3] Vienna was home to people from across the Austro-Hungarian Empire—Hungarians, Czechs, Poles, Serbs, Croats, Slovenes, Jews—as well as native Austrians. They concentrated within distinct neighborhoods in Vienna but, perhaps with the exception of the Yiddish speakers in Leopoldstadt, these never became so isolated as to resemble ghettos. Vienna was a place in which conversation and debate flowed.

Not, however, where you might expect—in the university. The University of Vienna had an effective monopoly as the capital's only major academic institution. Within the philosophy faculty, the empiricists (Schlick, Carnap, Kraft) were a minority, and most courses were on the history of philosophy. The university also had its own philosophy society in which the empiricists were, again, poorly represented.

We might have an idealized image of a university as a haven of tolerance and equality. In fact, the University of Vienna in the first few decades of the twentieth century was a bastion of conservatism, not just in the politics of those who taught there but in the rules and ethos by which it was governed. For example, as in many European countries, by tradition there was a remote relationship between academics and their students. Professors were not seen as approachable and did little to encourage interaction. Schlick was typical enough. He would lecture sitting down and made no effort to captivate his listeners. In one note Schlick tells Rose Rand, who wants to discuss the use of the seminar room, that she can talk to him about it "only during my official office hours."[4] And she was a Circle member! Popper described how those who taught him mathematics and philosophy were regarded as demigods. "They were infinitely beyond our reach," he recalled. "There was no contact between professors and students who had not qualified for a PhD dissertation. I had neither the slightest ambition to make, nor the prospect of making, their acquaintance."[5]

Academic jobs were hard to come by and carried considerable prestige, yet post–World War I professorial wages were barely adequate to get by on. Working conditions too left much to be desired. The lecture rooms were cold and overcrowded—some students had to sit on the floor, others on the windowsills. Basics like paper were in short supply; the library could not afford foreign works.

Students in the university belonged to fraternities. After World War I, and with the student body now containing many ex-soldiers, these became much more hostile to outsiders, particularly minorities. Many fraternities offered membership only to those who could prove their Aryan purity and campaigned for a reduction in the number of Jewish students. On Saturday mornings the fraternities would march through the campus, and wise liberals and nonobservant Jews made themselves scarce. The university was a self-policing zone, and if you were roughed up it was futile to cry for help.

The typical academic started out on their career by becoming a *Privatdozent*, a title that still exists in some German-speaking universities. It is conferred on an academic only after they have received a higher doctoral degree, the habilitation. Somehow—an ingenious trick this— the university authorities managed to imbue the Privatdozent position with status while leaving it unpaid.

Still, it was the normal starting position for an academic career. When Carnap arrived in Vienna in 1926 it was to be a Privatdozent in philosophy. Philipp Frank, Kurt Gödel, Felix Kaufmann, Viktor Kraft, and Karl Menger all began as Privatdozent, as did Moritz Schlick (in

Rostock). The title gave the holders the right to lecture, so it was a mainstream route into the academic world and, despite the absence of a stipend, much sought after.

There was no guarantee that brilliance would be enough to earn you the title. For instance, Schlick was mistaken when he thought that it would be a simple task to obtain a *Privatdozentur* at the university for Herbert Feigl. There were two problems: Feigl was a Czech citizen, and he was of Jewish descent. In any case, the lack of any secure income made the position too precarious for some. Although Felix Kaufmann earned his habilitation and Privatdozent status, in the end shortage of money forced him to take a job, which he did, very successfully, managing an oil company. He was not lost to the Circle entirely. He was able to combine his work with publishing articles and with regular attendance at Circle evenings. For those wishing to stay in education, secondary school teaching offered a backup route and one taken, for example, by Popper.

The many intellectual circles in Vienna, of which the Circle was only one, were not officially part of the university but drew many of their members from it. Indeed, they flourished precisely because the official lectures in the university did not lend themselves to free discussion. Philosopher Heinrich Gomperz ran a discussion group; it convened at his home on Saturdays and covered economics, politics, and psychoanalysis as well as philosophy. It was occasionally attended by Carnap, who also went to a Wednesday-night circle run by the eminent psychologists Karl and Charlotte Bühler. Sigmund Freud held a regular gathering at his apartment on Wednesday night. The constitutional lawyer Hans Kelsen had a circle, as did Otto Bauer, the leading theoretician of Austro-Marxism.

For those with the energy and inclination there were circle meetings every day, often twice a day.

There were left-wing circles and right-wing circles and some circles were more socially progressive than others. The Geist circle, which included economists Friedrich Hayek and Oskar Morgenstern, did not welcome women. Schlick's circle was more inclusive. (Schlick cared less about the background of those he would invite into his group and more about their talent and attitude: a man of old-world gentility, he could not abide boorishness, as Popper discovered to his chagrin.) The circles overlapped, so that some people were members of two or more. Naturally, the ubiquitous Neurath popped up in several. The biggest overlap with Schlick's circle was Karl Menger's.

———

Karl Menger was the son of Carl Menger, the founder of the Austrian school of economics, which emphasized motivations and actions of the individual (as opposed to the group). From Carl a squiggly line, through other Viennese economists such as Ludwig von Mises and Friedrich von Hayek, can be traced to the economic policies and political outlook of Margaret Thatcher and Ronald Reagan.[6]

It seems clear that Karl was in fact the offspring of an affair between his father and a much younger woman, Hermine (Mina) Andermann, who managed his extensive library and published short stories. Mina was born Jewish in Galicia but raised as a Catholic and baptized in her mid-twenties. Karl was baptized at birth under the name Andermann, only becoming Karl Menger in 1911, aged nine. His father had asked Emperor Franz Josef to have his son declared as legitimate. The emperor's ready assent may have been related to the fact that Carl had been personal tutor to his son (Crown Prince Rudolf).[7]

Karl inherited his father's political outlook and was himself interested in economics, although for this multitalented student writing was also an appealing career option—as a young man he had written plays, one of which was even read by novelist Arthur Schnitzler. In the end he studied physics at the University of Vienna. But it was only when he heard Hahn lecture on the mathematics of curves and dimensions—and the apparently insuperable difficulties of defining what curves were—that Menger's professional trajectory became set. "I left in a daze; for I clearly saw that curves were different from surfaces and solids. Should I not then be able to make precise *how* they differed and to *define* curves?"[8]

Karl Popper, a fellow math student, thought it obvious that Menger was a genius. Despite bouts of serious illness including, in 1921, tuberculosis, Menger received his PhD by 1924 and was awarded a fellowship to Amsterdam working alongside Dutch mathematician L.E.J. Brouwer, whose lecture in Vienna would reignite Wittgenstein's passion for philosophy. Brouwer was humorless and high-strung with a "hollow-cheeked face, faintly resembling Julius Caesar's."[9] For Menger it did not prove a happy collaboration—Brouwer sought out quarrels, and there was a bitter dispute about whether Brouwer's account of dimension theory had sufficiently acknowledged Menger's work. The young post-doctoral student was relieved when an opportunity arose to return to Austria. A post in Vienna as an assistant professor of geometry had opened with the departure to Königsberg of Kurt Reidemeister.

A year after returning to Vienna, Menger established his Mathematical Colloquium, modeled on Schlick's circle. It focused strictly on mathematics and continued for eight years until 1936. Although it never achieved the fame of the Vienna Circle, it was a significant presence on the Viennese intellectual landscape. In Menger's circle, students and professors would discuss their own work or a development in mathematics elsewhere. Hans Hahn, Olga Taussky, and some other Circle members would turn up. Kurt Gödel rarely missed a meeting. Tarski would sometimes travel to Vienna from Warsaw just to attend. Popper regarded his involvement in this group as the pinnacle of his intellectual life in Vienna.

Just as the Vienna Circle was under Schlick's leadership, so the Mathematical Colloquium was very much under Menger's. Although circles tended to be loose gatherings, invitations were usually given only by the circle convener. That was why, beyond the university and the circles, another Viennese institution, requiring no invitation, no ticket, and no qualifications, was so fundamental to the city's flourishing.

————

The coffeehouse. A place to read the newspaper, to catch up on the gossip, to be alone but not lonely, to sit with friends, to play cards and dominoes and chess, to conduct business, to become embroiled in a heated political row, to ponder curve theory. Viennese apartments were in short supply, and typically small, dark, and cold. The coffeehouses offered an appealing alternative to home. They varied, of course. Not all of them had marble tables, not all of them had deep leather chairs and heavy chandeliers. They offered their own choice of pastries. Yet all were run on similar lines, governed by a similar set of informal rules. The coffee itself was served with a glass of water. The papers—sometimes an astonishing selection, including the foreign press—were stacked on bamboo holders. One visitor to Vienna, William Beveridge, the director of the London School of Economics, was sitting in a café in 1933 when he read a story in the evening paper about Jewish academics being dismissed from their jobs in Nazi Germany. This report would nudge him into setting up a life-saving organization (of which more later). The coffeehouses were open in the day and in the evenings, patronized by the busy and the idle. You could nurse a coffee for as long as you wished without incurring the wrath of the waiters. Feeling indulgent? Listen to the options and treat yourself with *ein Stück Apfelstrudel oder Sachertorte*. In a Viennese novel of the time, one character is asked by another whether he ever gets fed up dawdling in the coffeehouse. Not at all, he says:

> Sitting in cafés is a barrier against the enforced activity which makes our lives miserable. . . . People like us always have the mistaken feeling that they are wasting time, missing something irretrievable. . . . As if a man had a set of things to get done in a set amount of time. . . . [It's] the harmful influence of our materialistic generation, a generation of physical labor and advanced technology. . . . But the minute you enter a café, you're on holiday—the yoke is lifted from your shoulders, snapped in half.[10]

A condescending British visitor blamed the coffeehouse for Viennese lassitude. "There is no city in the world where it is more pleasant to sit considering what to do next, and that, doubtless, is why, when all is said, its inhabitants do so little."[11] But Austrian novelist Stefan Zweig venerated the Viennese coffeehouse as "a sort of democratic club to which one bought admittance for the price of a cup of coffee."[12]

There was a degree of distortion in that. The working classes tended to frequent taverns rather than coffeehouses, though the coffeehouses

themselves varied in plushness. Coffeehouse patrons were often middle-
class, and the coffeehouse was a predominantly male space. An exception was the cashier, (*Sitzkassiererin*), usually a woman. A nineteenth-
century Vienna travel guide described how, "[e]nthroned behind the
bar, among the bottles and glasses is that ambassador of the fairer sex,
the cashier. She is always a very sweet-tempered, accommodating representative of her sex."[13]

Vienna could boast more than a thousand coffeehouses. Much has
been written about them: they were not mere symbols of the city's vi-
brant creative life; they were its linking ducts and pipes. For our story
their importance is the particular role they played in the Vienna Circle.
The University of Vienna provided the essential bedrock to scholarly
life in the city with its seminars and lectures and its academic salaries.
However, because of its formality and stuffiness, its anti-Semitism and
its conservatism, the most exhilarating discussions routinely took place
beyond its walls.

Different coffeehouses came to be known for specific fields and professions. Café Weghuber was popular among actors and actresses. Freud
and some psychoanalysts met in Café Landtmann. Until it closed at the
turn of the twentieth century, Café Griensteidl was frequented by writers such as Arthur Schnitzler and Hugo von Hofmannsthal. They mi-
grated after World War I to the Café Herrenhof, favored by authors
Robert Musil and Joseph Roth, although the future Nobel Prize winner
Elias Canetti preferred the Café Museum.

Between 1907 and 1912, when the precursor to the Vienna Circle
(Hahn, Frank, Neurath, and, less frequently, von Mises) gathered, Café
Central, with its beautiful domes and arches, was probably one location,
though they may have been too engrossed in the philosophical problems arising from relativity theory to take much notice of the regulars,
who included polemicist Karl Kraus, architect Adolf Loos, and a Russian émigré, Lev Bronstein, who would pass the time there playing chess
and would become better known after returning home, under his assumed name, Trotsky.

Later, when the Vienna Circle had become formalized, the cafés were
still where members would retire to continue the Thursday-evening

discussion or gather when a foreign friend of the Circle was in town. Cafés Reichsrat, Schottentor, Arkaden (on the Reichsratstrasse), and Josephinum were all popular, particularly Josephinum, which was close to Boltzmanngasse. The Herrenhof, the writers' retreat, was a favorite of Neurath, who joked that the coffeehouse atmosphere was worthy of observation and analysis, just as anthropologists observe and analyze "the life of the natives somewhere."[14] Neurath could be found at the Herrenhof several times a week, and consequently it began to attract others from the Circle. It had a contemporary feel, being better lit than the Central. One Circle visitor from abroad, Norwegian philosopher Arne Naess, recalled that talk in the coffeehouses was more animated than at Circle meetings in Boltzmanngasse. "It was not easy for me to break into the fast discussion. Sometimes I would suddenly and unexpectedly say, *Im Gengenteil*, 'On the contrary.' There would then be a second's astonished silence and I could proceed at leisure."[15]

Poet Peter Altenberg gave his address as Vienna, First District, Café Central, and in the coffeehouses there was the tradition of the Regulars' Table (*der Stammtisch*), understood to be reserved for the same people at the same time on a particular day. These groups might be closed, a bit cliquey. But the wider ambience was friendly—this was not usually a place from which individuals were socially excluded. Intermingling was vital to the intellectual fecundity of the coffeehouse. Here the mathematician could swap stories with the journalist, and the businessman could converse with the historian. Across much of *Mitteleuropa*, the coffee shops were social adhesives, binding individuals and groups—and nowhere more so than in Vienna. They offered a setting in which, amid the coffee fumes and the cigarette smoke, views could be floated and theories exchanged.

That openness was particularly appealing to Viennese Jews. According to one historian, the coffeehouse served as "a secular version of the synagogue: Jewish men could meet there either after or, increasingly instead of, going to the *Shul*."[16] One comprehensive study of coffeehouses in Vienna and elsewhere states that in the Viennese coffeehouse, "new or second-generation Jews were dominant."[17] Inside the coffeehouse it was easy to conjure up the image of a cosmopolitan utopia, in which ethnic or religious background was no barrier to a club or job. Within the coffeehouse walls, outside hierarchies were flattened. Students and librarians could debate math, logic, language, and philosophy on an equal footing with salaried professors.

And who could object to the coffeehouse? What could be more harmless?

In fact, the image of the effete Jewish intellectual whiling away hours in abstract argument rankled both anti-Semites and Zionists alike. In his speech to the Zionist Congress in 1898, one of the founding fathers of Zionism, Max Nordau, imagined a future of muscular Jews toiling in the fields of the Holy Land in place of the "coffeehouse Jews"[18] of the Diaspora. Meanwhile, for conservatives, the abstract ideas drifting through the coffeehouse appeared far from benign. In Vienna, and elsewhere, the first three decades of the twentieth century was a period in which new ways of thinking, new ways of seeing the world, were subverting the existing order.

Logical empiricism was linked to this movement, which came to be known as "modernism." The Right—social as well as political conservatives—deemed it a menace.

8

◄○►

Couches and Construction

Ornament and Crime

—ADOLF LOOS

THERE SHE STANDS, in profile, wearing a full-length, off-the-shoulder, white gown and a pained expression. Her dark, arched eyebrows and black hair are set against her pallid skin. It is not a joyful image. The subject seems weighed down, anxious. You would not guess that this portrait was commissioned to mark her wedding. Although her face may not be familiar, the style is unmistakably that of the modernist artist Gustav Klimt.

Circles and coffeehouses were transmission mechanisms. And some of the ideas they spread came to coalesce in Vienna under a new, loose, unorganized movement, "modernism." Often, the Circle is written about as though it were somehow an autonomous group, operating in isolation and unaffected by the prevailing cultural and intellectual trends. In fact, the Circle was profoundly influenced by modernism, which in various ways penetrated almost every aspect of Viennese cultural life.

That woman in the flowing white dress was Ludwig Wittgenstein's sister, Gretl (Margaret). Klimt, you'll recall, was a recipient of Karl Wittgenstein's artistic patronage. He must have felt indebted; no doubt he wanted to please his benefactors. But Gretl detested the painting and banished it to the attic.

In fact, by Klimt's standards, it is relatively sober and restrained. Some of the art produced by Viennese painters, by far the three most significant being Klimt, Egon Schiele, and Oskar Kokoschka, has the power to shock over a century later. Adolf Hitler was certainly shocked by it. His own paintings, decently enough executed, though that is an

FIGURE 2. Portrait of Wittgenstein's sister, Margaret Stonborough, by Gustav Klimt (1905).

awkward technical judgment for critics to concede, are of flowers, grand buildings, courtyards, and churches, which for the most part he tried to depict as faithfully as possible. He drew principally on nineteenth-century styles: there was nothing experimental about his brushstrokes or portrayals.

Klimt and Schiele, by contrast, depicted the human form as it had never been revealed before; there was a deliberate overcoming of inhibition. Their eroticism was bound to provoke; provocation was an objective, not a side effect. Here was their insolent response to the stiff-lipped, straitlaced, bourgeois Catholicism of the society in which they had been raised.

Bourgeois Catholicism was not their sole target. The eighteenth-century Enlightenment had been a period characterized by confidence in the power of reason. Individual and societal problems could be overcome through human ingenuity and scientific progress. But in the nineteenth century Charles Darwin had forced mankind to relegate itself, to see itself as part of the animal world—not entirely distinct from it. Modernism placed an emphasis on the animal, on the emotional and the irrational parts of our psychological and physical makeup, on our sexual and primeval urges.

In the explicit representation they gave to sex and the body, the artists were in good company. In fiction there was a similar pushback against prissiness, from the likes of novelist Robert Musil (in, for example, his book *Young Törless*) and playwright Arthur Schnitzler. One of Schnitzler's plays, *The Round*, was banned by the censors for being pornographic.

All these expressions of a new cultural mood, a willingness to confront and unmask our base instincts, must themselves be understood within a wider context, the new "science" of psychoanalysis. Shortly after *The Round* was written, Sigmund Freud produced his *Three Essays on Sexuality*. The influence between Schnitzler and Freud was two-way. Freud posted a revealing letter to Schnitzler in 1922, as Schnitzler was about to turn sixty years old.

> I shall make a confession to you which I will ask you to be good enough to keep to yourself. . . . I have plagued myself over the

question how it comes about that in all these years I have never sought your company. . . . I think I have avoided you from a kind of awe of meeting my "double." . . . Your determinism and your skepticism . . . your deep grasp of the truths of the unconscious and of the biological nature of man . . . and the extent to which your thoughts are preoccupied with the polarity of love and death; all that moves me with an uncanny feeling of familiarity.[1]

Although the manifestations of modernism varied according to its artistic expression, be it literature or art or the atonal music of Arnold Schoenberg, the self-consciousness with which acts of creation engaged with their own form was a common theme. The modernist novelist, no longer content with just trying to depict a world, became intrigued by the way in which novels are themselves constructed, and then began to experiment with this structure. Modernist musicians, poets, and artists all became introspective, lifting up the bonnet, examining how their art form functioned, and then choosing to expose inner workings to the listener, reader, or viewer.

The Circle was not straightforwardly modernist. After all, logical empiricism believed in science, logic, and reason. Nonetheless, links with modernism are easy to discern. The logical empiricists were interested not just in doing philosophy, but in the prior question, *What is philosophy?* They became more self-conscious about the activity in which they were engaged. Traditionally, metaphysics was supposed to provide some insight into the world beyond what was available to the senses. The logical empiricists rejected that, and in so doing reimagined the nature and role and limits of philosophy.

Then there was language. At least in Vienna, modernism had a preoccupation with language and its use. Journalist Karl Kraus, in particular, a remarkable stylist and unparalleled polemicist, adopted rigid rules for the use of language; he held a withering contempt for those who could not or would not live up to his standards. To be fair, he was harsh on himself too. He was known to agonize over the placing of a comma. What mattered was that language be clear and be stripped of unnecessary ornamentation.

The channel through which Kraus spread his gospel and castigated the language transgressors was the journal *Die Fackel* (*The Torch*), which he founded in 1899. That his fellow scribblers in other publications were so loose with their words and prone to hyperbole, half- (and sometimes full-) blown lies, unintentional and (far worse) intentional ambiguity, was proof positive to Kraus that Austria was living through an era of moral degradation and cultural inertia.

The Circle did not go this far. But they shared Kraus's fixation with language and obsession with clarity. Some of their philosophical foes were targets precisely for the sins of writing in an abstruse style and shrouding their arguments in jargon. The prose of their enemies might impress with surface profundity, but more often than not it lacked depth and substance. Kraus's influence spread through Viennese society. A month after his death on 12 June 1936, Margaret wrote to her brother Ludwig: "Strange that Karl Kraus's death has hit so close to home for me. 'Close to home' is of course a stupid phrase."[2]

———

Modernism had expression, too, in architecture—and once again the impact of this movement could be observed on the Circle.

The buildings around Vienna's most famous street, the Ringstrasse, constructed in the second half of the nineteenth century, had arisen with little sense for any unifying harmony, though they had in common arrogance and a desire to make a statement. The Viennese had always liked their arches and columns, their colorful frescoes. Beyond the Ringstrasse, the architecture had particularly drawn on gothic and baroque styles. Buildings were ornate, flamboyant; inside and outside, walls were viewed as canvases for embellishment.

The modernist drive in architecture was a response to all that. In Vienna its finest expression was the Looshaus, by architect Adolf Loos, opposite the elaborate Hofburg Palace. All straight lines and completed in 1911, it was hated so much by Emperor Franz Josef that he kept the curtains closed on the window that faced it, or so the story goes.

Nonetheless, the new aesthetic flourished. In part this was because of the exigencies of the age. In the aftermath of World War I, there were appalling housing shortages across Europe. In 1921 Paul Wittgenstein implored his brother Ludwig, then teaching in Lower Austria, to occupy a room in one of the Wittgenstein properties (Neuwaldegg); otherwise "we run the risk of the housing authority placing some stranger in the house."[3] As the government of Red Vienna initiated its ambitious building program, a central concern was what sort of housing should be constructed. Among the Circle it was, of course, Neurath who most engaged with this issue. He was a socialist steeped in theory but far more interested in practice, and Vienna had no shortage of practical problems. Later, when he opened his statistics museum, Neurath asked Philipp Frank's brother, Josef, one of the country's leading architects, to help design it.

In December 1926, Neurath was present at the opening ceremony in Dessau, central Germany, of the art and design school known as the Bauhaus, founded by Walter Gropius. The Bauhaus look was characterized by clean lines, a lack of ornamentation, and a belief that function should dictate form. Neurath returned twice to Dessau to lecture; the first time, in 1929, he spoke about pictorial statistics and how from straightforward pictures it was possible to convey complex information.

He encouraged Feigl to visit that same year. Later, Carnap lectured there too. Carnap's talk in a roomful of designers and architects was entitled *Science and Life*. "I work in science," he began, "and you in visible forms: the two are only different sides of a single life."[4] Reinforcing the link between Vienna and Dessau, two Bauhaus students traveled to Vienna for work experience in Neurath's museum.

For the Bauhaus, ideology and economics were interwoven. Building materials were not easy to come by and few people could afford to finance new private homes, so the condemnation of wasted space was motivated by both aesthetic and pragmatic considerations. The Bauhaus believed that design should lend itself to mass production. One slogan from Adolf Loos, who shared their vision for the future of architecture, was "Let's repeat ourselves incessantly." A famous talk by Loos was entitled "Ornament and Crime." Mass production had a downside, a new age of alienation, for industrialization had irrevocably altered the relationship between the producer and the product.

Logical empiricism and the Bauhaus—particularly during the period from 1928 to 1930 under its second director, Hannes Meyer—were kindred spirits, eager to tear up the fusty old and replace it with their down-to-earth new. No respecters of tradition, they revered science and embraced progress. They both pushed a unifying agenda. While several influential logical empiricists were set on uniting the sciences, Walter Gropius proposed a unity between art and craft; all the arts, including architecture, were to be brought under one metaphorical (and no doubt flat) roof. The building of the future would involve an egalitarian fusion of skills, a joint effort of architect, sculptor, painter, and craftsman. Any snobbish hierarchy of the past was to be swept away.

It is intriguing, and surely not coincidental, that a central text in the positivist canon, Carnap's *The Logical Structure of the World* (*Der Logische Aufbau der Welt*) has a bottom-up architecture to it (Carnap fashions his complex logical system from elementary experiences), as does the *Tractatus*. Wittgenstein and Loos were well acquainted and recognized in each other kindred spirits. For his sister Hermine's fiftieth birthday, Wittgenstein presented her with a signed copy of a Loos book (*Spoken into the Void*). "You are me,"[5] Loos once said to Wittgenstein. This was not about just a parallel approach to their respective disciplines, though that they had. The *Tractatus* is a work impatient of explanation and skinned to the bone. It can be seen as a pursuit of an ornament-free language—in which every element expressed the logic of language and thereby of the world (unlike ordinary language, which obscures its structure with its many redundancies—or ornaments).[6]

But there was a more direct connection between them. From 1926, Wittgenstein devoted almost two years of his life to the building of his sister Gretl's house on a street in Vienna's Third District, Kundmanngasse. During this period he took to describing himself as an architect, though he had no formal training. The official architect was his friend Paul Engelmann, a student of Loos. In practice, Wittgenstein himself was behind much of the detail—the doorknobs, radiators, window locks—his orders driven by an obsessiveness for harmony and precision that nobody could match. At the end of the process, when he had frayed the nerves of all those who worked on the project, he demanded that the ceiling of one of the rooms be raised three centimeters.

The Loos influence is apparent in its focus on simplicity, its plain decoration. Gretl approved, but Wittgenstein's eldest sister, Hermine, labeled it logic-become-house (*hausgewordene Logik*). This should not be mistaken for a compliment.

The aesthetic sensibility that created the building at Kundmanngasse was evident in how Wittgenstein conducted himself. He led a dramatic, rich, and varied life, but one without adornment. His rooms in Cambridge were kept spartan. Long before his work on his sister's home he lectured Bertrand Russell on how furniture had to be simple. Fussiness was impure.

Neurath also subscribed to this new aesthetic, although when he was involved in Viennese public housing he took a less rigid attitude to homely comforts. But elsewhere, the aesthetic emerged in other surprising ways. Beards, for example, were no longer à la mode—deemed unnecessary facial clutter. After Neurath became convinced that ornament was mostly objectionable, he felt obliged to shave off his beard (the same explanation may account for the mysterious disappearance of Hahn's moustache).

———

Sigmund Freud's impact on modernism has already been alluded to. Freud was not the first person to argue that humans were driven by unconscious motives; this thought was anticipated by several others, including Schopenhauer and Nietzsche. But he was the first to investigate the phenomenon systematically. And as the founder of the psychoanalytic movement, in which psychological problems were alleviated or resolved through a dialogue between patient and analyst, he introduced several ideas that continue to frame debates in psychoanalysis today. They include the role of sexual desire in our feelings and actions, and the function of dreams (which Freud interpreted as wish-fulfillments).

Freud also shaped the practice of psychoanalysis, introducing the patient's couch and techniques such as the method of free association,
which encouraged patients to discuss whatever came into their mind,
so as to make the unconscious more transparent and to bring repressed
thoughts to the surface. Freud ran a circle of his own. On Wednesday
nights, a group of (mainly) faithful followers met at Berggasse 19, Vienna
IX. Freud had moved to Berggasse in 1891 and for forty-seven years it
served not just as his home but also his place of work. It was in Berggasse that he installed his short, comfortable couch, covered with Oriental rugs, on which his patients would recline. To avoid eye contact, he
would talk to them while sitting to one side.

By the 1920s, Freud had earned an international reputation, but nowhere was he more celebrated than in his home city. In 1924, he was
made an honorary citizen of Vienna. Two years later, on his seventieth
birthday, all the main newspapers paid homage with lengthy articles to
his pioneering achievements. In the 1930s the city council even contemplated renaming Berggasse as Sigmund Freud Gasse—a proposal Freud
himself thought preposterous.

His attitude reflected his complex relationship with Vienna. He may
have been honored by the city, but he was acutely sensitive to its pervasive anti-Semitism; the university took years to grant him the full professorship he manifestly deserved. Nor had his success protected him
from the upheavals in the economy. The hyperinflation in the 1920s was
no respecter of celebrity; it gobbled up his savings along with everyone
else's. With banknotes becoming almost worthless, he asked one Hungarian periodical to pay for an article in potatoes. He began to take on
many more foreign patients—particularly English and American—who
could afford to pay and, even better, in a currency that did not depreci-
ate between the beginning and the end of the session.

That foreigners would travel to Vienna for sessions of therapy might
strike one as peculiar today. But, if you could afford the journey and
accommodation, the Austrian capital was *the* place to head for self-
understanding or to resolve mental anguish. It was *the* home of psychoanalysis and the city where its most experienced, most revered

specialists practiced their art. Or would it be more accurate to say that they practiced their science?

It was never discussed formally in Circle meetings, but inevitably, the status of psychoanalysis was a topic of interest to Circle members. Was psychoanalysis a science? If so, what made it so? Freud certainly regarded it as a science. It was not metaphysics—the unconscious was not, as it were, unreachable; it was there to be discovered and exposed. Many in the Circle, such as Schlick and Feigl, were sympathetic. In 1932, Neurath and some younger Circle members attempted to translate Freud's psychoanalytic claims into "scientific" language, linking it directly to human behavior.

Several Circle members were themselves psychoanalyzed, including Bergmann and, later in the United States, Carnap. In musing on Wittgenstein's hostility toward him, Carnap conceded that he had no adequate explanation, "probably only a psychoanalyst could offer one."[7] Bergmann in particular was heavily influenced by Freud. In the preface to a collection of essays he mentions the terror he feels at the thought of book-writing: "Some causes of this terror probably belong in the psychoanalyst's study."[8] Teaching in the US after the war, he would insist that his students become familiar with Freud's work and always took pride in trying to figure people out. "He was a follower of Freud to the nth degree."[9] One Circle member, Heinrich Neider, subsequently claimed that numerous members of the Circle were in analysis, though even from its pioneering days there was some stigma attached to the process, and it was not something openly discussed. Walter Hollitscher would later write a book on Freud, drawing connections between psychoanalysis and sociology.

Visitors to Vienna and the Circle from abroad also took advantage of the local expertise to have themselves mentally checked out. Arne Naess, from Norway, was analyzed by a collaborator of Freud, Dr. Edward Hitschmann, to whose practice he would walk every morning at 8:00 a.m., keeping up the routine for eighteen months. "We were both somewhat astonished to find that I have suffered from a pronounced childhood neurosis."[10]

Frank Ramsey entered analysis in 1924 with Dr. Theodor Reik, a well-known psychoanalyst and disciple of Freud. For Ramsey, psychoanalysis was the central reason for being in Vienna; it was not just mental pampering, to be indulged in between philosophy. His aim was to recover from a doomed infatuation with a flirtatious married woman, Margaret Pyke, a decade his senior. Once freed from his hang-ups he would, he thought, become cleverer.[11] He reported back to his mother: "Being analysed is different from what I expected in being, at any rate at first, much more exhausting and unpleasant."[12] Ramsey told the overweight Reik that he, Reik, was the ugliest man he had ever seen. "Everyone has to say that before we can get started,"[13] Reik replied. Reik had Ramsey write back to his parents to obtain important information, such as his early bowel movements as a child.[14] Later Reik irked him by asking to borrow the *Tractatus* and then declaring that the book's author, Mr. Wittgenstein, "must have some compulsion neurosis."[15] But one of Ramsey's friends reported that despite the tension between doctor and patient, the sessions had worked to cure Ramsey of his lovelorn state. "He's abandoned Mrs. P[yke]; has taken on a new lady with whom (though, before, the idea had filled him with repulsion) he proceeds to the furthest limits. . . . Perhaps we'd better all go on to Reik."[16]

This was Ramsey's second trip to Austria, following his visit to Wittgenstein in Puchberg in 1923, and he got to know Wittgenstein's sister Gretl. Only then, after seeing her home with its numerous reception rooms, did he come to grasp that the family was "colossally wealthy."[17] Gretl took him to the opera, and he dined with the family regularly. A fellow guest at one dinner was Hans Hahn, and Gretl also introduced him to Schlick, who "didn't seem to be much of a philosopher, but [was] a very nice man."[18] He returned to Puchberg to see Ludwig at least twice, but their discussions were not often fruitful. "It is such hard work for him, like pushing something too heavy uphill."[19] He reported back to Keynes in a letter that Wittgenstein was refusing all financial support from his family, even Christmas presents.

Meanwhile, his psychoanalysis continued for six months, after which he returned to Cambridge. A talk given by Ramsey in November 1925 to the Apostles, a small, secretive, self-congratulatory and self-appointed group of the brightest Cambridge students, is an indication of how deeply Freudian thinking had already penetrated elite and progressive British society. Taking for granted their familiarity with the new discipline, Ramsey delivered a classically Oedipal explanation of his philosophical concerns: "In my own case I think that my interest in philosophy and all kinds of criticisms, which is much greater than my interest in constructive thought, is derived from a fairly well repressed infantile rivalry with my father and my wish to kill him. This means that I can never get any great satisfaction from philosophising, never anything like the pleasure I should have got from killing my father, which my conscience or rather my love for him forbade me to do when I was small."[20]

The idea of the unconscious was welcomed in Cambridge. It was interpreted as sanctioning a liberalization of the existing and repressive sexual mores. It offered balm to sexual guilt. That was at an individual level. At the same time, if Freud was right that we were governed by drives of which we were largely unaware, then there were disturbing implications for institutions and governments—persuasion was unlikely to be achieved through the power of reason alone, and destructive urges might propel us into conflict.

So seriously did Ramsey take Freud and psychoanalysis that they became the cause of a heated argument with Wittgenstein that led to a fracturing of relations between the two men—who then had no contact for two years. This was the reason that Schlick had to serve as middleman between Ramsey and Wittgenstein when they had an exchange about "identity" in 1927. The row occurred during a visit Wittgenstein paid to England in 1925 when both he and Ramsey stayed at Keynes's house. It was a tense time, with Ramsey preparing for his wedding, and with the house guests stuck inside because of the rain. Ramsey felt psychoanalysis had cured him of some of his sexual anxieties and held Freud in the highest regard. Wittgenstein, on the other hand, though impressed by some of his work, thought Freud had moral deficiencies. What evidence he had to condemn Freud's character is unclear. There is no record of his ever having met Freud, but he had personal connections, particularly through Gretl, who took her son to be psychoanalyzed by Freud (on account of his stutter) and who was then analyzed herself in 1937. A year later, following the Anschluss, she helped Freud flee to England.[21]

Despite Wittgenstein's reservations about Freud, he still regarded himself as a fan and viewed his achievements as extraordinary. Even in disagreement, he always felt that Freud was worth reading, and he particularly admired his imagination. There is evidence that at one stage Wittgenstein even considered becoming a psychiatrist himself.

That Freud had an influence on Wittgenstein's own thinking is without doubt, though the degree of influence is a topic for scholarly debate. Still, he was preoccupied with various issues raised by psychoanalysis, and the topic surfaces throughout his writings. What do we mean by the subconscious? How should we regard psychoanalytic explanations of dreams and jokes? Were there parallels between the aims of psychoanalysis and the aims of philosophy?

The answer to the last question was yes, and Wittgenstein drew several parallels. Philosophical puzzles can cause anguish, a feeling that can be relieved once they are correctly diagnosed. As he put it: "The philosopher's treatment of a question is like the treatment of an illness."[22] As with psychoanalysis, the philosopher can help by bringing to consciousness that which lay in the subconscious. And the philosopher, like the psychoanalyst, could expect to have to overcome some resistance.

The deepest concern Wittgenstein had with psychoanalysis was what was to count as a correct psychoanalytic interpretation of a patient's condition, and whether psychoanalytic questions were open to definitive answer. One could imagine a psychoanalyst telling a patient that her dream represented repressed anger at her father; could the psychoanalyst be right, even if the patient was skeptical of the explanation? And what of a related concern: if the patient assents to an explanation, must we take this as the final word? Would patient assent to the psychoanalytic interpretation "solve" a dream? Wittgenstein suggests not: he worries that a patient may be charmed by a particular explanation or, in other words, taken in by it. Indeed, it was precisely because Freud's work was so alluring that Wittgenstein felt it posed a danger. At one point Wittgenstein raises the possibility that there might be two competing explanations that are nonetheless both valid.

Suppose Taylor and I are walking along the river and Taylor stretches out his hand and pushes me in the river. When I ask why he did this he says: "I was pointing out something to you," whereas the psychoanalyst says that Taylor subconsciously hated me. . . . When would we say that Taylor's explanation was correct? When he had never shown any unfriendly feelings, when a church-steeple and I were in his field of vision, and Taylor was known to be truthful. But, under the same circumstances, the psychoanalyst's explanation may also be correct.[23]

It was for these reasons that Wittgenstein had qualms about Freud's brash boasts. "Freud is constantly claiming to be scientific. But what he gives us is *speculation*—something prior even to the formation of a hypothesis."[24] The analyst, in giving us a story to account for our dream, is engaged in an act of persuasion. But science was not persuasion: if we are trying to show that the earth goes around the sun, rather than vice versa, it would seem odd to call this an act of *persuasion*.

The standing of psychoanalysis was a live issue for the Vienna Circle and remains contentious. But in the early part of the twentieth century it was not considered obvious that psychoanalysis had stronger claims to being scientific than, say, parapsychology. Just as there was no shortage of psychoanalysts in Vienna, so too spiritual mediums flourished. Neither Hahn nor Carnap was willing to dismiss parapsychology out of hand. Hahn himself attended many séances at which mediums would profess to be in contact with the spirits of the dead.

His presence at these events drew the contempt of his brother-in-law Otto Neurath. But Hahn always maintained, reasonably enough, that the claims of parapsychology had to be investigated. It was not inconceivable that some humans possessed powers that others did not. Perhaps parapsychology was not science: if so, this had to be demonstrated not merely asserted. Carnap took Hahn's side.

The problem of demarcating science from pseudo-science was one to which the Circle would return. There was a difference between bad science—for example, a laboratory experiment conducted chaotically and with poor measurements—and something being acceptable but not empirical, not science. Poetry belongs to the latter category, astrol-ogy to the former. And psychoanalysis? Wittgenstein seems to waver between these two options, though leaning toward the view that it isn't science at all. The problem of demarcating science from pseudo-science was one to which the Circle would return. And the status of psycho-analysis would be mentioned in the Circle's most important document.

9

Schlick's Unwelcome Gift

"Renunciation of metaphysics!" As if *that* were something new!

—LUDWIG WITTGENSTEIN

I have always been for the womans.

—OTTO NEURATH

SCHLICK WAS A HIGHLY sought-after academic, one whose presence would bring distinction to any philosophy department. In early 1929, he was offered an attractive, well-paying professorship at the University of Bonn. He had been in Vienna since 1922 and was now feeling it was time to move on. He was increasingly frustrated that the University of Vienna was so short of money, and that there were no jobs for his protégés Feigl and Waismann. The Bonn post was tempting, and he was close to accepting it. The university made no serious attempt to dissuade him with a financial counter-offer.

Fearful of losing him, supporters, and board members of the Ernst Mach Society (Verein Ernst Mach) wrote him a letter. The society had been formed in 1927 by the Austrian Freethinkers, a group of radical socialists opposed to the power of the church and its belief structure. The aim was to promote scientific education to ordinary Austrians through publications, talks, and tours. The link between the Vienna Circle and the Freethinkers was, as might be expected, the Circle's best-connected member, Otto Neurath. In November 1928, when the Ernst Mach Society had its public launch, the Vienna Circle effectively took it over: Neurath and Carnap became secretaries, Hahn vice president, and Moritz Schlick president.

Were he to leave, the letter to Schlick said, "the world conception propagated by the Ernst Mach Society . . . would suffer a profound and grievous loss indeed."[1] It was a flattering and direct appeal and it did the trick. The German professor turned Bonn down out of a sense of loyalty to his new home and a feeling that his project in Vienna was incomplete. He did, however, accept a temporary position at Stanford University on the West Coast of the United States. Stanford held many attractions. Schlick was an American-phile, but he had not been to the US since he married his American wife, Blanche, a quarter of a century earlier. The invitation was for the summer term, and Schlick was both a sun-worshipper and desperate to have a break from teaching and administration.

In the months that he was away, and without letting him know, members of the Circle began to draw up what they called a manifesto. It was to serve as a campaigning tool to spread their beliefs, and it was to be presented to Schlick upon his return, to honor him, and to thank him for remaining with them in Vienna.

The manifesto went through various iterations. Its chief authors were Neurath and Carnap and Feigl, with input from Hahn, and to a lesser extent from Waismann and others. It was probably Carnap's idea, and Carnap and Neurath signed off on the final version. Entitled *The Scientific Conception of the World: The Vienna Circle* (*Wissenschaftliche Weltauffassung: Der Wiener Kreis*), it states in the preface that it was only when Schlick was faced with the opportunity to leave that he and others realized that there was such a thing as the Vienna Circle conception of the world.

Once they saw that they had a new approach to philosophy, they wanted to show it off. Philipp Frank later wrote, "As every father likes to show photographs of his baby, we were looking for means of communication."[2] In this document, the name *Wiener Kreis* appeared for the first time. This was Neurath's label, designed to conjure up pleasing Viennese connotations, the Viennese waltz, the Vienna woods, "and other things on the pleasant side of life."[3]

The manifesto set out a long list of intellectual precursors to the movement. It identified Leibniz, Hume, Comte, Mach, and Boltzmann and, from more recent times, Einstein, Russell, and Wittgenstein as the "leading representatives of the scientific world-conception." As for the Circle itself, not a single member, the manifesto stated, was "a so-called 'pure' philosopher; all of them have done work in a special field of science."

What united them? What was distinctive about their beliefs? According to the manifesto, the Circle's basic orientation was science free from metaphysics. The aim was to provide a better understanding of the aims and methods and claims of science than currently existed. "The scientific world-conception knows *no* unsolvable riddle." Their targets were the "pseudo-problems": a genuine problem was empirical, or it was nothing. The claims of psychoanalysis were among those singled out. "If someone asserts . . . the primary basis of the world is the unconscious . . . we do not say to him: 'what you say is false'; but we ask him: 'what do you mean by these statements?'" The Circle combined its empiricism and positivism on the one hand with logical analysis on the other. Ordinary language can often mislead us. The role of philosophy was to clarify problems with the use of the new tools of logical analysis. In doing so, it could help secure the foundations of physics, geometry, biology, and the social sciences.

It is worth highlighting two aspects of the manifesto in particular. The first was its tone. It was not a modest affair. The Circle stood for modernity against the forces of tradition, and its task was "removing the metaphysical and theological debris of millennia"—not errors committed by a few contemporaries but those that had bedeviled philosophy from its inception.

The second was its activism. The manifesto claims a link between the Circle and attempts to bring about new economic and social relations and educational reform. These endeavors, the manifesto claimed, were "regarded with sympathy by the members of the Circle." A link was drawn between the philosophy of the Circle and the use of rational planning to bring about socialism. As Philipp Frank would put it, "The whole original Viennese group was convinced that the elimination of metaphysics not only was a question of a better logic but was of great relevance for the social and cultural life."[4]

It was in this spirit—of wanting to reorganize social life in a rational way—that the manifesto concluded with its most memorable phrase, "The scientific world conception serves life, and life receives it." There followed a list of Vienna Circle members in alphabetical order: Gustav Bergmann, Rudolf Carnap, Herbert Feigl, Philipp Frank, Kurt Gödel, Hans Hahn, Viktor Kraft, Karl Menger, Marcel Natkin, Otto Neurath, Olga Hahn-Neurath, Theodor Radakovic,[5] Moritz Schlick, Friedrich Waismann. A separate list, of those "sympathetic to the Vienna Circle," includes the names of Frank Ramsey, Hans Reichenbach, Kurt Reidemeister, and Edgar Zilsel.

The Vienna Circle had now entered the public domain and was now no longer just a private academic seminar. That would make it more influential, but also more threatening to the state, and so, more vulnerable. As Carnap finished typing the final version of the manuscript in July 1929, a thunderstorm broke out.

———

Many of us will have had the awkward experience of receiving an unwanted gift from a friend or family member: a thoughtless present that we have no interest in receiving. Often this will be the result of a failure of imagination, perhaps the giver presuming that what he or she enjoys is enjoyable for everyone.

The manifesto was such a gift. The stridency and confidence of the manifesto was in tune with the times; the influence of Karl Kraus is immediately apparent. Still, a little reflection should have given the authors pause. It was not the approach of the mild-mannered man it was written to honor and to whom it was dedicated. Schlick had returned from the US and was holidaying in Italy when he received his bound copy, sent through the post by Carnap. Though touched by the gesture, he felt uneasy. Although he had by now presided over the Circle for five years—and in a 1923 letter to Bertrand Russell he described the Circle as a working union of philosophers—he had become perturbed by the idea of philosophy as team sport. He viewed the Circle as a set of like-minded philosophers meeting to thrash out problems but without losing their individuality: their group was not a gang or squad. He disliked conflict. He also opposed agitation: he thought it was enough to pursue the truth and was optimistic that the truth would win out. He was the Circle's most apolitical member, whilst the manifesto was a blatantly political document, penned by three highly politicized individuals. Cynics might assume that here was an attempt to hijack the Circle, to integrate it into the socialist movement. But it is more likely to have been the product of naïveté and, on Neurath's part at least, irrepressible exuberance.

Until the publication of the manifesto, those who attended Circle discussions had no need to see themselves as belonging to a movement. But from that moment, fissures within the Circle began to deepen. With hindsight, we should see the manifesto as marking less the Circle's public establishment and more the beginning of its end. Schlick was not alone in finding the content and/or the tone irksome. There had been no time to ask for permission from each of those whose names were listed. Objectors included Menger (who requested that he now be listed only as an associate, not a member of the Circle), Viktor Kraft, and Kurt Gödel—the latter began to show up to meetings less frequently. No one objected to the manifesto more than Wittgenstein. It was the lack of humility that most vexed him, the bellicose tenor. That was a matter of style. But he also opposed the substance. Waismann had been in contact with Wittgenstein about the manifesto, and Wittgenstein wrote back to Waismann. "Just because Schlick is no ordinary man, people owe it to him to take care not to let their 'good intentions' make him and the Vienna school which he leads ridiculous by boastfulness. When I say 'boastfulness' I mean any kind of self-satisfied posturing. 'Renunciation of metaphysics!' As if *that* were something new! What the Vienna school has achieved, it ought to *show* not *say*."[6]

Wittgenstein was not clubbable, nor was he a committee man. "The philosopher is not a citizen of any community of ideas. That is what makes him a philosopher."[7] The Cambridge Apostles had several times tried to co-opt Wittgenstein into their secret society. This had not gone well. His objections were many, including loathing the display of cleverness as an end in itself. And although Wittgenstein's own writings

brooked no uncertainty, he abhorred any self-satisfaction or overconfi-
dence in the writings of others. As for the project to unify the sciences,
including the social sciences, this was not one for which he felt any
sympathy.

———

The Circle now set about pushing its agenda. It did so through various
mechanisms. One was the Ernst Mach Society. The majority of talks,
including from Carnap and Neurath, were delivered by philosophers
from the Circle. Not all. Philipp Frank's brother, Josef, the modernist
architect, spoke about architecture and Marxism, whilst the Social
Democrat politician Otto Bauer also gave a talk. One of the Society's
functions was to give thoughtful members from the political Left a plat-
form from which to air their ideas and receive public feedback. An
added bonus for nonacademics was that addressing the society served
to burnish their intellectual credentials.

Beyond the Ernst Mach Society, there was the logical empiricists'
journal. In 1930, Hans Reichenbach (from the Berlin Circle) and Carnap
took over *Annalen der Philosophie* (*Annals of Philosophy*). They renamed
it *Erkenntnis* (*Knowledge*) and would act as its editors for almost a decade. The opening edition had an article by Schlick entitled "Die Wende
der Philosophie" ("The Turning Point in Philosophy"). It set out what
he thought the role of philosophy should be: although science provides
solutions to real problems, "philosophy is the activity by means of which
the meaning of statements is clarified and defined."[8] Schlick was convinced that they were living "in the middle of an altogether final turn in
philosophy."[9] In a later article, Schlick distinguished the logical empiricists from the metaphysicians. He argued that empiricists do not tell
metaphysicians that they are wrong but rather that they assert nothing
of any meaning. That is, they do not contradict the metaphysicians;
rather, they simply fail to understand them. And of course the reason that
they fail to understand them is that there is nothing to be understood.

Over several years, *Erkenntnis* would feature many important articles
and debates, covering all the areas of interest to the Circle. The

protocol-sentence debate (more on this later) played itself out on the pages of *Erkenntnis*. The verification principle (again, of which more later) was first aired in print in *Erkenntnis*, in an article by Waismann. The journal published articles from all the main members of the Circle and provided a forum in which aspiring philosophers could begin to establish their names. An article from Rose Rand drew on her doctoral work about a Polish logician, Tadeusz Kotarbiński. *Erkenntnis* was also the first journal in which Karl Popper published. The confident tone of the Circle is captured in an article by Carnap that appeared in the journal in 1931: "Can it be that so many men, of various times and nations, outstanding minds among them, have devoted so much effort, and indeed fervor, to metaphysics, when this consists in nothing more than words strung together without sense?"[10] Yes, said Carnap, it could be.

Then there was a series of books, under the title *Schriften zur wissenschaftlichen Weltauffassung* (*Writings on the Scientific World-Conception*), and a series of international conferences. The first took place in Prague in September 1929 with a crowd-pulling title, the First Conference for the Epistemology of the Exact Sciences. This was funded in part by the government of the Czechoslovak Republic, whose president, Tomáš Masaryk, was himself a philosopher, and it was jointly organized by the Ernst Mach Society and the Society for Empirical Philosophy in Berlin, with some of the administrative burden falling on Philipp Frank, long based in Prague. Five thousand copies of the manifesto had been printed, and liberally handed out to attendees. Several core Circle members, including Carnap, Frank, Hahn, and Neurath, gave talks. Meeting alongside this conference was another for mathematicians and physicists, who sat in on sessions but were wary of the philosophers and shocked by Frank's contention that modern science and traditional philosophy were incompatible. Frank's wife was in the audience for his address: "It was uncanny to listen. It seemed to me as if the words fell in the audience like drops into a well so deep that you cannot hear the drops striking bottom. Everything seemed to vanish without leaving a trace."[11]

Over the next few years, until the outbreak of World War II, there would be a number of such gatherings—in Königsberg; Prague (again);

Paris; Copenhagen; Cambridge, UK; and Cambridge, US. The conferences performed many functions, but they were explicitly part of an
outreach program, bringing the Circle's approach to the wider world.

Conferences were run traditionally. That is, there were delegates and
discussions and papers—one or two of which were of historic importance. In the follow-up conference to Prague, in Königsberg, 5–7 September 1930, focusing on the foundations of mathematics, both Carnap
and Waismann were speakers, the latter giving an exposition of Wittgenstein in "The Nature of Mathematics: Wittgenstein's Standpoint." In
ordinary circumstances this might have been expected to be *the* talking
point of the conference. There were rumors that the great man's ideas
were evolving and here was a chance to hear the latest news from his
messenger on earth. But Königsberg was also where a short but seminal
paper was delivered by Kurt Gödel.

Circle members had had some forewarning. Carnap and Gödel
would meet in a coffeehouse every few days. They were together in
Vienna in the Café Reichsrat from 6:00 p.m. to 8:30 p.m. on Tuesday
26 August 1930. Feigl and Waismann were there too. Carnap's diary
entry that day is a model of understatement. Gödel had shown him
some "problems with the proof of consistency."[12] It was a result that is
now widely regarded as being the most important in twentieth-century
logic. In essence, Gödel was showing that whatever axioms were posited
as the foundation blocks of mathematics, there would inevitably be
some truths within mathematics that could not be proved.

A mere twenty-four years old, Gödel was a diffident young man and
it was only in the final session of the conference, on 7 September, as part
of a roundtable on the foundations of mathematics, that he publicly
revealed his incompleteness finding. There was no fanfare, and it was
understandable that most delegates were nonplussed. Gödel would expand his claims in *Erkenntnis*, but it is said that only one man in the
Königsberg audience that day immediately grasped the nature of his
accomplishment—John von Neumann, an extraordinary Hungarian-
born polymath. He was a pioneer in (among other topics) set theory,
quantum theory, game theory, and computational studies. Later he
would help in the development of the atomic bomb. He was only two

years Gödel's senior, but had already published over thirty weighty papers. He now buttonholed Gödel, and over the next few weeks the two men corresponded. In that time, the magnitude of what Gödel had proved had become evident. It is now regarded as one of the most significant—if not *the* most significant—breakthroughs in logic.

————

Present too at Königsberg were Professor Stanislaus Jolles and his wife, Adele. They were the couple with whom Wittgenstein had stayed during his spell in Berlin, 1906–08. Their relationship with their lodger had been affectionate; Stanislaus felt protective and paternal toward "Little Wittgenstein," as they called him. But, as so often with Wittgenstein, there had been a rupture, and, typically again, it seems to have arisen from Wittgenstein's perception that his hosts had fallen short of his exacting standards: he had adjudged some aspect of their behavior inauthentic, which, for Wittgenstein, was a capital offense.

The Jolleses had heard a little about Wittgenstein since then, but by 1930 had lost touch. After attending the conference, Adele was moved to write to the man she had known when he was a teenager. "We went again, for the first time in many years, to a scientific congress, in Königsberg, and there I met a number of Viennese from the learned fraternity, and found out in this way that our former friend—'our ex-friend' would be a ruder but more accurate expression—'little Wittgenstein' had after all turned into something more than a village schoolmaster and was very highly thought of there. Now, whether or not this is a matter of indifference to you or even unwelcome, I *have* to tell you how exceptionally, really exceptionally, pleased I was."[13]

Wittgenstein posted a long letter in reply. It mirrored other letters he would write over his lifetime in its confessional tone, in owning up to personality failings and asking for forgiveness. To Adele he said that he and the Jolleses lacked a mutual understanding, yet he now recognized that this was trivial compared to the virtues of gratitude and loyalty. He confirmed, however, her suspicion that the good opinion of professors of philosophy and mathematics was a matter of indifference to him.

In 1934, the conference returned to Prague, but this time plans were afoot to change the title. At a side meeting in Prague, attended by Frank, Carnap, and Neurath, a decision was taken to launch a series of gatherings under the rubric of the Unity of Science movement, aiming to bring together scientists of both the natural and the human world—physicists, chemists, biologists, and social scientists. The first full international Unity of Science conference took place in Paris at the Sorbonne in 1935, backed by grants from the French government and some French foundations. It was a star-studded event, with 170 participants and an opening address delivered by Bertrand Russell. He later called it a remarkable and encouraging occasion:

> My first impression, on seeing the opening session, was one of surprise; surprise that there should be in the world so many men who think that opinions should be based on evidence. My second impression, on hearing the papers and discussions, was one of further surprise, to find that the opinions advocated actually conformed to the rule: I did not discover any of the signs of unfounded and merely passionate belief which, hitherto, has been as common among philosophers as among men.[14]

Among the figures from the Vienna Circle were Schlick, Carnap, Frank, and Neurath. Reichenbach came from Germany, Charles Morris and Ernest Nagel arrived from the US (Chicago and New York, respectively), while the neo-Marxist group of thinkers who have become known as the Frankfurt School sent along the cultural theorist Walter Benjamin. In all, twenty countries were represented, and the sessions were the meat and drink of logical empiricism; language and pseudo-problems, induction and probability, the philosophy of mathematics. A. J. Ayer gave a paper on the Analytic Movement. But the revelation was Alfred Tarski from Poland. Both Carnap and Popper had discussed Tarski's work on truth, and Carnap persuaded Tarski to present it in Paris. The paper caused so much buzz that an additional session was hastily arranged to discuss it further.

Tarski argued that the notion of truth as applied to ordinary languages inevitably entangles us with the Liar Paradox and sentences such as *This sentence is false*. But he argued that we *can* give a consistent account of the notion of truth as applied to sentences in restricted, ambiguity-free, idealized languages modelled on those used by mathematicians. We can theorize about such a formalized language L "from the outside," in a so-called metalanguage that allows us to talk about being a true sentence of L. How do we do this? For some limited but still interestingly rich languages L, Tarski shows how to construct in our metalanguage a theory that entails correct so-called biconditionals of the form *S is true (in L) if and only if p*, where S is replaced by a sentence of L, and P is replaced by a sentence that means the same as S (i.e., the same empirical content). Arguably, Tarski's technical theory then defines "true (in L)," while bypassing debates about, for example, the relationship between propositions and worldly "facts." Success for Tarski is demonstrating how truth can be a useful and meaningful concept, without entangling us in contentious metaphysics. However, his theory was contentious even at the time—and remains a subject of debate; some believe that he does not really sidestep metaphysical debates about truth, but just smuggles them in a word/world relation through the back door.

Four years later Tarski was at the Unity of Science conference in Harvard. His decision to attend probably saved his life—for he was not in Poland when war broke out. Indeed, among the benefits of such conferences were the friendships and connections they fostered across nations. These were to prove invaluable, and not just for Tarski. Charles Morris, who would be instrumental in importing Vienna Circle ideas into the US, urged the German-speaking philosophers to learn and then write articles in English as a means of getting positions at US universities: he helped with translators and publishers, and personally wrote to friends and colleagues across the US to identify jobs for the empiricists. In Paris, Ayer and Popper met for the first time. Susan Stebbing, who would later be of life-saving assistance to several members of the Circle, came from London. Ayer witnessed a conversation between her and the Circle's most voluble member. "One of my most pleasant memories of this congress is that of watching Otto Neurath being gallant to Miss Stebbing, speaking to her in English and saying, 'I have always been for the womans.' It was the only occasion on which I saw her at a loss."[15]

Beyond the conferences, there was another project afoot, spear-headed again by Neurath, who had always believed in the unity of science. That is, he saw the existing division of science, into biology, chemistry, physics and so on, as purely practical. Fundamentally these various branches were engaged in the same enterprise—understanding the physical world. That was true too of the social sciences; humans were as much part of the physical world as anything else. Neurath was not alone. A similar thesis is manifest in a book Felix Kaufmann published in 1936 on the methods of the social sciences. The gap between the natural and social sciences was exaggerated, he argued. What they had in common—such as the central place of prediction—was more important than what divided them. At Paris there was a vote to approve an ambitious series, an International Encyclopedia of Unified Science. The allusion to the French *Encyclopédie*—the colossal Enlightenment project in the second half of the eighteenth century, which had aimed to document all of the world's knowledge—needed no spelling out. Never one to aim low, Neurath planned 200 volumes as well as 10 supplemental volumes of a "Visual Thesaurus." The first title, *Foundations of the Unity of Science*, would appear in 1938 and include contributions from Bohr, Carnap, Morris, and Russell as well as Neurath himself. John Dewey, the American philosopher and educational reformer, was persuaded to participate by Neurath despite Dewey's initial skepticism about logical empiricism and his rejection of the idea that there existed atomic facts or atomic propositions. (Neurath visited Dewey in his home and in faltering English earnestly declared "I *swear* we don't believe in atomic propositions.")[16] Carnap and Morris became Neurath's coeditors, with the University of Chicago as publisher. His rousing address at the Paris conference ended with the words, *"Vivent les nouveaux encyclopédistes."*

10

Strangers from Abroad

What would Wittgenstein say here?

—MORITZ SCHLICK

IN THE 1929 Christmas holiday, just a few months after the publication of the Circle manifesto, Wittgenstein was back home in Vienna. He met Schlick and Waismann on 22 December, and they discussed the meaning of the quantifier *all*.

> I shall first speak of the ordinary "all," e.g. "All men in this room are wearing trousers." How do I know this? The sentence means "Professor Schlick is wearing trousers, Waismann is wearing trousers, Wittgenstein is wearing trousers, and no one else is present." Every complete enumeration must end with the words "and nothing else." What does this mean? There is a conception here according to which one says: "Mr. Carnap is not in this room, Mr. . . . etc."[1]

Wittgenstein's animosity toward Dr. (not Mr.) Carnap meant he had already been excluded from the room. Wittgenstein met Schlick and Waismann at least six times over that Christmas period. There were more meetings in 1930 and then again in 1931. Sometimes these would occur in Schlick's house; other times they would take advantage of the extensive Wittgenstein family properties and use the house in Neuwaldegg or the one in Argentinierstrasse, which was conveniently near Schlick's apartment. Occasionally Waismann and Wittgenstein would meet alone, but Schlick was nearly always present.

Waismann's principal function was prompt and note keeper. One philosopher later described his relationship to Wittgenstein as one of "glove puppet to controlling hand."[2] A plan had emerged for Waismann to summarize the ideas from the *Tractatus* in book form—for a series entitled Writings on the Scientific World Conception (Schriften zur wissenschaftlichen Weltauffassung)—and in a way that made them accessible. Meetings soon began to take on a more formal atmosphere. When Wittgenstein was in Vienna, Waismann would drop his other commitments, including family responsibilities, to spend as much time with him as possible. The (never-published) book was to be called *Logik, Sprache, Philosophie* (*Logic, Language, Philosophy*) and it became sufficiently far advanced to be advertised in the first volume of *Erkenntnis* in 1930. Wittgenstein was willing, even eager, to collaborate. Waismann knew shorthand, and the notes of his conversations with Wittgenstein were collected in school exercise books.

There were a few problems. One was the speed with which Wittgenstein's ideas were evolving, so much so that it was almost impossible to record a fixed position. Examples of thinkers with the courage and open-mindedness to repudiate their earlier academic contributions are rare, especially when, as in Wittgenstein's case, the original work has attained a hallowed status. But that is, in effect, what Wittgenstein did. His philosophy was developing into an entirely different way of understanding the relationship between language and the world. As a result, an expository book on the *Tractatus* seemed inappropriate. Schlick was at Stanford during the 1931–32 winter, so Waismann and Wittgenstein met alone—eighteen times. Wittgenstein sent Schlick a letter expressing concern that "a lot of things will be presented quite differently from the way I think right."[3]

Eventually the "right way" would find expression in Wittgenstein's posthumously published *Philosophical Investigations* (1953). His picture account of language from the *Tractatus* was shelved. Instead of asking what a sentence pictures, we should focus on its use.[4] Words, in particular, can have a variety of uses. The reason why we so often land ourselves in philosophical muddle is that we do not pay close enough attention to normal usage. We try to deploy language in alien ways. We try, as it were, to take language on holiday, when we would do better to leave it at home. We ask strange questions, such as *Can I know I am in pain?*, without recognizing that our own sensations are not something we can "know," since knowledge presupposes the possibility of doubt. This new approach to language sees it as embedded in a way of life—philosophical problems take on an anthropological flavor. Language cannot be studied in isolation. We must observe the rules it follows in practice.

Among Wittgenstein scholars, the extent to which Wittgenstein's latter philosophy is foreshadowed in the *Tractatus* remains a topic of contention. But one way of summarizing Wittgenstein's philosophical evolution is this. In the *Tractatus* he had a monolithic conception of language and a monolithic conception of the correct philosophical method. That is, there was a single way of dissolving philosophical pseudo-problems. But by the end of his life he had embraced a pluralistic conception of language and was open to employing a range of philosophical methods to dissolve pseudo-problems. From the perspective of later Wittgenstein, the author of the *Tractatus* was himself trapped in a kind of philosophical illusion.[5]

An anecdote Wittgenstein himself repeated illuminates why and how he came to rethink philosophy. He was in Cambridge talking to his friend Pierro Sraffa, an Italian Marxist economist. Wittgenstein was explaining that a proposition (e.g., *the cat is on the mat*), and what the proposition was about (the cat being on the mat), must have the same logical structure. Sraffa flicked his chin with the back of his fingers, so they made an arc, an Italian gesture of contempt. "What is the logical form of that?" he asked. What lesson did Wittgenstein take from this question? That understanding a gesture requires understanding not its logical form (whatever that could possibly mean) but its use, when it is deployed, what it is designed to convey. Sraffa's gesture led Wittgenstein to acknowledge that language could be used in multiple ways.

With Wittgenstein's growing doubts about his earlier views on language and logic, a new plan for the Waismann book was concocted around 1932. It would be coauthored and would explain Wittgenstein's recent thinking. But the second problem was Wittgenstein's jealousy; his guarded ownership of his own ideas. This needs accurate characterization. It was not that he showed any desire for fame or fortune (which in any case he had once possessed before intentionally shedding it); he did not seem to have the usual author's thirst for a wide readership. However, if his ideas were to be disseminated, then it was imperative that they not be misinterpreted. This became a fixation for Wittgenstein. His other obsession was that they not be appropriated and presented by someone else as *their* thoughts.

Poor Waismann was in an impossible position: having to put tumbling ideas into stationary form. An indication of Wittgenstein's low regard for Waismann is given in a letter he wrote to a friend in April 1932. He talks of how hard he, Wittgenstein, is working and, without bothering to identify Waismann, describes taking "some stuff to a man who is writing a book on philosophy."[6] At other times, in other letters, he spells Waismann's name incorrectly. In 1937, a year after Waismann published *Einführung in das mathematische Denken*, a book about mathematics from a Wittgensteinian perspective, Wittgenstein wrote to a friend from Norway, "I haven't read Waissman's [*sic*] book and I'm not going to."[7] Waismann was a highly original thinker but by nature more sheep than shepherd; still, there was something shocking about the degree to which he subordinated his interests to those of Wittgenstein, and the ingratitude with which his efforts were rewarded.

Others were also at the receiving end of Wittgenstein's wrath. In May 1932, Wittgenstein read a paper of Carnap's, "Physicalist Language as the Universal Language of Science," which had appeared in *Erkenntnis*. It bore, he was convinced, an uncanny resemblance to his own ideas. He fired off a letter to Schlick complaining that he would "soon be in a situation where my own work shall be considered merely as a reheated version (*zweiter Aufguss*) or plagiarism of Carnap's."[8]

There was an irony here, given Wittgenstein's explanation in the preface to the *Tractatus* for not identifying his sources; "[I]t is indifferent to me whether what I have thought has already been thought by another."[9] But he was not shy about chastising others. Writing to Schlick on 6 May 1932, he drew one of his striking metaphors: "If I have an apple tree in my garden, then it delights me and serves the purpose of the tree if my friends (e.g. you and Waismann) make use of the apples; I will not chase away thieves . . . but I am entitled to resent that they are posing as my friends or alleging that the tree should belong to them jointly."[10]

In theory the book project with Waismann was still ongoing. By the early 1930s Wittgenstein was often meeting Waismann and Schlick separately. In the summer of 1933 he spent a holiday with Schlick in Italy. A year later, in 1934, he saw the opening of Waismann's draft book, and was horrified. Waismann was already finding the collaboration a frustrating process. As he put it to Schlick, "Wittgenstein has the marvellous gift of always seeing everything as if for the first time. But I think it's obvious how difficult any collaboration is, since he always follows the inspiration of the moment and demolishes what he has previously planned."[11]

The book meetings came to an end. It meant, at least, that Waismann was free to publish a book in the form he wished, without the fear that any tyrant would wield a veto.

———

By this stage a new set of younger members had joined Circle discussions. The dates in which they first joined are not documented, but they included Gustav Bergmann, Walter Hollitscher, Marcel Natkin (who immigrated to Paris in 1929), Heinrich Neider, Rose Rand, Josef Schächter, and Olga Taussky. The preoccupation with language, meaning, and clarity had truly taken hold. A dryly amusing account of how discussion proceeded was later given by Arne Naess. "A participant put forth an opinion, using a sentence T. A second participant, probably thinking the opinion is not tenable, interferes, saying '*Würden Sie die Formulierung U akzeptieren?*' ('Would you accept the formulation U?') A special opening gambit was invented by the young Walter Hollitscher, 'That is perhaps not a happy formulation.'"[12] Core to their project was to establish what was to count as *sinnlos* (meaningless). Menger became irked by Waismann, who had the habit "of designating as meaningless everything that went beyond whatever it was that he was asserting."[13]

Between November 1932 and March 1933, Rose Rand ran what we would now call a color-coded spreadsheet in which she noted down which of six Circle members—Schlick, Waismann, Carnap, Neurath, Hahn, Kaufmann—either agreed with particular propositions (blue), disagreed (red), or found meaningless (green). Neurath and green was a common combination.

Nonetheless, Wittgenstein continued to hold a mythical status within the Circle. Of course, the Circle members had been discussing Wittgenstein for years, so this fact appeared far more startling to newcomers, particularly foreigners, than to the old guard. After the Circle had gone so provocatively public with its manifesto, philosophers outside Austria began to take note. The Circle had received regular visitors from Berlin (for example, Carl Hempel) and Prague (Philipp Frank). Now some of the most brilliant young philosophers from further afield became curious enough to travel to Vienna to witness this revolutionary movement for themselves. They would return whence they came, to pollinate their home culture with positivist ideas.

From England arrived a young, amusing, sharp-witted, mildly autistic Oxford graduate, A. J. Ayer. In Oxford Ayer had studied under Gilbert Ryle, a young don who would later become best known for his book *The Concept of Mind*, an attack on the idea (emanating from Descartes) that the mind and body are two separate entities and that mental phenomena are nonphysical. Ryle ridiculed this notion, coining the phrase "the ghost in the machine" to mock the claim that something nonphysical occupied and interacted with something physical.

Ayer had had no dealings with the Circle members, and just one previous encounter with Wittgenstein. As Ryle's protégé, he had been taken by his mentor to Trinity College Cambridge to visit Wittgenstein in his rooms in Whewell's Court. It was late 1932. They sat in the plain deck chairs that Wittgenstein supplied for guests and those attending his seminars. The meeting went well, based on a misunderstanding. Wittgenstein asked Ayer what he was reading, and the young Englishman replied *La vida es sueño* (*Life Is a Dream*), by seventeenth-century Spanish playwright Pedro Calderón de la Barca, before adding that he had found it hard to understand. Wittgenstein admired this self-effacement. He always thought it right that one had to struggle to grasp the profundities of great art; but Ayer had simply meant that his Spanish was too rudimentary to allow for easy comprehension.

Before beginning a lectureship in Oxford, Ayer had planned to spend a few months in Cambridge to study under Wittgenstein. It was Ryle who persuaded the twenty-two-year-old Ayer to travel to Austria instead. He, Ryle, had run across Schlick at a philosophy conference in Oxford in 1930 and been much impressed by him. Going to Vienna would be good for Ayer, Ryle thought, and if Ayer brought back a report of developments there, it would benefit philosophy too. Vienna, he suspected, was where the philosophical action was. He wrote Schlick a letter praising Ayer's intellectual capabilities for Ayer to deliver personally.

Ayer had recently married Renée Lees (in a religious Catholic ceremony the militantly atheistic Ayer would regret agreeing to for the rest of his life). As soon as they had settled into their lodgings in the Fourth District, he paid Schlick a visit at his home in Prinz Eugen Strasse. He recorded his impressions. "He has an American wife of a homely type who looked like a German *Hausfrau*, whereas he has the suave appearance and manner that I had come through my film-going to associate with an American senator."[14] On receipt of the letter from Ryle, Schlick not only arranged for Ayer to be allowed to attend lectures at the university, he also invited him to sit in on Circle gatherings. This he did, from December 1932 to April 1933. He later recalled his impressions of other Circle members. Neurath was charming and funny, "a large man, running to fat in middle-age, with a white puffy skin, reminding me of a marshmallow."[15] Gödel was "dark and small and silent and self-contained."[16]

Lack of confidence was not one of Ayer's shortcomings, but because he was operating in a second language and at a high level of abstraction, his contributions to Circle discussions were minimal. What he did (and what he always excelled at) was soak up ideas. He was predisposed to embrace logical empiricism: his great philosophical hero was the Scottish archempiricist David Hume. For the Circle, he would prove a vital messenger, though not one they entirely appreciated. Many people in the Anglo-American world would first become acquainted with the Circle through Ayer, but his polemical style did scant justice to the nuances and internal disagreements within Vienna.

Ayer himself had a marvelous time there. He felt liberated and, although it was no longer the Viennese fashion, grew a beard, which he knew he would have to shave before returning to Christ Church Oxford, since the senior common room was a puritanical place and "will certainly not tolerate it."[17] He gave a vivid description of the city. He loved:

> the crowded tramways; the cafes where you could sit indoors for hours over a single cup of coffee reading the newspapers which they provided; the cellars where for very little money you could drink litres of white wine of the newest vintage; the unpretentious night clubs; the popular dance-halls, where you could ask strangers for a dance. It was at one of these dances that I first realized with a shock of excitement that I might be attractive to other girls besides Renée, and attracted by them. I danced with a girl only once and never saw her again, but the memory stayed with me. She may, indeed, easily have had another motive; as a foreigner I might be supposed to be comparatively rich. In fact, we had little money to spare. On the days when I went to the University, I used to lunch alone at a near-by restaurant, and I seldom could afford anything but boiled beef and noodles, for which I had little liking then and none at all since.[18]

———

A. J. Ayer overlapped for five weeks in Vienna with another out-of-towner who initialized his name. W.V.O. Quine had recently earned a Harvard doctorate on some aspects of *Principia Mathematica*. Ayer was a decent linguist, who within several months had achieved a respectable degree of proficiency in German. But Quine was much quicker still. He picked up languages, including German, with ease, so much so that he could understand Schlick's lectures and by January 1933 was able to address the Circle in German and then participate fully in a ninety-minute discussion. At that meeting he first saw Ayer.

Born in 1908, Quine was two years Ayer's senior. He had been raised in Akron, a medium-size town in Ohio, and came across Bertrand Russell's writings while at Oberlin College. One of the appeals of Harvard, where he decided to pursue his graduate studies in 1930, was that Russell's coauthor of *Principia Mathematica*, Alfred North Whitehead, had been teaching there since 1924. Within two years Quine had acquired a PhD, after which he won a travel fellowship for the academic year 1932–33. In 1930 he had befriended Herbert Feigl, who was on a scholarship at Harvard, and it was Feigl who urged Quine to go to Vienna.

Quine would later move on to Prague, where, as we shall see, Carnap had transferred. Carnap would become his mentor: Quine said he quickly discovered "what it was like to be intellectually fired by a living teacher rather than by a dead book."[19] In Vienna Quine was not particularly happy. His lodgings were basic, though they included the cost of a bath (which elsewhere was extra). He was surprised that elevators in apartments cost money. Like Ayer, Quine was in town with his wife (Naomi), and the Quines and Ayers often socialized together.

Ayer and Quine were just two of a number of foreign visitors. They arrived from Italy and Argentina and one philosopher, Tscha Hung, from China. Ernest Nagel also came from America. There were several philosophers from Berlin, including, of course, Hempel. Tarski from Warsaw gave some lectures in Vienna in February 1930 and became a regular visitor, and there were philosophers from Scandinavia too, including Arne Naess.

Ayer, Quine, and Naess were all struck by the veneration for Wittgenstein within the Circle. Ayer wrote that "Wittgenstein is a deity to them all, not mainly on the strength of the *Tractatus* which they consider a slightly metaphysical work ('metaphysical' is the ultimate term of abuse) but on the ground of his later views which I myself (again the insufficiency of my German) have not been able to learn from them fully."[20] Bertrand Russell, according to Ayer, was now downgraded by the Circle to being merely "a forerunner of the Christ (Wittgenstein)."[21] In one of Quine's letters home, the American said he had written to Wittgenstein. His use of language is instructive: "I want an audience with the prophet."[22] This may have been tongue-in-cheek; still, nobody, not even Quine, would have described Carnap, for example, as a prophet. Supporters of Carnap and critics of Wittgenstein might say that that was because Wittgenstein's style lent itself to multiple interpretations. Arne

Naess, who attended the Circle seminars in 1934, recalled that Schlick did not talk much but "When a discussion led us into an impasse he might ask, 'What would Wittgenstein say here?'. When somebody offered a quotation from Wittgenstein's writings or from his appearance in seminars or private conversations, it was clear that only very, very clever interpretations could be accepted. Like interpreting Ibsen in Norway."[23]

Since members of the Circle only had access to Wittgenstein's latest thinking through Waismann and Schlick, it was to be expected that they—Waismann in particular—became *the* acknowledged authorities on Wittgenstein's philosophical positions, "the (correct) Wittgensteinian view."[24] They would report on their meetings as though delivering messages from the Oracle of Delphi. Of course, Waismann was acutely sensitive to Wittgenstein's fear of misrepresentation. At meetings he would caution his remarks with: "I shall relate to you the latest developments in Wittgenstein's thinking but Wittgenstein rejects all responsibility for my formulations. Please note that."[25]

His interpretations of Wittgenstein were picked up by others and quoted in papers and at conferences. In this way, as in Chinese whispers, Wittgenstein's influence grew. But since the mysterious philosopher himself was rarely seen, and certainly not at philosophical conferences, questions began to be raised—only half in jest—about whether he really existed.

It was Waismann who first introduced Wittgenstein's thoughts on what became a key tenet of the Circle—verificationism.

———

Wittgenstein had explained his ideas on verification to Waismann and Schlick in late 1929 and early 1930, and Waismann then made them public in an article he wrote for the first volume of *Erkenntnis*. Verificationism offered a criterion for what was meaningful. Its proponents were motivated by the desire to make all domains of inquiry scientific, and so banish metaphysics from the domain of "meaning." It claimed that unless something was open to being verified it was meaningless.

This needs some unpacking, not least because in the early 1930s there was some confusion about how the verification principle was to be understood. Slowly it became clear that there was a distinction between a Carnap version of verificationism (adopted by Neurath, Frank, and Hahn) and a Wittgenstein version (adopted by Schlick and Waismann). Putting to one side analytic statements that are true by definition (*All bungalows have a single floor*), the Carnap version stated that whether a synthetic sentence—e.g., *God is all-powerful*—was "empirically meaningful" or "cognitively empty"[26] depends on whether there were criteria for verifying it. The Wittgenstein version was that the meaning *consisted* in the conditions of its truth. What is the meaning of *The moon is made of raspberry yogurt* or *Water boils at 100 degrees centigrade*? According to Wittgenstein, these claims are to be *understood* in terms of what would have to be the case in the world were they true.

In the end the Carnapian version won out.

It is difficult to exaggerate how radical a position verificationism was. *The moon is made of raspberry yogurt* is a testable statement. It is meaningful, but false. There are ways of checking its veracity. But fairly standard statements about God—such as *God is everywhere, God is all-powerful*—fail at least one rigid interpretation of the verificationist test. They have the surface appearance of sense but, according to the verification criterion of meaning, they are in fact nonsense. Not nonsense like a string of random squiggles or sounds such as *xysvotp og dcplqz*. But a type of nonsense nonetheless.

This is not to preclude the possibility that they may have cultural meaning—clearly certain nonverifiable phrases are intoned all the time in churches and mosques and synagogues and temples. But they have no cognitive meaning, they have no truth value.

Much the same can be said of aesthetic and moral statements. Moral claims such as *Killing innocent people is wrong* do not lend themselves to being tested. Nor do aesthetic judgments. Art connoisseurs might have a heated dispute over the claim *Gustav Klimt was a finer artist than Egon Schiele*. Disputes over the aesthetic value of a piece of music, or of a film, play, building, or poem, are commonplace. When we engage in such debates we believe we are exercising our critical judgments. We may even take a harsh view of those who think differently: we may regard them as stupid, or vulgar, insensitive, or imperceptive. The Circle held that, in an important sense, these aesthetic disputes should not be characterized as pointless but, once again, as meaningless.

Accompanying various statements about God, aesthetics, and ethics down the garbage chute were several metaphysical disputes with which philosophers had long engaged. Take Immanuel Kant's well-known dichotomy between the "phenomenon" and the "noumenon." The phenomenon is a thing as it appears to us; that table looks to me to be rectangular and black. But appearances can be deceptive, and in any case depend on our faculties—we cannot detect sounds that a bat can detect; we cannot see what eagles see. But Kant also coined the term *noumenon*. This was the "thing in itself" (*Ding an sich*). The thing in itself exists independently of all experience of it. We cannot access it directly: we can speculate upon it, but ultimately knowledge of the noumenon necessarily eludes us. The Circle's verdict: nonsensical. We cannot empirically test claims about the noumenon.

Skepticism about whether other people have thoughts and feelings (e.g., can I really know you feel pain?) became much more straightforward questions about how I can verify your thoughts and feelings (e.g., do you say that that you are in pain?, are you bleeding and/or screaming?).

Other long-standing debates were also dissolved by the verification criterion, including that between monists and pluralists—Is the world one thing or many? And that between the materialists and the idealists—Is there a world independent of our mind, or does the world take place entirely within our mind? Both sides in both debates have long and distinguished pedigrees. But what empirical test could conceivably settle the matter either way? And what of grandiloquent claims made by Georg Wilhelm Friedrich Hegel, among others, that history has "a spirit" and is moving inexorably in certain directions? How could this be tested? Carnap delivered some lectures in October 1934 in which he gave examples of metaphysical claims.

"The Essence and Principle of the world is Water," said Thales; "Fire," said Heraclitus; "the Infinite," said Anaximander; "Number," said

Pythagoras. "All things are nothing but shadows of eternal ideas which themselves are in a spaceless and timeless sphere," is a doctrine of Plato. From the Monists we learn: "There is only one principle on which all that is, is founded"; but the Dualists tell us: "There are two principles." The Materialists say: "All that is, is in its essence material," but the Spiritualists say: "All that is, is spiritual." To metaphysics (in our sense of the word) belong the principal doctrines of Spinoza, Schelling, Hegel, and—to give at least one name of the present time—Bergson.[27]

Within the Circle, the sense of satisfaction in slaying philosophical leviathans from history was overwhelming.

11

The Longest Hatred

> If any city in the world could claim to be the cradle of modern political anti-Semitism it is Vienna.
>
> —PETER PULZER[1]

BEING A UNIVERSITY librarian was not Friedrich Waismann's dream job. He had held it since 1930, but the salary was only 480 schillings and he had to supplement his income by giving private lessons, including to one of Wittgenstein's nephews. He would far rather have been a university teacher. In fact, any fair-minded assessment of his qualities would have deemed him eminently suitable for such a role. He may not have been the most original thinker, but he published several weighty papers. He had a first-rate mind, with an unusual capacity both for identifying the crux of a problem and for simplifying and making accessible complex ideas. He was conscientious and helpful, and would have made a diligent instructor. He was trained in mathematics and physics, and so, not intimidated by the new philosophy. Indeed, he embraced it.

But Waismann had two fundamental flaws, which in the eyes of the university authorities outweighed his manifest virtues. The first, and most basic, was that he had developed an irrational fear of being examined or judged, so had delayed taking his doctor's degree. Hence the need to accept the role of librarian.

The second was that he was Jewish.

To understand the history of the Vienna Circle is impossible without acknowledging its Jewish element. The majority of members were Jewish or half-Jewish. They included Bergmann, Feigl, Frank, Hollitscher, H. Hahn, O. Hahn, Kaufmann, Neurath, Rand, Schächter, Taussky, and Zilsel. Menger's mother was Jewish. Popper and Wittgenstein were of

Jewish origin, as were some important visitors to the center such as Ayer and Tarski. Hans Reichenbach from Berlin was half-Jewish. Others, like Viktor Kraft and Carl Hempel (also from Berlin), could not ignore or escape anti-Semitism because they had Jewish wives.

Jews had gained the right to reside in Vienna after the 1848 revolution, and had been granted full civil rights in 1867. In that year the Vienna census registered only 6,000 Jews. By 1936, the Jewish population of Vienna numbered around 180,000, or 9 percent of the population, the highest population in the German-speaking world: in Europe, only the cities of Warsaw and Budapest were home to more Jews. The most dramatic increase in Jewish numbers had occurred in the second half of the nineteenth century, but the figures continued to rise until the collapse of the Austro-Hungarian Empire at the end of World War I.

Friedrich Waismann was born in Vienna, his father having come from Odessa in Ukraine, then part of Imperial Russia. He was a difficult Jew to categorize. Crudely put, Vienna's Jews could be split into two, the ties and the caftans. The *Kaftanjuden* were more religiously observant, more traditional, much poorer, and tended to be recent arrivals from the eastern fringes of the Austro-Hungarian Empire, particularly from Galicia, an area that now straddles Poland and Ukraine. The Galician Jews had begun to arrive in the late nineteenth century, but the numbers accelerated with the outbreak of World War I when Tsarist troops marched into Galicia. The Cossacks were the most violently anti-Semitic of the Russian troops. There was a devastating pogrom in December 1918. Fearing other pogroms, hundreds of thousands of Jews fled. Included among them was the family of future Circle member Rose Rand. Although many would eventually return to their homes, at least 35,000 stayed in the capital. They crammed into particular parts of the city, Leopoldstadt (second district) and, a bit further north, Brigittenau (twentieth district). These eastern European Jews were proud of their distinctiveness and wanted to retain it: those few who abandoned the community brought shame and dishonor to their families.

The tie-Jews, the *Krawattenjuden*, were better off and more assimilated into Viennese life. Many had come from Czechoslovakia and Hungary a generation (or two) earlier. Olga Taussky was only three when her family moved to Vienna from Moravia, but her father, an industrial chemist, was representatitive of a type. The Krawattenjuden revered German culture, and religion was likely to play a more peripheral role in their lives. Berlin meant more to them than Jerusalem; they were more likely to read Schiller than the Talmud. They were more ambitious for their children to enter the *Gymnasium* than a yeshiva. The Gymnasium was a gateway to the university, which itself was the route to paradise, also known as the bourgeoisie.

Waismann had dispensed with most of the rituals of Judaism—in that sense he could be classified as a tie-Jew—but, like Rose Rand, whose origins were also in eastern Europe, his financial position was precarious. Rand was left stateless by the collapse of the Austro-Hungarian Empire. Similarly, although Viennese-born, Waismann did not have Austrian citizenship and as a foreigner had to find "foreign fees" for his university studies. But the Vienna Circle was dominated by wealthier Krawattenjuden. They were almost all secular (Josef Schächter, a rabbinical scholar, was unusual in this regard); logical empiricism and religion were not natural bedfellows.

The Circle was by no means exceptional in having such a strong Jewish presence. Jews played a disproportionate part in many other areas of Viennese life, in finance, business, the arts, and the liberal professions. Already by the 1880s they accounted for more than half of the city's doctors and lawyers. In 1936 they made up 62 percent of the city's lawyers, 71 percent of its newspaper editors, and almost 100 percent of its advertising executives.

Some professions were far harder for Jews to enter, particularly those controlled by public officials. The civil service was a profession almost entirely blocked to Jews. In 1934, there were only 700 Jews among Austria's 161,000 civil servants. Meanwhile, Friedrich Waismann exemplified the difficulties at the University of Vienna. As has been described, when Moritz Schlick was being considered for the chair in the inductive sciences in 1922, the university committee of professors checked to see whether he was Jewish. Two years later one of the Austrian papers published a list of Jews teaching in higher education: a not-so-subtle signal to society at large that the Jews surely had enough of a presence in the university already.

In 1923, the right-wing German Students Union in Vienna proposed that all books by Jewish authors be branded with the Star of David. (They also published a list of professors who for political and other reasons they deemed undesirable; it included Schlick.) In 1930, an official attempt by the university rector to limit the number of Jews failed after it was ruled unconstitutional. Still, Jews had to be significantly more qualified than non-Jewish candidates to be awarded a post; even renowned Jewish scholars were denied promotion. That their Jewishness was a hurdle to advancement was not usually made explicit, and by its nature was almost impossible to substantiate, but it seems likely that, in addition to poor Waismann, Bergmann (who retrained as a lawyer because of academia's anti-Semitism), Feigl, Popper, and Zilsel were all discriminated against. Every one was of a higher caliber than others who had been appointed to the university when they were not. Poor Zilsel was not awarded his habilitation; the claim was that his work was insufficiently philosophical, but other factors probably contributed: a Marxist and a Jew, he had the two blackest marks against him.

———

Anti-Semitism was a protean beast, and Viennese Jews found no successful strategy to dodge it. When something went wrong, the Jews were always to blame. Defeat in battle? Blame the Jews. Inflation? The fault of the Jews. Abhor modernism? It originated with the Jews. Otto Weininger, a Viennese writer and philosopher, wrote that "the spirit of modernity is Jewish, no matter how one looks at it."[2] The new, the breaking of taboos, the transgression of convention, all this terrified traditionalists, who naturally attributed the undermining of the status quo to the Jews. The newspaper of the Christian Social party, the *Reichspost*, covered the Jewish problem from every angle in each section of the paper.

There was a rich tapestry of stereotypes: the war profiteer, the grasping capitalist, the scheming puppeteer, the subversive communist, the fawning subordinate (Waismann?), the oily scrounger, the lascivious decadent. The wealthier Jews ("money Jews") were loathed for their power. The professionals and intellectuals ("ink Jews"; Waismann again) were detested for their influence. The Jews from the east ("beggar Jews") were despised for their poverty and exotic difference. At the end of World War I, there were severe shortages of both food and fuel, and the new refugees were held culpable for exacerbating the hardship. In Vienna, there were shouts of "*Hinaus mit den Juden!*" ("Jews Get Out!"). In the Austrian hinterland, outside Vienna, where there were far fewer Jews, anti-Semitism was stronger still.

An unfortunate truth is that the middle-class Jews shared some of the disdain of non-Jewish Austrians for the new Yiddish-speaking arrivals. Those middle-class Jews had worked hard to achieve respectability, to establish themselves in polite Christian society. The poor peddlers and cattle dealers—the men with their beards and black fur hats, the women with their *Sheitels* (ritually prescribed wigs)—were an embarrassment, an all-too-visible reminder of the life *they* had left behind and were eager to forget. And, as anti-Semitism grew ever uglier, some middle-class Jews developed a sneaky suspicion that perhaps the *Ostjuden* were at least partially to blame. Writer Joseph Roth, himself an "eastern" Jew, identified and diagnosed the pathology. "One doesn't want to be reminded of one's grandfather, who was from Posen or Kattowitz, by some stranger who has just arrived from Lodz. That is the ignoble, but understandable, attitude of an endangered *petit-bourgeois* who is just about to climb the rather steep ladder to the terrace of the *haute bourgeoisie* with its free air and magnificent view. Looking at a cousin from Lodz, one can easily lose one's balance, and fall."[3]

Of course, bigotry was scarcely a new phenomenon: it had been alive and well in the Austro-Hungarian Empire. Karl Lueger, the charismatic mayor of Vienna who presided over the city during the fin-de-siècle era and who is credited, among other achievements, with bringing it spring water through a network of pipes, boosted his popularity by running cynical and vicious anti-Semitic campaigns. He labeled Jews "God murderers" and inveighed against Jewish capitalists. When a Jewish deputy objected to Lueger's provocations, he responded that anti-Semitism would "perish, but not until the last Jew had perished."[4] He had friendly dealings with individual Jews but is credited with the quote, "*Wer ein Jud ist, bestimme ich*" ("I'll decide who is a Jew"). Lueger was greatly admired by a homeless artist in the city, Adolf Hitler, who described him as "the most ingenious mayor who has ever lived among us."[5] So when it came to anti-Semitism, Vienna had form. As one historian has put it, "If any city in the world could claim to be the cradle of modern political anti-Semitism it is Vienna."[6]

Still, until the Empire collapsed, Viennese Jews at least felt they were one minority among many, and that their own mixture of political, cultural, and religious loyalties could happily coexist. Austro-Hungarian Jews mostly embraced World War I as a chance to display their patriotism. After the war, playwright Arthur Schnitzler wanted to reemphasize his tripartite identity "as an Austrian citizen of Jewish race committed to German culture."[7] In this, he typified the attitudes of the community into which most of the Vienna Circle Jews were born—families who were loyal to Emperor Franz Josef and worshipped at the altar of Beethoven.

Postwar Austria felt provincial, more Catholic, less cosmopolitan, not such a comfortable place for Jews to be. Matters were not so desperate that they felt the urge to emigrate. Most would have sympathized with Sigmund Freud, who wrote on Armistice Day 1918 that he would remain in Vienna, though the empire was gone. "I will live on with the torso and persuade myself that it is the whole [*Ich werde mit dem Torso weiterleben und mir einbilden, dass es das Ganze ist*]."[8] Nonetheless, Jews now felt themselves to be conspicuous and exposed.

In theory, the Treaty of Versailles allowed citizens to opt for a state in which they were not living but that was more appropriate for their "race" or "nation." In practice, however, this freedom was only selectively granted. Around 75,000 German-speaking Jews from states that had been part of the Habsburg Empire were refused Austrian citizenship after Austria's Supreme Court declared that they were not "racially" German.

Some Austrian Jews responded to the new, menacing realities by deepening their religiosity, in defiance of the contempt, taunts, and sneers of hostile elements within the Christian population. But among those of a more secular orientation there were several reactions. A minority turned to Zionism, a movement established by a charismatic Viennese journalist, Theodore Herzl, who thought it was hopeless to pursue civil equality at home and insisted that only in a Jewish state would Jews be free of anti-Semitism (this utopia would of course contain an abundance of coffeehouses). Others, reluctant to embrace the Zionist political project, nonetheless possessed a Jewish cultural identity that became, if anything, even more pronounced in the teeth of inescapable anti-Semitism.

Freud and Schnitzler both fell into this category. Freud was an avowed atheist who still regarded himself as Jewish and who collected Jewish jokes and anecdotes. "I can say that I am as remote from the Jewish religion as from all others; that is to say, they are highly significant to me as a subject of scientific interest; emotionally I am not involved in them. On the other hand, I have always had a strong feeling of solidarity with my people and have also fostered it in my children. We have all remained in the Jewish confession."[9] Likewise, Arthur Schnitzler felt deeply Jewish, though again there was little Jewish ritual in his daily life. His grandmother fasted and prayed on the holiest day of the year, Yom Kippur, but the rest of the family did so, "mainly for her sake, and after her death solely out of a feeling of reverence for her."[10]

But in the multidimensional taxonomy of Jewish identity there was another category, the assimilationists. The assimilationists wished to integrate into the wider culture and were willing, indeed sometimes keen, to abandon their Jewish links and identity. And it was to this group that most of the Jewish figures linked to the Circle belonged. Certainly they were almost uniformly hostile to religion. Herbert Feigl wrote that his father was an outspoken atheist, which "made my own emancipation from Judaism (at age eight) quite easy" (*emancipation* being a pointed choice of word). But for the assimilationists not only did religion play a minor or nonexistent role, they barely identified themselves as Jews. A number went so far as to convert to Christianity. Indeed, no major city in Europe had such a high conversion rate as Vienna, though conversion remained rare. The converted included Gustav

Mahler, Karl Kraus, and Victor Adler, the founder of the Social Democratic Party. Popper, whose parents converted to Lutheranism, always believed assimilation offered a solution to anti-Semitism. Both Hans Hahn and Otto Neurath were from mixed marriages; their Jewish fathers converted, as did Menger's mother. Menger would never have considered himself a Jew.

There were certainly practical reasons to convert. For a Jew and a non-Jew to marry, one or the other had to convert, and why would the non-Jew adopt outsider status? Conversion was also a pragmatic step if one wanted to advance in the civil service. Abandoning the Jewish faith could help in other professions. Mahler's wife, Alma, claimed that Gustav was baptized because "he was afraid lest otherwise he might find it difficult as a Jew to get his engagement in Vienna."[11]

Protestantism was the faith of choice for Jewish converts. It was, after all, the creed of the Enlightenment; Catholicism was perceived to be more backward-looking and more contaminated by anti-Semitism. There was rarely much religious sincerity in the conversion, though this varied from individual to individual, family to family. However, even the skeptical felt more comfortable clothed in the identity of a Jewish-Protestant-atheist than an atheist of the Jewish-Catholic kind.

In shedding links to the old religion, assimilated Jews adopted a new religion—education. The obsession with study would propel many Jews to positions of social respectability. Otto Neurath's father, political economist Wilhelm Neurath, supported himself through his education and taught himself Latin. His personal library contained 13,000 volumes. "Science, in Neurath's case was secularized Judaism," writes historian Steven Beller. "His son, Otto, inherited this."[12] Karl Popper too benefited from growing up in a household with a major library, though estimates differ on whether it fell short of or surpassed the Neurath collection.

―――――――

The condition of semiliberation may have been the perfect incubator for Jewish success. Jews were free to study, but blocked from many routes to social standing. To achieve, they had to overachieve.

Nonetheless, the degree to which the Jewish factor was central to Vienna's intellectual and cultural flourishing in the first three decades of the twentieth century remains a contentious topic among historians. Certainly Jews were massively overrepresented among the cultural and intellectual elite. Equally, there were numerous notable non-Jews, including Austria's three most significant artists, Klimt, Schiele, and Kokoschka. Talk of "Jewish Vienna" used to drive the Vienna-born art historian Ernst Gombrich to distraction. He complained that of the Viennese artists of the era "it goes against the grain to enquire whether any of them were Jews or of Jewish extraction. I prefer to leave that enquiry to the Gestapo."[13]

The Jewish element in Viennese affairs was the subject of a satirical book imagining the city without its Jews. The life of the author, Hugo Bettauer, captured some of the contradictions in Jewish identity and his death eerily presaged a similar death that would mark the end of the Vienna Circle. Bettauer was born into a Jewish family but as a young adult in 1890 was baptized a Lutheran. He was a prolific, best-selling novelist, and several of his books were adapted into films. He was also a journalist and publisher of magazines; both his books and magazines contained sexually explicit material.

His best-known work appeared in the year Moritz Schlick arrived in Vienna, 1922. Within two years, *The City without Jews* had sold a quarter of a million copies. It describes a political demagogue, Dr. Karl Schwertfeger, who bore a none-too-subtle resemblance to Karl Lueger, and who rises to power through attacks on Jews. The neat solution is to expel the Jews, who are blamed for all the problems of postwar Vienna. Then one day, at one o'clock, whistles proclaim that all the trains carrying Jews have left, and church bells ring out to celebrate.

But life in the now *Juden-frei* space is not as blissful as the mayor or the city's inhabitants envisaged. Vienna becomes dull, its spirit and energy vanished. Almost immediately the city begins to disintegrate. Chic shops go bankrupt for want of custom from fashion-minded Jewish women. A customer sits in the Café Imperial complaining to the headwaiter that the place is now so empty "a fellow could freeze next to the stove."[14]

Bettauer's erotic publications had enraged elements of conservative Austria. *The City without Jews* cemented his infamy. At 3:00 p.m. on 10 March 1925, Otto Rothstock, a young dental worker with extremist right-wing views, walked into Bettauer's office and with a gun fired five times. Bettauer was rushed to hospital but died from his wounds two weeks later. At his trial, Rothstock said that it was important to remember that Jesus had come into the world to do battle against Jewish publishers, the sons of Satan. He accused Bettauer of ridiculing German culture and said he felt no remorse. Although he was found guilty, his lawyers claimed he was mentally unbalanced. The judge agreed, and Rothstock was sentenced to a spell in a mental hospital. Later he was assessed to be sane and was allowed to join the army. That judicial outcome, too, would curiously foreshadow another.

———

How people identify themselves does not always correspond with how they are identified by others. It was all well and good for Bettauer to proclaim himself Lutheran, but identity is a two-way street. In Austria, while you could declare your exit from, or indifference to, Judaism, that did not make others indifferent to your Jewish origins. The assimilationist Jews did not project their Jewishness onto the external world, but in the non-Jewish world they remained Jews. Converts, and children of mixed marriages, were by and large still regarded as Jewish. (To that extent, the Nazis' 1935 Nuremberg Race Laws, which defined a Jew by blood, were simply a formal codification of what in Vienna was ordinary practice.) As a schoolboy, Popper, despite being raised in a nominally Protestant household, was subjected to so much anti-Semitic abuse by one particular teacher that he moved schools.

In Vienna, if you were Jewish in origin, whether or not you had converted or had a strong Jewish identity, you were likely to live in the same neighborhoods as other Jews, be in professions popular among Jews, and, crucially, socialize with other Jews. There is scant evidence that Otto Neurath regarded himself as Jewish, or even reflected much on the Jewish predicament. Yet he moved predominantly in Jewish circles. The same could be said for Popper. Historian Eric Hobsbawm, raised in Vienna, wrote that although his family was "entirely unobservant, we nevertheless knew that we were, and could not get away from being, Jews."[15]

Indeed, Vienna was arguably the most race-conscious city in Europe. A culturally pervasive notion was essentialism, that race was linked not just to physical but also to psychological traits. In the twenty-first century, researchers have put the case for implicit bias, unconscious prejudice, being a powerful and malevolent force. Intriguingly, this bias seems to affect the minority population as well as the majority. Thus, there is evidence that African Americans in the United States carry around the same kinds of prejudices against other African Americans that whites do.[16] Where prejudice is in the air, everyone inhales it to a degree, even its victims. We should not, therefore, be overly surprised that some members of the Circle, even some Jewish members, held attitudes toward Jews that would make us uncomfortable if articulated today.

David Bakan, an American psychologist, wrote of Gustav Bergmann:

> Bergmann was a refugee who was deeply wounded in his soul by the Nazis. I have seen many such people but Bergmann's injury was the worst I have seen. He had become profoundly anti-Jewish. He renounced his Judaism. I had been told that if he were sent a Jewish New Year's card he would send it back. His view was that the only way the Jews could prevent repetition of their various historical persecutions was in a relentless assimilation. This meant that no Jew should ever marry a Jew.[17]

Bakan did not know Bergmann until after the philosopher's emigration to the US following the Anschluss, and his presumption that it was only with the rise of the Nazis that Bergmann developed such views is unlikely and unsubstantiated. There were plenty of Viennese Jews, especially among the assimilated middle-class, who maintained a highly ambiguous attitude to their ethnic origins. Perhaps most notorious was Otto Weininger, who wrote the misogynistic and anti-Semitic *Sex and Character (Geschlecht und Charakter)*. Weininger thought there were male and female aspects to our character: the female part was linked to instinct, the male to creativity and intelligence. Jews were essentially feminine: "Women and Jews are pimps, it is their goal to make man feel guilty. Our era is not only the most Jewish, it is also the most feminine of all eras."[18] Jews lacked moral instincts and, like women, had little sense of individuality. There was much more in this vein; arrant nonsense that was guzzled up by half the intellectuals in Vienna, many of whom regarded *Sex and Character* as a work of lapidary brilliance.

On 3 October 1903, Weininger rented a room in the same building in which Beethoven had died; no coincidence since he was preoccupied with the nature of genius. In the room that same evening, he fired a loaded pistol into his chest. Just twenty-three years old, he died the following day. In his final year, he had converted to Christianity.

His funeral was attended by Karl Kraus, another convert with anti-Semitic leanings. Kraus had written an anti-Zionist polemic, *A Crown for Zion* (*Eine Krone für Zion*), lampooning Herzl and arguing that only total assimilation could bring true Jewish liberation. Kraus directed particular antipathy toward the *Ostjuden*. He said he had an aesthetic repugnance to Yiddish as a language and thought it impure (notions of impurity, contamination, and disease were commonly connected to Jews). Schnitzler, that proud Jew, nonetheless held the Jews partially culpable for being so hated and in too weak a condition to respond to the onslaught against them because of their "excessive objectivity" and "a certain inclination to self-analysis."[19]

Wittgenstein was another to hold an essentialist view of Jews. The Wittgensteins were an unusual case in that their Jewishness was buried through at least two generations and it played little part in Ludwig's upbringing. Even so, he later began to question whether he had deliberately masked his origins. To various close acquaintances in England, in January 1937, he delivered some painful confessions. Discomforting as much to those who had to listen to them as to Wittgenstein himself; they included an admission that he had allowed people to suppose he was less Jewish than he was.

Wittgenstein was in the habit of recommending Weininger's *Sex and Character* to various friends. No doubt he found its emphasis on brutal honesty—with oneself and with others—appealing, and its uncompromising style chimed with his own. The characteristics

Wittgenstein associated with the Jewish people were the usual centuries-old slurs: Jews were secretive and liked money. Ironically, the most original philosopher of the twentieth century was also convinced that Jews were incapable of originality. "Even the greatest Jewish thinker is no more than talented (myself for instance)."[20]

It was the least original statement he ever delivered. Kraus and Weininger had expressed the same judgment about Jewish thinking. That Jewish thought was especially parasitic upon that of others was taken for granted by many Austrians. It is therefore not surprising that so many critics of Mahler's music in fin-de-siècle Vienna condemned the compositions of this Jewish convert to Christianity for being derivative, or that Wittgenstein thought Mendelssohn derivative.

To Karl Popper's credit, he never took these ludicrous racial claims seriously. But he too retained a highly ambiguous attitude toward his Jewish origins. His parents might have been born Jewish, but according to the religion stated at his birth, he was not. As an atheist he always resented being classified as Jewish. In his retirement year a request by the *Jewish Year Book* to include him met with a brutal and scathing response. Popper told them that he did not believe in race, and so, "I do not see on what grounds I could possibly consider myself a Jew."[21] He abhorred racial pride, which he considered "not only stupid but wrong, even if provoked by racial hatred. All nationalism or racialism is evil, and Jewish nationalism is no exception."[22]

Throughout his life, Popper remained a cosmopolitan; people should see themselves as citizens of the world, he thought. Yet Popper too seems to have swallowed some vials of Viennese poison. He may have thought all nationalism was objectionable, but he was particularly intolerant of one version of nationalism—Zionism. And in *Unended Quest* (1976) he advances the peculiar argument that given the power of anti-Semitism in Austria, the most effective way for a Jewish socialist to promote the socialist cause was to have stayed out of politics altogether. To have become so prominent in professions like journalism was equally unwise.

The virulent strain of anti-Semitism in Vienna needs to be understood in the context of the casual anti-Semitism that existed in other countries. Austria was merely an outlier in this phenomenon. In this regard, the views of some of the visitors to Vienna and the Circle from abroad are instructive. Frank Ramsey, who had gone to Vienna to be analyzed, sent a letter back home describing his first impressions. "I like my analyst, although he is a Jew (but all the best ones are)."[23] In his autobiography, meanwhile, W.V.O. Quine confesses to have thought about three of his friends—fellow stamp collectors—"What a pity . . . that they are Jews."[24]

———

This, then, was the atmosphere in which the Vienna Circle operated. The lives of almost all those associated with the Circle were directly affected by anti-Semitism, and several others affected indirectly. But to what extent it influenced their ideas is harder to pin down. Some scholars, notably Malachi Hacohen, have made the case for a powerful link. Hacohen, a biographer of Karl Popper, claims that many of Popper's intellectual projects and commitments, including hostility to nationalism, a defense of the Enlightenment, and the advocacy of an open society, are part of his engagement with his Jewishness. Jews were the most loyal of Habsburg subjects. Certainly Popper, and Circle members, saw the Habsburg era through rose-tinted, rearview glasses. After World War I they felt that the Jews stood out: in the golden age of the empire it was different: everyone stood out.

Though they could scarcely remain unaware (with the exception of the otherworldly Kurt Gödel, as we shall see) of the ubiquitous anti-Semitism, none of them foresaw where events were headed. There were reasons to get out of Austria, including career progression, but even when the Nazis came to power in Germany, the thought that their lives might be at risk seemed, to most, preposterous. Neurath was an obvious exception because of his active political engagement. But for others the temptation was to give a positive spin to developments, rather like Freud, who when he heard that in Berlin in 1933 his books had been put to the flame, said, "In the Middle Ages they would have burnt me; nowadays they are content with burning my books."

12

◄○►

Black Days in Red Vienna

"CARNAP EXPECTS YOU"

SHORTLY AFTER THE manifesto was published, the Austrian economy, still punch-drunk from World War I, took a knockout blow. The October 1929 Wall Street crash triggered a worldwide depression. Between 1929 and 1932, Austria experienced a catastrophic decline in production of 40 percent, while unemployment increased to over a third of the population.

The collapse not only hit every city, town, village, and hamlet in Austria, it exacerbated long-standing tensions between the capital and the provinces. Elsewhere in the country the left-wing municipal politics of Vienna were despised. Vienna was a red island, surrounded by regions that were more uniformly Catholic and conservative and politically in the grip of the Christian Social party. In May 1919, a referendum had been held in Voralberg, Austria's most westerly province, and, though their wishes were ignored, more than 80 percent of its people voted to join the Swiss rather than remain part of what was sometimes called "the Jewish state of Vienna" (*der Wiener Judenstaat*). Sigismund Waitz, who was to become archbishop of Salzburg, described the Vienna government as "the rule of Satan."[1] The Vienna Circle would come to be identified as on the urban, socialist, Jewish, and godless side of this unbridgeable divide.

Satanic rule was to survive a while longer. But across the border in Germany, the Nazi party was gathering strength, emboldening their Austrian counterparts. In April 1932, the Austrian Nazis performed well in local elections: before that they had been a fringe movement. In May, a young, inexperienced, diminutive politician, Engelbert Dollfuss, a Christian Socialist, became federal chancellor. Eight months later, Adolf

Hitler became the German chancellor, further ramping up political pressure and mistrust in Austria. When the unions announced a strike in protest against wage cuts for railway workers in February 1933, Dollfuss dispatched the army to crush it. On 4 March, he first called an emergency session of parliament, and then suspended parliament. Direct presidential rule was declared on 7 March.

Viennese Austro-Marxism was over: the short-lived era of Austrofascism had begun. Press freedoms were curtailed and the Constitutional Court dissolved. The German National Socialist Workers' Party was banned. The new regime felt itself to be closer to Catholic Italy than to Protestant Germany. Mussolini and Dollfuss soon established a strong political rapport. Hitler responded by introducing a fee for all German tourists wanting to visit Austria.

In Vienna there was no lull in the unrest, with regular bombings and outbreaks of violence. The Nazis were gathering strength. Karl Menger watched as young Nazis marched through the streets. "I found it almost impossible to concentrate and rushed out hourly to buy the latest extra."[2] Schlick told Menger he read the newspaper extras from morning to night. The university was often closed as a result of disturbances, though both Schlick and Menger had keys to get in, and so their respective circles could continue. Inside the deserted building, wrote Menger, away from the strife and fanaticism on the street, it was like "a quiet oasis."[3] Menger had a mischievous streak. He later told a student how he had managed to escape the attention of an especially irritating and aggressive student by referring him to an "expert" down the corridor: a Nazi colleague. When not closed, the university itself became a battleground. There were regular demonstrations and scraps. The writer Hilde Spiel describes the time she "arrived on the scene as a Jewish student was beaten up and thrown down the University steps, to lie bleeding at the bottom."[4]

For a fortnight in February 1934, fighting between the security forces and paramilitary groups on the Left (the Schutzband) threatened Austria once again with full-blown civil war. Hermine Wittgenstein wrote to her brother Ludwig, "We hear constant gunfire and I don't understand how the reds were able to stockpile enough weapons to fight for days on end."[5] Across the country, around two hundred civilians lost their lives. On 1 May, after the Left had been crushed, Dollfuss introduced a new constitution, creating a one-party state (the Fatherland Front), pro-nationalist, pro-independence, anti-Nazi, pro-Catholic.

The Austrian Nazis' response came three months later. On 25 July, 1934, ten Nazis disguised in army uniforms raided the Chancellery building and, in what turned out to be a botched coup attempt, Dollfuss was assassinated. Hitler was not behind the coup, but an irate Mussolini assumed German involvement. He pledged the Austrofascist regime military support and ordered Italian forces to the Austrian border. There was a personal explanation for Mussolini's outrage: by coincidence Dollfuss's wife and children were staying as guests at his villa in the Adriatic resort of Riccione.

Although there were minor eruptions throughout Austria, the coup was quickly suppressed and a new chancellor was appointed: the former education minister, Kurt Schuschnigg, a decent but aloof and, as it turned out, naïve man. The ban on the Nazi party remained, but over the next few years there was a dramatic shift in the military balance of power between Italy and Germany. Blithely contravening the Treaty of Versailles, Hitler ordered the rebuilding of the German army, navy, and air force. In March 1936, German tanks moved into the Rhineland, which had been designated a demilitarized zone—to only muted protests from the French and British governments.

Then France and Britain inadvertently conspired to push Italy into German arms. In October 1936, the two fascist governments would sign what became known as the Rome-Berlin axis. But the turning point had come a year earlier, in October 1935, when the Italians, pursuing a new colonial agenda, invaded Abyssinia (now Ethiopia), deploying aircraft and poison gas. The invasion was a month before the UK general election, and the question of how to respond to Italian aggression became an election issue. The Westminster government pushed for League of Nations sanctions on Italy, a policy that had unintended and disastrous consequences.

Italy's relationships with both Britain and France were frayed, even though the sanctions were so tepid (excluding, for example, oil) that they fatally undermined the credibility of the League. The League had been set up just fifteen years earlier, with a mission to maintain world peace through collective security. A leaked plan between the British foreign minister and the French prime minister, the Hoare-Laval pact, in December 1935, in which Mussolini was offered much of Abyssinia in exchange for Italian opposition to any future German attempts to annex Austria, only served to reinforce the popular perception that neither France nor Britain was genuine in their determination to resist aggression and to uphold the principle of collective security. When the plan became known to the public, the resulting outcry forced both Samuel Hoare and Pierre Laval to resign.

Despite the overwhelming superiority of their weaponry, the Italians did not occupy the Abyssinian capital, Addis Ababa, until May 1936. By then it was evident that in Britain the policy of appeasing fascism had taken its grip on the body politic. And the momentum toward a closer relationship beween Germany and Austria had become unstoppable.

————

On 24 February 1934, a fortnight after the end of Austria's brief civil war, and with the country now a one-party state, Moritz Schlick received a police summons. They had some questions about the Ernst Mach Society. What did the club do? What were its politics? It was thought to be a leftist front: was this accurate? In any case, they were closing it down.

In the following month, Schlick wrote three letters in support of the Ernst Mach Society, explaining its origins and making the case for its being politically neutral. The claim that the club backed activities against the state was "absolutely untrue."[6] The political affiliations of its members were never interrogated, because they were irrelevant. That a few members of the Circle were on the Left was mere happenstance. In each of the three letters, to Vienna's police headquarters, to Vienna's security commissioner, and to the federal police, he used the same phrase. The club was "absolutely unpolitical" (*absolut unpolitisch*). As further evidence that the Club was nonpartisan and that Schlick himself was no subversive, he pointed out that he had become a member of the

Fatherland Front (though this was now expected of all civil servants, including university staff).

It did no good. The Ernst Mach Society was disbanded on 6 March 1934. The authorities now went after Waismann, Schlick's faithful librarian. He received a note on 10 February 1936. "According to ordinance of the Ministry of Education of the 29th of January 1936, ZL. 2818/I1, no future employment of Dr. Friedrich Waismann, who has worked as librarian at the Department of Philosophy of Vienna University since 1930, is foreseen in that capacity. Further monthly instalments of the remuneration at the level of a librarian are to be withheld from the person of that name." Schlick weakly protested, writing to the philosophy faculty dean that since Waismann could no longer be employed as a librarian he, Schlick, must insist on replacing him with an appropriately qualified candidate. This was a matter of principle, Schlick explained. The nature of this principle was not clearly spelled out. It appears to have been that Schlick be allowed an assistant.

Waismann, having already been deprived of his meager librarianship earnings, now also lost his teaching job in adult education. So did Zilsel, who was arrested and held in custody, though quickly released; he later found work at a high school. Neurath's beloved enterprise, the International Museum of Society and Economy, was closed down too, its information regarded as dangerously accessible and provocative.

Neurath had been sufficiently far-sighted about political developments to make provisions for just such an eventuality. His museum had worked with organizations in the Netherlands and in July 1933, shortly after Dollfuss had declared he would rule in Austria without parliament, Neurath established the International Foundation for the Promotion of the Vienna Method of Visual Education in The Hague. This fed Neurath's expansionist appetite and, more practically, provided a possible route of escape if events in Austria took an even nastier turn.

In February 1934, Neurath was in Moscow on one of his regular trips to the communist propaganda institute modeled on his museum, Izostat. About to return home, he received a telegram from his lover and collaborator, Marie Reidemeister: "Carnap expects you." This was prearranged code; it meant, head to Prague. The police had raided his office and rifled through his personal files. She added, "Letters forwarded to Philipp." This meant he was to go to the home of Philipp Frank, also in Prague, and she would meet him there.

From Prague he arranged for the transfer of the institute's belongings to The Hague, which he reached via Poland and Denmark. Marie and Olga, his blind wife, joined him soon after. His arrival was hardly given the red-carpet treatment. Sharing a long border with Germany, the Dutch were keen to stress their neutrality and not to be seen as a haven for Jewish or political refugees. Neurath, a Jewish political refugee, was doubly suspect.

———

Why could Austrofascism not tolerate the Circle?

Was logical empiricism inherently socialist?

The 1929 manifesto insisted there was an explicit link: "The Vienna Circle believes that . . . it fulfils a demand of the day: we have to fashion intellectual tools for everyday life, for the daily life of the scholar but also for the daily life of all those who in some way join in working at the conscious re-shaping of life." There could be no doubt that this reflected the sentiment of at least one of the authors. Otto Neurath was the most politically engaged member of the Circle. He was always the Circle member most in tune with the ideology of Austro-Marxism, and for him there was a direct connection between logical empiricism and socialism. While the new apparatus of logic was to be used by the Circle to transform philosophy, so the technical, rational planning of the Austro-Marxists, thought Neurath, could and would transform society.

Neurath might be called a Marxamite: that is, he was half a Marxist, half a Benthamite. Jeremy Bentham, eighteenth-century British philosopher and founder of utilitarianism, had proposed that actions be judged by whether they produced the greatest happiness of the greatest number, and had produced a framework for measuring this happiness, a "felicific calculus." Neurath too thought there should be a way of measuring happiness, and that this should be used to interrogate the rationale for social policies. Later in life he would become known as the sociologist of happiness. The happiness that meant most to him was where it was in the shortest supply, in poor and struggling lives. He was a level-headed, technocratic Marxist, interested in data and other forms of evidence, in testing and discovering what worked. What was the best way to feed, clothe, educate, and house people? He embraced the term *social engineer* to sum up his own activities. "He looked at everything— ideas as well as facts—through an often distorting lens of socialist philosophy."[7]

But within the Circle, he was far from alone in his political orientation. Most figures in and around the Circle were left-wing. The two other principal authors of the manifesto, Carnap and Hahn, also had strong socialist leanings. Hahn extended his concern for the oppressed to the animal world (he once physically hauled to the police a coachman who had maltreated his horse). Feigl was on the Left, Philipp Frank was a committed socialist, so too were Edgar Zilsel (Zilsel had joined the Social Democratic Party in 1918) and Walter Hollitscher, a young communist who in discussions regularly quoted Marx. There were personal links between the SDAP and the Circle, including Josef Frank, Philipp's brother and the moving force behind Vienna's housing program.

That most of the Circle had leftist leanings was no shock. There was the Jewish element. The founder of the SDAP, Victor Adler, was of Jewish origin as were several of its other leaders; the SDAP was the least anti-Semitic of the political parties and commanded the vast majority of Jewish votes. That did not make it prejudice free, far from it. In Austria, electoral success was predicated on bigotry. It was merely a question of degree: the full acid or the milder acetic kind. Within the SDAP anti-Semitism was less blatant than within the Christian Social party, which in turn practiced a far milder version than the fascists.

Still, the SDAP was the natural political home for most Circle members. It should be recalled that several members of the Circle had seen action in World War I. War can politicize soldiers and civilians alike. In 1914, Carnap had been caught up in the wave of war euphoria; by the end, like another soldier, Hans Hahn, he had become a pacifist and a socialist. Hahn had been wounded in the lungs. In Bonn, before he took

up the chair in Vienna, he caused a minor scandal by handing out pacifist leaflets. Neurath's commitment to socialism also came out of the war.

The left-wing instincts of the Circle found expression in a variety of
ways. It was most conspicuous in adult education. In the 1920s and early
1930s adult education was a thriving sector. Adult education lecturers
had more license to address a range of topics eschewed in the stuffy
university, and the lecturers themselves were often drawn from groups
that were, to a greater or lesser extent, shut out of the university—Jews,
women, socialists.

Almost all members of the Circle taught at the adult education centers, the *Volkshochschulen*, at one time or another, and several, Feigl,
Hahn, Kraft, Neurath, Rand, Waismann, and Zilsel, taught regularly.
Neurath lectured on the planned economy, on housing, and on urban
design. Zilsel ran many courses, including one on the cult of personality.
His book, *The Development of the Concept of Genius*, was dedicated to
the People's University of Vienna. Schlick and Carnap gave lectures too.
Gustav Bergmann was actually inducted into the Circle after attending
evening classes on philosophy and mathematics delivered by Waismann. Hahn, the head of the Union of Socialist University Teachers,
publicly espoused the cause of adult education and school reform in
newspaper articles. He objected to the lowly status of students and the
lofty disregard in which academics held them.

Wittgenstein, though he did not himself teach in adult education, was
swept up in the reform movement. When he taught in village schools
in southern Austria, he adopted the methods of the reform movement;
pushing pupils to work out answers for themselves, rather than being
spoon-fed. For the very best pupils he was clearly inspirational. His passion for education is shown by the *Wörterbuch für Volksschulen*, a spelling dictionary for elementary schools, which he wrote out for his pupils
and which was published in 1926.

The involvement of Circle members in adult education was neither
entirely ideologically motivated nor entirely selfless. Several Circle philosophers found their academic careers blocked either because of their
adherence to logical empiricism, or their ethnicity, or both. The *Volk-
hochschulen* offered an alternative to the university and a much-needed

source of income. The conservative establishment regarded it as subversive.

But adult education was not the only intersection between Circle members and politics. Neurath wrote articles for *Der Kampf*, the journal of the Social Democrats. In one issue, in 1928, he entered into a debate about proletarian lifestyles. SDAP attempts to shape preferences, discouraging tobacco, encouraging women to wear their hair bobbed, were, he argued, trivial and silly: these were just temporary fashions and had nothing to do with the class struggle. Hahn also supported *Der Kampf* by contributing articles, as did Zilsel, who wrote about the sociology of philosophy and science, and the social roots of romantic ideology. The journal reciprocated by consistently championing the role of science in modern society and trumpeting scientific breakthroughs. The public face of the Circle, the Ernst Mach Society, was another channel for the dispersal of left-wing ideas. Members of the public could show up to lectures on the connection between Marxism and modernist architecture, for example, or the link between Marxism and the Unity of Science project. Well-known left-wing figures, most notably Austro-Marxism's leading intellectual, Otto Bauer, addressed the Society.

––––––

To give the impression that the Vienna Circle served as some kind of intellectual front line for the Social Democrats would, however, be misleading. Neurath pushed for the Circle to take a more explicitly combative stance, but on this he was overruled. He was forced to concede that other Circle members were not, nor were they required to be, committed to the cause. This was even made explicit in the manifesto: "Of course not every single adherent of the scientific world-conception will be a fighter. Some, glad of solitude, will lead a withdrawn existence on the icy slopes of logic; some may even disdain mingling with the masses and regret the 'trivialized' form that these matters inevitably take on spreading."[8]

The irony was that by the time Schlick received a police summons to be questioned about the Ernst Mach Society, it had indeed become much more apolitical. With extremist right-wing sentiment bubbling to the surface in the early 1930s, and with the SDAP revealing itself as vacillating and timid, the Society chose to shun confrontation, refocusing its lecture program toward the range of abstruse topics debated by the Circle members themselves each Thursday evening. Out went social policy and Austro-Marxism; in came talks about the problem of induction, the meaning and significance of protocol sentences, and the status of ethics. Not uncontentious, but not directly threatening, either. There had always been aspects of logical empiricism that militated against a doctrinal approach. It was vital for the Circle that the findings of science were not preempted; science would take us down paths that could not always be predicted in advance. They adopted a neutral stance with regard to what scientists would someday discover.

Although even the most apolitical of citizens could not ignore the rise of extremism in Austria, several members of the Circle were, initially at least, largely disengaged from the political scene. They included Waismann, who was both distrustful of Marxism and dubious about the scientific claims of social science. Others were on the Left but wary of inserting politics into philosophy. Carnap represented this attitude, at least from around 1928, when he adopted the position that absolute-value statements were cognitively meaningless. A letter he wrote to Bertrand Russell, however, wonders whether Russell's socialism and his work in logic were related. "Is it mere coincidence that the people who achieve the greatest clarity in the most abstract area of mathematical logic are also those who oppose, clearly and forcefully, the narrowing of the human spirit by means of affect and prejudice in the area of human relations?"[9]

The most vociferous champion of a separation of philosophy and politics was Moritz Schlick. It was only natural that Schlick, a gentile from a patrician family, financially and socially secure, would not be as sensitive as others to the impending political catastrophe. He had started off on the Left, but by the late 1920s he was certainly no socialist. He also believed that the Circle should, as a matter of policy, remain impartial in the political arena. He thought the links between the Circle and the Ernst Mach Society were worrying and gave a misleading impression.

In his quietly effective way, Schlick pushed through his own agenda. A reading of the Circle's minutes makes it clear that in Boltzmanngasse, at least, the Circle did not discuss Politics with a capital P. The world may have been imploding around them, but there was no debate about the shootings of 15 July 1927. Constitutional democracy may have been under threat, but paramilitary groups, hyperinflation, and the rise of unemployment were never on the agenda. Hitler's appointment as German chancellor in January 1933 was front page news internationally, but apparently only to be discussed later in the coffeehouse, after the proceedings in Boltzmanngasse had been brought to a close.

———

The puzzle, then, is why the nationalists and the Nazis regarded the Circle as such a pernicious force, as the Circle was to quickly discover after the 1934 coup. Across the border in Germany, the Berlin Society—whose interests were so closely aligned to the Circle's—was winding up. Many of its members went into exile, including the Society's leader Hans Reichenbach, who took a job in Istanbul in 1933. (The Turkish leader, Ataturk, wanting to energize the University of Istanbul, was quick to employ refugee professors from Nazi Germany—Reichenbach's lectures were delivered in German and translated into Turkish.) In 1935, a new physics institute was established in the German university city of Heidelberg, led by Philipp Lenard, a Nobel Prize–winning physicist. Lenard opposed relativity theory on the grounds that it was Jewish physics. Significantly, a speech at the opening targeted "the so-called Vienna Circle." It was described as a "club of mostly persons of foreign race, largely of Near Eastern and oriental race," and it was propagating a new logic that "distinguishes itself from Aryan logic."[10]

There was a rationale to this hostility. For if there was nothing inherently socialist about logical empiricism, there was something inherently antifascist and anti-Nazi about it.

The varied intellectual roots of Nazism included a romantic German nationalism, German blood fused with German soil in a mystical bond. This ideological strand was deliberately, unashamedly antirational:

magic and sentiment were privileged over experience and reason. In the search for truth, emotion was more reliable than dry intellectualizing. Nazism was steeped in nostalgia and tradition, and a commitment to what was called *völkisch* thought was integral to it. Many political thinkers, such as Jean-Jacques Rousseau and Karl Marx, had identified a malaise within modern man, an alienation brought about by urbanization, industrialization, and specialization, the wrenching of the worker from the land and from the product of his labor. One way of understanding *völkisch* ideology is as a response to that challenge: it acted as a balm against individualist anxiety, by stressing the group, the race, the people. *Das Volk.* There were the individuals, and then there was the set of individuals, and this set of individuals was to be understood as something more, something greater, than its constituent parts.

Among the *Volk*, however, there were some special individuals. Part of the romanticism of *völkisch* ideology was the glorification of genius, particularly German genius, exemplified by Goethe and Beethoven. This genius was nurtured in, and arose out of, a uniquely German spirit. Geniuses were in a category all their own: they could and should play by different rules than ordinary mortals. They were to be held to different standards, with special duties and obligations. They possessed some indefinable, transcendental gift.

There were some powerful and influential proponents of "social" values within the University of Vienna—most particularly Othmar Spann, a sociologist and economist. Spann ran his own circle, was a popular lecturer and a prolific writer, and had many disciples. In some ways he went even further than *völkisch* thinkers. He held that the whole precedes the parts and that only the whole was truly real—the individuals within it were not.

———

These, then, were some ideological strands underpinning fascist and Nazi ideology.

And logical empiricism stood in opposition to each of them. Positivism was an outgrowth of the Enlightenment. It revered science and technology, which represented progress. It embraced modernism, which many conservatives regarded as decadent and destabilising. It attacked tradition, which conservatives believed was the bedrock of community. It was contemptuous of superstitious thinking. Although there was nothing explicitly pro-democratic about logical empiricism, it was implicitly anti-elitist. The priestly caste claimed some special insight into God, while the metaphysician claimed some special understanding of the world beyond appearance. It is easy to see why the declaration that all knowledge was empirical—and so, potentially open to examination by all—was perceived as threatening both to the church and to a certain kind of philosophical thinker.

Logical empiricism was also skeptical about the ontological status of the group: the base unit for explaining action was thought to be the individual. This thesis, methodological individualism, went back at least to Carl Menger's *Principles of Economics* (1883) and would later be more fully developed by, among others, Karl Popper. It was absurdly misinterpreted by British Prime Minister Margaret Thatcher, who notoriously claimed that there was no such thing as society. Of course, the methodological individualist did not hold that society did not exist. What they believed was that society was not a causal agent. If you wanted to explain why an action took place you should do so by identifying why one or more individuals had acted in a certain way. A class of people does not cause action; individuals within a class cause action. Positing a causal whole, a group, that was somehow over and above the elements from which it was made, was metaphysical nonsense.

In fact, the problem with metaphysics went further. In a pamphlet Hahn wrote in 1930,[11] he called it "world-denying" and a way of conning or appeasing the masses. If we were forced to confront the idea that the empirical world constituted our only reality—and that there was no true reality behind this veil of appearances—then social reform would take on an added urgency. We would have to confront the here-and-now. We could not, for example, take solace in the promise of an afterlife. He proposed a version of Occam's Razor: that we should not endorse more principles or assumptions than was necessary to explain the problem at hand. And he linked this to democracy and the attack, for example, on the divine right of kings.

As for the deification of genius, this was subjected to a sustained critique by Edgar Zilsel. Like almost all the Circle members, Zilsel loved music; he also loved literature. But he was more interested in the art than in the artist. He traced the rise of the cult of genius to the erosion of, and threats to, a religious worldview. We were, the claim was, in need of new gods to replace those abandoned. As we have seen, the Circle was not immune to its own romanticism of genius, and the person most associated with that label, Wittgenstein, was himself preoccupied with what it meant to be a genius. In a letter to Bertrand Russell on 16 August 1912, he wrote that Beethoven and Mozart were "the actual sons of God."[12] Wittgenstein was tortured by incompatible fears: on the one hand that whatever qualities were demanded of genius, he did not possess them; and on the other, that since he was a genius, he was required to interact with the world in a particular way. Zilsel insisted the notion of genius was shrouded in metaphysical obscurity.

Carnap delivered a couple of revealing talks in the first half of 1934, one in Brno and the other in Prague. The sketchy notes for these are now housed in Carnap's archive in Pittsburgh. He argued that it would be a mistake to conclude that just because statements are meaningless they are "without effects." On the contrary, pseudo-sentences can generate powerful emotional responses. He went on to claim that governments can profit from cultivating in particular a sense of sanctity and the sublime. It is no coincidence that those countries in which the dominant class is most opposed to social change—including Germany and Austria—are also those in which mythology and metaphysics are most prevalent. "The masses," Carnap said, are the main target for metaphysical bamboozlement because metaphysics keeps them in their place. The message from his talks was that metaphysics was not merely an academic matter, it was political weaponry, *Kampfmittel*.[13]

"Metaphysical" remained the favored insult of the empiricists. They were scornful of all metaphysics, including fascist metaphysics. They were also hostile to religion. The link between religion and fascist ideology remains a topic of historical controversy. Incontrovertible, however, is the fact that millions of ordinary citizens in Germany, Austria, and elsewhere, saw no contradiction between a belief in God and support for fascist or Nazi governments. For the majority of Austrians, regular church attendance was the norm. The Vienna Circle, on the other hand, denounced most statements about God as cognitively meaningless. Almost all the Circle philosophers were secular; some were avowedly antireligious. As a young man, Karl Menger had made an entry in his diary: "God has outlived himself."[14] This was written before the Circle was formed, but it neatly sums up sentiment among many Circle members. Carnap, who always worked incredibly hard, made a point of working on Sunday apparently out of atheistic conviction.[15] And we should recall Feigl's description of abandoning his faith as one of "emancipation." (Gödel was an exception—he later claimed to have proved God's existence through logic).

So, against *völkisch* ideology, disparaging of romanticism, suspicious of tradition, critical of the glorification of genius, pro-modernism, pro-individualism, and above all dead set against metaphysics. The Circle was also, as we have described, heavily Jewish and left-wing. This was obviously not a basket of ingredients likely to appeal to Austrofascists or German Nazis.

13

Philosophical Rows

> The Nothing itself nihilates.
>
> —MARTIN HEIDEGGER

TO UNITE A GROUP, it helps to have a common enemy. Hostility to Kant united the Circle but, long dead, he was not the most satisfactory of foes. There was, however, one figure who aroused their universal contempt. To this day he divides philosophers, with some regarding him as one of the great philosophical titans of the twentieth century. To members of the Circle, however, he was a portentous fraud. On one occasion there was a reading at the Circle of Martin Heidegger's writings on death: "the merriment elicited by the attempts to resolve the posed task of transcribing the text into scientific language was tumultuous and universally shared."[1] A. J. Ayer reported of the Circle that they regarded all contemporary German philosophers as "rogues or fools. Even to think of Heidegger makes them sick."[2]

Born a few months after Wittgenstein, in 1889, Heidegger studied at the University of Freiburg, taught at Marburg, and then returned to Freiburg. Notoriously, he joined the Nazi Party and, after Hitler came to power, prevented his former teacher, Jewish philosopher Edmund Husserl, from entering the university. There is incontrovertible evidence, much of which has come to light since his death in 1976, that Heidegger was an enthusiastic Nazi and an ideological anti-Semite. Popper rightly thought him "a swine" and "a swindler."[3] It was said of Carnap that he "read Heidegger much as the devil would read the Bible."[4]

In fact, it was Carnap who took on Heidegger most directly.

On 24 July 1929, a year after Heidegger succeeded Husserl in the chair of philosophy at Freiburg, he delivered his inaugural lecture, "What is Metaphysics?" It was just over two years since he had published the tome that made his name and for which he is still primarily known, *Being and Time.* In it he had addressed the question of what "being" is; what is it for something to be? The investigation of "Being" was not principally a scientific one. He argued that humans should not be seen as something apart from the world, but as part of the world. The convoluted prose made the *Tractatus* seem like a children's picture book, but like the *Tractatus* the book was soon hailed as a work of genius.

There was a corresponding question to what it was to be—what it was not to be. Heidegger had always been interested in what he called the Nothing. The ultimate metaphysical question, he believed, was "Why is there Something rather than Nothing?" And Heidegger made the case that our awareness of death was what made freedom and authenticity possible. The "What is Metaphysics?" lecture included the phrase "the Nothing itself nihilates" (*"Das Nichts selbst nichtet"*). An uncorroborated but plausible story has it that the lecture was followed by silence, before one brave soul put a question: "Mr. Heidegger, what is metaphysics?" (*"Herr Heidegger, was ist Metaphysik?"*), to which Heidegger responded, *"Gute Frage!"* ("Good question!").

In 1932 Carnap published an essay in *Erkenntnis,* "Overcoming Metaphysics through Logical Analysis of Language,"[5] in which Heidegger and his 1929 lecture were the prime targets. He took the classic logical positivist line. At first glance statements about "spirit" or "the absolute" look as if they are saying something; we may even be persuaded that they are on to something profound. We may feel the same when Heidegger asserts, "the Nothing is prior to the Not and the Negation." But, asks Carnap, "Where do we seek the Nothing? How do we find the Nothing? . . . What about this Nothing?—The Nothing itself nothings."[6] Here was where verificationism was needed. Metaphysical propositions could not be verified, even in principle. The claims made by metaphysicians were therefore not wrong but senseless. They were not best characterized as deep or as shallow but as rubbish. They had no cognitive meaning. They should be understood as statements groping toward certain feelings. But feelings were more effectively captured through the arts, through poetry or music. It's fine to do metaphysics as a poet (Carnap used the example of Nietzsche) but not as a scientist. His caustic verdict was that "metaphysicians are musicians without musical ability." The real task of philosophy was not to grapple with metaphysical questions, but to bring some logical clarification to the method and statements of the sciences.

Heidegger's political outlook had yet to reveal itself. Whether or not there is a link between his philosophy and his politics is a contentious matter, and one vigorously denied by his philosophical devotees. Certainly not all metaphysicians were fascist. At the 1934 Congress in Prague, there was a skirmish between the empiricists and Hans Driesch, an expert in the embryology of sea urchins. Driesch was no Nazi (the Nazis would force him to retire), but someone who wanted to retain a place for metaphysics and who rejected the notion that life can be explained entirely as physical or chemical phenomena. In his plenary session he explored the idea of vitalism, of there being a force that cannot be reduced to physical stuff. One or two empiricists objected, and the following day Schlick delivered a lecture entitled "On the Concept of the Totality," which was taken as a rebuke to Driesch, and pushed the Circle line that there was no whole, distinct from the sum of its parts.

———

By the time Carnap's diatribe against Heidegger had appeared, Carnap had left Vienna for the German-language university in Prague. This was a route taken two decades earlier by physicist Philipp Frank, another figure associated with the Circle. The philosophers at the university opposed the appointment, but Frank had cunningly pushed for a chair in the science faculty (as opposed to the philosophy faculty) on the grounds that a philosopher was required to help make sense of the developments in the natural sciences. In this way, he bypassed the objections.

Initially, Frank had hoped the chair would be taken by Hans Reichenbach, but he complained that the salary was too low for him and his family to survive. Carnap took up his new post in 1931. Life in Prague was not to prove as intellectually stimulating as in Vienna, and a depressingly small number of students turned up at his lectures—often only five people, one of whom was Elizabeth Stöger. He had met her in Vienna: She called herself ina, always with a small *i*—a made-up name. They married in a civil ceremony on 5 March 1933, with Philipp Frank serving as the witness and (because Carnap did not understand Czech) translator. Carnap, ever the logician, kept interrupting the proceedings to ask for clarification of a particular statement, eventually forcing an outburst from Frank. "Do you want to get married or not? If so, just answer and don't ask questions!"[7] Maybe it was middle age, or maybe it was because this union was a happy one, but Carnap apparently no longer indulged in extramarital affairs (although there is evidence that ina herself was not entirely faithful). With the Carnaps' relocation, Prague, along with Berlin and to a lesser extent Warsaw, became another strategic garrison of the Circle.

In January 1931, while still in Vienna, Carnap had developed a fever. He had one particularly unpleasant night, but in his agitated state had thought up the basis of *The Logical Syntax of Language*, his second major work. This he would write up in Czechoslovakia, but the Circle was presented with the ideas in nascent form.

The project was to develop a formal language that would provide the tools to define basic logical notions, such as analyticity (*All bachelors are unmarried men*) and logical consequence (*From 1. For all x's, if x is a mammal then x is warm-blooded and 2. For all z's if z is a whale then z is a mammal, to 3. For all x's, if x is a whale then x is warm-blooded*). We can separate the rules of language from the claims that can be made about the world once these rules are adopted. Only after the logic and the language have been established is it possible to make claims about knowledge of the world.

The most important intellectual move in the book was its Principle of Tolerance. While still maintaining that logic was vital to philosophical inquiry, and that the logician must state clearly the rules of the game, Carnap now held that there was not one true logic. We were free to adopt any framework we wished. "In logic, there are no morals.

Everyone is at liberty to build up his own logic, i.e. his own form of language, as he wishes. All that is required of him is that, if he wishes to discuss it, he must state his methods clearly, and give syntactical rules instead of philosophical arguments."[8]

What made one framework superior to another was not that it was "true" while the other was "false," but that it was simpler, or more useful. There were clear affinities here with the American pragmatist tradition represented by thinkers like William James, John Dewey, and Charles Sanders Peirce, who held that theories or beliefs were to be evaluated according to whether they worked, their practical application.

Neither Frank nor Carnap could be described as "escaping" or "fleeing" Vienna. They moved for what in normal times are normal reasons—pay, career advancement, a change of scene. The first man who left for other than day-to-day motives was Herbert Feigl. Schlick believed that Feigl could secure a *Privatdozentur* at the university. But Feigl was the most clear-sighted of the Circle. Two years before the Nazis came to power in Germany, and before his thirtieth birthday, he had concluded that there was no future for a young Jewish academic in Austria. After a fellowship at Harvard, he took up the offer of a job at the University of Iowa and set sail, with his new wife Maria, in 1931. Several times over the next few years he would return to Vienna during the summer holidays. He would never again, however, call Vienna home.

Feigl had not been long in the States when he published an article (with an American philosopher, Albert Blumberg) in the *Journal of Philosophy*. It was entitled "Logical Positivism: A New Movement in European Philosophy," and it introduced the Circle's ideas to an American readership. It is the first known use of *logical positivism*, a term that did not please everyone. Frank, for one, objected, perhaps because he disliked all "isms." But he also acknowledged the importance of being able to attach a term to an intellectual approach. "[A] long life among views and theories has shown me that if we want a view to be regarded as a respectable tree in the garden of opinions it must have a label just as much as the elms and oaks in our public gardens."[9]

Feigl had represented the Circle's future. Hans Hahn embodied its past. He had established the Circle's prototype in the first decade of the century through his discussions with Frank and Neurath; he had been instrumental in bringing Schlick to Vienna; he had helped shape the Circle's agenda as its most passionate advocate of Russell and Whitehead's *Principia Mathematica;* his voice had been influential in the wording of the manifesto. During a lecture at the university in the summer of 1934, Hahn collapsed with stomach pain. It was cancer. The significance of his premature death following a botched emergency operation is difficult to overstate. In an obituary published in *Erkenntnis,* Frank described him as the real founder of the Vienna Circle.

Meanwhile, Hahn's former student Kurt Gödel had established a link with the Institute for Advanced Study in Princeton, visiting there between October 1933 and May 1934 and again in 1935. He was becoming increasingly detached from Schlick's circle. So, by the mid-1930s, the Circle had effectively lost four of its key members in three years, blows from which it would never recover. Mathematician Olga Taussky also departed—becoming a Fellow at Girton College Cambridge in 1935.

————

Splits within the Circle, which had always existed, had begun to deepen. The manifesto certainly played a role in this. To give the impression that the Circle had ever been a cozy and united alliance of like-minded individuals would be misleading. There were both profound disputes and marked personality clashes. Going public served to exacerbate arguments, for in a sense there was now more at stake. If members belonged to a club that *overtly* stood for a set of specific ideas, then they had a greater interest in ensuring that these ideas mirrored their own.

Some differences had long existed. Although almost all Circle members became convinced that, drawing on Wittgenstein and Ramsey, they had solved the problem of mathematics—that mathematical truths were a type of tautology—Gödel had sat quietly at Circle meetings without believing a word of this. He was a mathematical Platonist, an "unadulterated Platonist,"[10] in Bertrand Russell's description. There were truths "out there," thought Gödel, that were not constructed by human minds. They existed independently of minds, and could be discovered by mathematicians.

Not surprisingly, Gödel took a more skeptical approach to Wittgenstein than did some others in the Circle. Attitudes to Wittgenstein were a source of tension. While Schlick and Waismann revered Wittgenstein, Gödel was among several bemused by the cult-like deference he inspired in his acolytes. Neurath was another prominent skeptic. When the Circle discussed Wittgenstein's philosophy he would repeatedly bellow, "Metaphysics." To placate Schlick, who found these interjections annoying, Hahn proposed that Neurath simply say "M" instead. Neurath responded that he thought "it will save time and trouble if I say 'non-M' every time the group is *not* talking metaphysics."[11]

The most important personality clash within the Circle was between Schlick and Neurath. Two men could scarcely have been more different. Schlick was calm and reserved, happiest in a seminar room or reading quietly at home. Neurath was voluble and gregarious. Schlick was an apolitical abstract thinker, Neurath a Marxist man of action. Schlick was a compromiser, Neurath a polemicist and proselytizer. There was a degree of class tension, with Schlick the patrician German versus Neurath the workers' champion. They did not have boundless respect for each other's academic output. Neurath detected a mystical strain in Schlick's thought, influenced as it was by Wittgenstein. Schlick regarded Neurath as dogmatic and lacking rigor. Neurath was acutely sensitive to this charge; he feared that he was seen as a kind of jumped-up secretary, an organizer and campaigner but not a first-class thinker. In an unsent letter to Carnap, Neurath wrote, "Poor Schlick, depressed me . . . such an aggressive person, full of unfriendly habits."[12]

All this came to a head when Schlick turned down Neurath's manuscript that had been due to appear in the Writings on the Scientific World Conception series. It was on the scientific foundations of history and economics, and Schlick complained that it was pure propaganda and had too many sentences ending with exclamation marks! Neurath, in turn, accused Schlick of being a bourgeois thinker—for believing philosophy could remain aloof from the real world, and for denying the relevance to philosophy of social and political context—and threatened to sue him. In the end, Neurath was persuaded to shelve the book in favor of another one, on sociology. Although Schlick was used to entertaining people in his elegant flat, not once did he invite Neurath. He had too loud a voice, Schlick complained.

———

There was virtually no topic on which the Circle achieved uniformity. But the most public disagreement within the Circle was the protocol sentence debate.

This has to be understood in context. The logical positivist project can be seen as having two components. On the one hand, there was an investigation into the link between words and propositions. This was not merely of the "all bachelors are unmarried men" kind. This is a case of one term being reducible to or synonymous with another. But there are other kinds of relationships. For example, sometimes sentences logically follow from others (as in the conclusion that *If the pH strip turns red in the solution then the solution is an acid. The pH strip does turn red in the solution; therefore the solution is an acid.* Some sentences can be inconsistent with others. *Neurath has a beard* and *Neurath is clean-shaven* are contradictory; they cannot both be true.

But beyond the analysis of language, there is the link between language and the world. If we define words only in terms of other words, then we can never escape language: we are trapped in a linguistic circle. So, eventually we must make an escape and jump from language to the world. There must be some way in which words get their meaning not from other words but from the world. But words do not get their meaning from standing for objects in isolation. Words get their meaning in the context of a sentence or proposition and the way that proposition stands in relation to the world. And this is where protocol sentences came in.

There was mostly agreement that the protocol sentences on which knowledge and meaningful language were to be constructed were fundamental observation statements—*This object is blue.* But that is about as far as agreement ran. Between 1929 and 1936, members of the Vienna Circle engaged in a prolonged debate on these protocol sentences. This was played out in Circle meetings, within the pages of *Erkenntnis*, and elsewhere. What was to count as a protocol sentence? Did protocol sentences really exist? Were they open to doubt? What was the relationship between protocol sentences and the empirical world?

To what extent logical empiricism had foundationalist ambitions is a matter of dispute. Foundationalism means (roughly) that there are propositions that are true and certain, independently of other propositions—and the debate about whether knowledge could be put on rock-solid foundations goes back at least to Descartes in the seventeenth century. Within the Circle there was a dispute about whether protocol sentences provided solid foundations. Schlick and (initially) Carnap had foundationalist instincts. The idea was that with valid inferences, we could move from these secure basic statements, these protocol sentences, to more complicated ones. And ultimately all the sciences—including the social sciences—would be united by their common underpinnings. The *Tractatus*, of course, had constructed its edifice on the notion that complex statements were built out of simple statements, which in turn pictured some arrangement of simple objects—states of affairs.

Carnap's initial view was that protocol sentences captured immediate experiences and required no further justification or public confirmation. They were sense data—the things that are immediately present to my mind—like the redness of a tomato. He faced attack from two directions. His first opponent was Neurath. Neurath maintained that the observations had to be about the observable attributes of objects and the properties on which we could publicly agree. That a tomato was red or that a table or stick had certain dimensions was open to testing, to public scrutiny. That, in turn, was only possible if there was a language with a shared understanding of words and concepts and rules.

The debate between Neurath and Carnap was at its most heated from 1930 to 1932. In the end, Carnap conceded ground. Philosopher Hilary Putnam admired Carnap's willingness to change his mind: "for me Carnap is still the outstanding example of a human being who puts the search for truth higher than personal vanity."[13] But in so doing, Carnap was forced to acknowledge what Neurath had long asserted, namely that rock-bottom certainty was beyond reach. If protocol sentences were about the physical world (as opposed to sensations and impressions of that world), then it was always possible that they were mistaken. If I said, "That stick is bent," I might be wrong, for the appearance of its being bent might be a trick of the light.

Enter Moritz Schlick. Schlick wished to reclaim the certainty that Neurath and now Carnap were prepared to ditch. He presented his case in a 1934 essay, setting off a further round of argument. Schlick insisted that protocol sentences had to be about how objects *appeared* to a particular person and take the form of *here, now, this*—for example, *here, now, blue patch*. The *here* and *now* ensured infallibility. A sentence that refers to an experience in the past, say, might be vulnerable to a deceptive memory.

On the face of it this seems like an arcane disagreement, an angels-on-the-head-of-a-pin quarrel. In fact, for the Circle, it had far-reaching implications. The advantage of the Schlickian framework is that it begins with statements that cannot be refuted and that require no further confirmation. I cannot err in declaring "here, now, blue patch." If I can then build up from this to more complex statements, I do so in confidence that the ground on which the edifice is based is firm.

All well and good. But the drawback is that it is unclear how one can make the move from a subjective statement about me and my experience to a statement to which we can all assent. You might see a blue patch, but I might not. Such an account threatens to ensnare us into a kind of solipsism. Even worse, if all you can guarantee is the here and now, then you could not be sure that *here, now, blue patch* would hold five seconds later. Schlick's radical subjectivism, Neurath claimed, took protocol sentences down a cul-de-sac—it could never lead us to non-subjective claims about, say, the dimensions of the table or stick.

The logic of their respective positions required Schlick and Neurath to supply different accounts of knowledge. Since Neurath had granted that protocol statements could be declared invalid just like any other empirical statement, he had to explain how science progressed. He

proposed a metaphor for how our knowledge of the world was to be understood. He had used it before, and would use it again: it has become known as Neurath's Boat. We have to presume existing knowledge, he said. We cannot overturn all our assumptions at once—that would be nonsensical. But neither can we assume that there are any rock-solid foundations. We can always jettison bits of "knowledge" as we progress. "We are like sailors who must rebuild their ship on the open sea, never able to dismantle it in dry-dock and to reconstruct it there out of the best materials."[14]

Neurath's Boat was far from the foundational certainty Schlick craved. And wrapped up in this row was another disagreement about the nature of truth. Take the statement, *The tomato is red*. Is this true because it somehow resembles the world—does this combination of letters and sounds present an accurate account of reality? Neurath thought this account was nonsense. The Wittgensteinian idea, endorsed by Schlick, that a sentence, made up of words and sounds, could be checked against the world, could conform with reality by sharing the same form of structure, was mysterious or, to deploy his favorite jibe, metaphysical. The debate between Neurath and Schlick was characterized by hostility and mutual misunderstanding. In philosophical jargon, Schlick endorsed something close to a correspondence theory of truth. Neurath was not interested in what it meant for something to be "true" and instead adopted a coherence theory of *justification*. Statements could not be justified by contrasting them with stuff that was extralinguistic, thought Neurath, they could only be compared with other statements. For example, did they contradict other statements? If so, they could not coexist; something had to give. Schlick objected, in turn, that Neurath's approach opened the door to relativism. Since Neurath could make no sense of the notion that statements can accurately or inaccurately portray reality, Schlick claimed, all that seems to matter to him is that they fit together.

These fundamental intellectual differences exacerbated the tensions that had always been present in the Schlick-Neurath relationship. A 1934 essay by Neurath, *Radical Physicalism and the Real World*,[15] in which he mocked Schlick's "poetry"—Schlick had talked of his protocol

sentences being the source of "all the light of knowledge"[16]—was the definitive breach in their relationship. They never spoke again.

———

Alongside protocol sentences, the Circle's second major debate was about verificationism. If a statement was not analytic—true or false in virtue of its terms—then, according to the verification principle, it was only meaningful if verifiable. This was one crucial distinction between empirical and nonempirical inquiries and fields. It is what made many statements about ethics, aesthetics, and religion nonscientific and neither true nor false.

Earlier we noted a distinction between a Carnapian and a Wittgensteinian interpretation of the verification principle—the Carnap version stated that whether a synthetic sentence was cognitively meaningful depends on whether there are criteria for verifying it. The Wittgenstein version was that the meaning *consists* in the criteria.

There was a deeper problem still.

What counts as verification? As the logical empiricists attempted to get more precise about the verification principle, difficulties quickly began to emerge. Take statements about the past and the future. Had a member of the Circle in 1929 declared "a man will land on the moon in 1969," how could this statement have been verified? And what about claims about the past made by historians? These did not seem to be open to verification in the same way as scientific propositions. We can test the hypothesis that water boils at 100 degrees centigrade by boiling water. But what predictions are entailed by historical propositions, such as *Vienna was besieged by the Ottoman Turks in 1683*. Intuitively it feels like such a sentence makes sense! In which case, how does it achieve this status?

There were various suggestions. Clearly history relies on evidence, so one way to view the work of historians is to draw an analogy between their tools and the tools of the scientists. The scientist has a Petri dish, the historian has an archive. And the historian does make predictions of a sort. If Vienna was indeed besieged by the Ottoman Turks in 1683, one might expect this fact to appear in documents, including documents that have not yet been, but will be, unearthed.

That sounds like a plausible way out for the logical positivist. But do all statements about history really take this form? The claim *At 8:30 a.m. on 1 January 1920, Carnap shaved* appears to make sense—yet, a century on, there might be no evidence to support or refute it, and no prospect of any relevant evidence ever emerging.

What about the practical problems of verification? Suppose a Circle member had claimed water existed on the far side of the moon. Since space travel was not feasible in the 1920s and '30s, must they dismiss such a statement as meaningless? Initially, Carnap seems to have accepted this conclusion, but it was an unappealing route for many Circle members who came to agree that what mattered was that a claim was verifiable "in principle." It was not practicable to fly to the moon, but it was possible *in principle*.

But this then begged further questions. What did it mean to say something was possible *in principle*? For example, what of claims about the afterlife—the claim, say, that our souls will end up in either heaven or hell? Schlick and Carnap disagreed about whether such talk made any sense. Schlick thought that if there was life after death we would eventually find out, and thus some afterlife propositions were verifiable. Carnap (and Ayer) dismissed the notion that there could be thoughts held by a bodiless being.

Then, trickier still, how are verificationists to account for unobservables? Much of modern physics posits unobservables. That is to say, to make sense of certain phenomena in the world, scientists conjecture that there must be entities that, given the kinds of creatures we are, and the kinds of sensory apparatus we possess, we cannot directly perceive. They include atoms, electrons, viruses, radio waves. Astrophysicists believe the universe was created by a Big Bang. The Big Bang cannot, of course, be seen. Yet there is plenty of supporting evidence for it, including cosmic microwave background radiation. And surely we all want to say that the Big Bang theory is science. Could verificationists smuggle unobservables into their account of science and yet remain uncontaminated by dreaded and despised metaphysics?

Then there was a linked problem of probability. Modern physics implied that there were certain statements whose truth could only probabilistically be determined. What did this mean? And how could it be verified? Once again the logical empiricists were split.

Hans Reichenbach, from Berlin, pushed what is sometimes called a frequency account. That is, to say that a thrown die has a one-in-six probability of showing a 5 is to claim that over many throws, the die would land on 5 one in six times. Carnap wrote that "In our discussions on probability in the Vienna Circle, we took for granted the frequency conception."[17] In fact, the frequency approach faces various difficulties, including the problem of how to deal with single events. It seems to make sense to ask "What is the probability of an all-out nuclear war?" but this is either going to happen or it is not, and if it happens it is certainly not going to happen multiple times. Popper would later propose an alternative to the frequency account—propensity theory. He regarded probability as like a "tendency," or "disposition." A die has a one-in-six tendency to land on a 5. Unlike the frequency account, this has the virtue of being able to make sense of single cases, but spelling out what is meant by a tendency or a disposition has always proved problematic.

Another approach might be called "subjectivist." This holds that a statement about probability is a statement about a degree of belief. It is not about the world, but about knowledge of the world. If I say that the probability that the rolling die will show 5 is one in six, that is a reflection of my confidence, which would change if I discovered a relevant new piece of information (e.g., that the die was weighted). Bayesian probability is a variation of subjectivist probability. In the eighteenth-century, Thomas Bayes provided an account of how to represent probability given the available evidence. Carnap attempted to capture this in logical language—there was a logical relationship between a statement and the evidence for it. The probability that the die landing on 5 was one in six was given partial confirmation by evidence—for example, by its landing on 5 one in six times.

———

Protocol sentences, verification, probability   these were staples of Circle debate. But then there was ethics.

Ethics was a tricky one. Wittgenstein had proclaimed in the final line of the *Tractatus*, "Whereof one cannot speak, thereof one must be silent," encapsulating his verdict that ethics lay beyond language. This did not prevent people from straining to state ethical truths. But attempting to do so was like hunting phantoms, failure was inevitable. Ethics was ineffable, ethical statements were nonsensical.

It took the Circle a long time to recognize that they had misunderstood Wittgenstein's central message. Wittgenstein thought that the aim of founding ethics in rationality was doomed. The obvious—and yet incorrect conclusion—was that Wittgenstein regarded ethics as trivial. The opposite was the case. Ethical statements cannot be compared to the world and found to be true or false. So ethics cannot be said. But it can be shown.

In November 1929, Wittgenstein delivered a Cambridge lecture in which he expressed sympathy with those drawn to talk and write about ethics. "What [ethics] says does not add to our knowledge in any sense. But it is a document of a tendency in the human mind which I personally cannot help respecting deeply and I would not for my life ridicule it."[18] Trying to explain the *Tractatus*, he wrote on another occasion, "My work consists of two parts: the one presented here plus all that I have not written. And it is precisely this second part that is the important one."[19]

The Wittgensteinian notion that ethics was ineffable was one that even his loyal supporter Schlick contested. People clearly did make ethical claims, such as *Lying is wrong*: such claims are understood by philosophers and ordinary people alike. For the Circle, ethics was not meaningless in the sense that it was gibberish. But ethical claims were outside the net of things that were verifiable—you could not verify the claim *It is wrong to lie*. It was just that ethical statements did not have scientific meaning. This claim is sometimes called noncognitivism. Ultimately philosophy or science could not prove one value judgment superior to any other. The difference between the Circle on the one hand and Wittgenstein on the other can be put in this way. Most Circle members more or less agreed that when it came to ethics, there was a sense in which what was called for was silence. But for Wittgenstein, that silence was pregnant with mystical (Carnap and Neurath would say metaphysical) undertones.

Since ethics could not be verified, the Circle largely ignored it. But there were some attempts by Circle figures to analyze ethics from a logical positivist perspective. Perhaps the best-known attempt came from A. J. Ayer. He proposed that we understand ethical statements as being not commands but more like expressions. To say "Lying is wrong" is merely to express a disapproval of lying. This became known as the hurrah/boo theory. "Lying is wrong" is like mentioning lying and then wagging a finger; it is like saying "Lying, boo," just as to state "Generosity is a virtue" is equivalent to saying "Generosity, hurrah!"

> Thus, if I say to someone, "You acted wrongly in stealing that money," I am not stating anything more than if I had simply said, "You stole that money." In adding that this action is wrong I am not making any further statement about it. I am simply evincing my moral disapproval of it. It is as if I had said, "You stole that money," in a peculiar tone of horror, or written it with the addition of some special exclamation marks.[20]

Ayer's approach was briefly fashionable. But in the aftermath of World War II—and as more and more details of concentration camps and killings emerged—many critics found abhorrent the notion that the charge of immorality was merely the utterance of a feeling, with no basis in objectivity. One well-known English philosopher, C.E.M. Joad, went so far as to accuse Ayer of inadvertently fueling fascism. Ayer's philosophy helped create a moral vacuum, wrote Joad, that was bound to be filled by irrational movements like fascism.[21]

A variation of "objectivity" in ethics was introduced by two Circle thinkers. One was Schlick, in his book *Problems of Ethics* (*Fragen der Ethik*, 1930). Deviating uncharacteristically from a Wittgensteinian position, he argued that to acknowledge the meaningfulness of ethical statements meant treating ethics as a branch of science. It is a purely theoretical matter: "If there are ethical questions which have meaning, and are therefore capable of being answered, then ethics is a science."[22]

How could that be? The solution was to give the topic an empirical spin. It made no sense to say that something was desirable. That was meaningless. It could not be connected to anything in the world. But it made perfect sense to say that something was desired. That was a statement of fact, which might be true or false. To understand ethics, then, was essentially an empirical project, an investigation into what humans want from life and how they can best achieve what they want. In that way, Schlick claimed, ethics was a branch of psychology. From this emerged directions and strategies for how human happiness or well-being could be maximized. This was not utilitarianism—the theory that we should act so as to maximize human happiness or well-being—because it was descriptive rather than normative. Schlick was identifying ethics, not prescribing it. The scientific investigator of ethics, thought Schlick, must constantly be on guard against the risk of becoming moralistic, for "there is no greater danger than to change from a philosopher into a moralist, from an investigator into a preacher."[23]

Karl Menger took this position on, publishing his own book on ethics in 1934. A mathematician, he decided to treat ethics as a branch of mathematics. Stripping out any normative element, he applied mathematical methods to group dynamics, to an analysis of what happened when you have one set of individuals with one ethical position and another set of individuals with a different position. The book had one significant impact: it was read by Oskar Morgenstern, an economist at the University of Vienna, and helped inspire the development of game theory, of which he was a founder.

Beyond the empirical treatment of Schlick and Menger, there was clearly a role for philosophy in ethics in the logical analysis of ethical statements—such as drawing out distinctions between means and ends. The philosopher could identify inconsistencies and make clear the nature of any factual disagreement.

Yet this was still not enough to resolve a puzzle at the heart of ethics, at least as it was understood by the logical empiricists. As we have seen, many Circle members had strong moral views. Neurath was not alone in being voluble about his opinions. Carnap was politically engaged throughout his life. But if the logical empiricists were convinced there was no truth about ethics, how could they take ethical matters so seriously? Some critics assumed that logical empiricism undermined ethics: one of Carnap's colleagues in Prague thought it so threatening to young minds that he pondered aloud whether to call on the authorities to put Carnap in jail.

The logical empiricist answer to this puzzle may not convince everyone but goes something like this. Ethics (as David Hume had declared) is ultimately a matter of sentiment and disposition. We humans are creatures with values, and our values do not always coincide. You may believe that equality is of the utmost importance, I may put certain rights above equality. That may result in disagreement—perhaps even heated disagreement. We may try to persuade each other in various ways, for example by citing evidence in support of our case. But in the end, there is nothing we can do to reconcile our disagreement, and there is nothing to be gained by my claiming that my values are true and yours false. We may simply have to live with our difference of opinion. In extreme cases, clashes over values might turn violent. But ethics is not about truth. It is not science. And philosophers have no special ethical insight. "I believe that . . . philosophy will not help us decide the value questions themselves in one way or another,"[24] said Carnap.

Does that drain ethics of its motivating force? No—or so the noncognitivist claims. My values are likely to be very important to me and I will want to see them applied. They reflect how I see myself and how I perceive the world. That they rouse me into action is entirely consistent with my ethical views being neither true nor false. It is perfectly legitimate for me to posit ethical judgments, so long as I acknowledge that they do not belong in the same category as empirical statements.

This, then, is the logical empiricist position. No doubt some readers will find it compelling; others less so or not at all. All one can point to is the fact that the empiricists themselves saw no tension in their taking strong ethical and political positions while at the same time holding that these positions were no more "true" than positions to which they ran contrary.

———

There were many other issues members of the Circle discussed—too many to go into, though a relatively minor one merits a note. There are several references in Circle writings about whether or not people should be divided into racial categories.[25] Obviously, for members of the Circle—a few of whom found themselves placed in a category to which they felt little allegiance and a weak or nonexistent identification—this was a highly personal matter. Broadly, the question was whether there was an empirical basis to the division of humans by race—whether propositions about racial groups picked out some observable difference. Nowadays, mainstream scientists claim there is no genetic distinction underpinning racial groupings, but the logical empiricists took a different stance. There seemed to be a consensus that race was not a pseudo-category; it did have empirical standing. Waismann even seemed to believe that racial dispositions could be inherited, and so race might be predictive of behavior.

But beyond the question of whether a racial taxonomy was meaning-ful, there was a subsidiary matter—was race a helpful way of dividing humans? What function did such a classification serve? In theory, Wais-mann at least, thought it could be helpful. But in practice, race categories had been embraced and deployed for entirely evil purposes by Nazis, Austrofascists, and later, in the American context, segregationists. Not surprisingly, therefore, there was opposition—sometimes strong—from, among others, Schlick, Carnap, Neurath, and Waismann—to their use. Here, then, was a distinction between the meaningfulness of a cat-egory and its purpose.

———

One final more fundamental debate needs mentioning. The Circle had begun with a common goal: to develop a philosophy of knowledge that was able to comprehend the latest revelations in physical science and in the process to slay metaphysics. This was the role of philosophy.

But now even this ambition began to divide the group. Since return-ing to Cambridge, Wittgenstein's thinking had evolved. This would see its fullest expression in the posthumous *Philosophical Investigations*. He came to regard philosophy as akin to a sort of therapy. He noted that people became bewitched and befuddled by certain questions—Could something be both red and green all over? If it was midday in Vienna, what time was it on the sun?—but, he now believed, these were not deep problems. They were puzzles that dissolved with an analysis of language. That something cannot be both red and green is not a meta-physical truth, but instead a grammatical one. It makes no grammatical sense to claim that something is red and green at the same time.

The idea that the task of the philosopher was to extract us from these linguistic traps was not one adopted by the Circle, but its influence was felt, particularly on Waismann, who alongside Schlick was the most loyal Wittgensteinian. Waismann insisted that philosophy could still assist in the progress of knowledge. Like his master, however, he now began to attend to how we use ordinary, natural language. Carnap was bored by the focus on everyday talk and continued to explore the logic of formal language.

On 4 November 1933, Schlick wrote to the English translator of *Fragen der Ethik*: "I am not going to have meetings of the 'Wiener Kreis' this winter. Some of our old members have grown too dogmatic and might discredit the whole movement." [26] The ruptures within the Circle were becoming irreconcilable. Their unity of spirit was splintering into factionalism, and their early optimism that together they could crush metaphysics was running into unyielding complexity.

Responsibility for destroying logical empiricism once and for all, however, was claimed elsewhere—by an outsider.

14

The Unofficial Opposition

I fear that I must admit responsibility.

—KARL POPPER

WHO KILLED LOGICAL positivism? It is a good question, and one Karl Popper poses in his intellectual autobiography, *Unended Quest*. Helpfully he also provides an answer: "I fear that I must admit responsibility."[1]

Born in 1902, Popper was nurtured in the same milieu as many Circle members. His father was a prominent lawyer whose family was from Bohemia; his mother came from a middle-class Viennese family. Both Jews, they converted to Lutheranism in 1900. As has been described, the family's savings, as with so many middle-class families, were wiped out by postwar inflation.

Popper was no prodigy. He initially began attending mathematics lectures at the university without having graduated from school, but found the content too difficult. He then returned to the university in 1922, taking an eclectic mix of courses but focusing on math. He had various false starts at a career: as an apprentice cabinetmaker, as social worker, and finally as teacher, for which he had enrolled in the Pedagogical Institute. It was there he met his future wife, Josefine Anna Henninger (Hennie). He first heard of the Circle around 1926 or 1927 from reading a newspaper article by Otto Neurath. During his teacher training, he continued to attend university courses, and he earned his doctorate in 1928, on psychological methods. It was an impressive piece of work. His teaching career—in math and physics—began a year later. In his spare time he was developing the thoughts for which he became famous.

It would take a conference of Freudians fully to comprehend Popper's complex relationship with the Circle, though Popper, a skeptic about psychoanalysis, would disdain their analysis. He was obviously the sort of talent the Circle would normally have pulled into its orbit. Popper claims in *Unended Quest* that he would have considered it an honor to have been invited. So why was no invitation ever forthcoming?

The answer was that offers lay in the gift of the mild-tempered Moritz Schlick, who abhorred conflict. He believed in civilized, urbane conversation. He thought Popper boorish, a grandstander, and an intolerant bully. He was not wrong. Popper was a forceful speaker but an antagonistic listener. Science, he would write, should move closer and closer to the truth. But in debate, truth for Popper always had a lower priority than victory. What mattered was that he both vanquish and belittle opponents. In private Popper had considerable charm and generosity, but in public he embodied the Nietzschean will to power. That this was driven by a deep insecurity is a hypothesis which cannot be tested.

Schlick's relationship with Popper was always strained. Schlick had been one of the examiners of Popper's PhD, which was passed despite containing a philosophical attack on Schlick's writings on physicalism—the view that everything that exists is physical, and that meaningful statements are all translatable into physical statements. Popper was probably the first philosopher to use the term *physicalism*; it was a doctrine supported by Neurath (who made use of the term himself in 1930) and then developed further by Carnap, in particular, but also by Schlick. However, it was Popper's other examiner, psychologist Karl Bühler, who acted as his champion, although even he was halfhearted in his endorsement, regarding the thesis as "clearly of a secondary and literary nature."[2] (This did not stop them from giving it the highest grade.)

It was one thing for Popper to criticize Schlick himself; it was another to disparage Schlick's idol. Popper's crucial error came at the Gomperz Circle (the discussion group led by philosopher Heinrich Gomperz), where in front of Schlick and several other Circle members, including Carnap, he delivered a talk containing a withering critique of Wittgenstein, delivered in his trademark trenchant and unyielding manner. Although in his personal interactions he was the ultimate dogmatist himself, he now accused Wittgenstein of dogmatism. Schlick stormed out halfway through. The irascible young man had effectively torn up his future entry ticket to the Circle. His approach to debate, Schlick concluded, was incompatible with the constructive and open-minded atmosphere he tried to foster.

———

Like Circle members, Popper was an empiricist: science had to be rooted in evidence. But, he came to believe, the Vienna Circle had the relationship between theory and evidence upside down.

Popper stressed that what he was interested in was not primarily about meaning—the difference between sense and nonsense. That issue bored him; questions about language in general he thought tiresome. While he approved of the project to clarify problems, the pursuit of total precision, he believed, was futile, and he adamantly opposed the notion, emerging out of Wittgenstein's later philosophy, that philosophical problems were essentially the product of linguistic confusion.

Rather than focus on language, his project was to demarcate science from pseudo-science, the empirical from the nonempirical. For example, he wanted to distinguish between astrology and the theory of relativity. It was not that one was true and one false. A scientific theory could prove false; a pseudo-scientific theory might be true. Nor was the issue that one was based on evidence and the other was not. Astrologers were not scientists even if they pored over charts and diagrams and made use of complex equations. Wherein, then, lay the difference?

Popper's key insight concerned inductive reasoning, the building up from individual facts to a general claim. The problem of induction went back to David Hume. Every day of my life the sun has risen in the east, so I conclude that tomorrow it will too. But according to Hume this inference has no rational justification. Another famous example concerns the black swan. You see a white swan, then another. You then formulate a theory that all swans are white. Suppose you see more white swans. Have you thereby shown that all swans are white?

No. In your research you may observe ten thousand swans, all of them white, and that still would not be sufficient. For the following day, you might see a black one. That suggests an asymmetry. No number of sightings of white swans can settle the hypothesis that all swans are white, but just one sighting of a black swan can disprove it. The Circle was not unaware of the problem of induction, of course—and mostly dealt with Popper's critique by turning to the idea of "confirmability." That is, even if something could not be conclusively proved, it could be supported by new evidence—it could be confirmed.

It was a defense that left Popper unconvinced. He said that we must overturn the old model of how science operated. Science progressed in the following way, he said: first scientists come up with a theory, then they set about testing it. The method is trial and error. The bolder the theory the better, for the more it is then open to refutation. Science makes predictions, and these predictions may not come to pass, in which case the theory has to be modified or jettisoned altogether. What distinguishes the empirical from the nonempirical, science from non-science, is precisely that science, unlike pseudo-science, is open to falsification.

Take psychoanalysis. Although throughout his life Karl Popper nursed a deep animus toward Wittgenstein, their critique of Freud bore striking similarities. Popper, like Wittgenstein, complained about the lack of agreed-upon criteria with which to judge the claims of psycho-analysis. Popper, like Wittgenstein, was not entirely dismissive of Freud—and far more supportive than is often acknowledged. Indeed, in *Conjectures and Refutations* he wrote that: "Much of [Freud's work] is of considerable importance," its theories "describe some facts, but in the manner of myths. They contain most interesting psychological sug-gestions, but not in a testable form."[3]

That was the key. Testability. Psychoanalysis had scientific preten-sions. What, then, would in Popper's terminology falsify a psychoana-lytic theory? If the analyst continued to insist that my dream should be interpreted as repressed anger at my father, there was ultimately nothing that could prove him wrong. Every action is capable of being given a psychoanalytic spin. If I become angry in an awkward situation, psychoanalysts can offer an explanation: if I remain calm, they can proffer an alternative explanation. This is not, insisted Popper, the scientific method.

In *Conjectures and Refutations* Popper recounted a conversation he had in 1919 with psychotherapist Alfred Adler about Adler's theory of inferiority. It's not the only Popper anecdote of this kind—centering on an intellectual dispute, with Popper emerging as wittily victorious. When Popper offered what he believed was a clear counterexample to the inferiority theory, Adler dismissed it. "Slightly shocked I asked him how he could be so sure. 'Because of my thousandfold experience', he replied; whereupon I could not help saying, 'And with this new case, I suppose your experience has become thousand-and-one-fold.'"[4]

———

In later life Popper would talk in grandiloquent terms about the so-called Circle "legend": the false idea that he had been a member of the Circle. Imagining himself as the subject of a legend was all of a piece with his megalomaniac disposition. It is true, of course, that he objected to some of the Circle's principal tenets. But his accounts of distancing himself from the Circle were historical distortions.

For one thing, it was premised on the false notion that the Circle was a homogeneous group and he alone was a critic. In fact, there were plenty of disagreements within the Circle, as we have seen. At the time only Neurath considered Popper's position to be entirely incompatible with the Circle. It was Neurath who labeled Popper—probably half tongue-in-cheek—as the Circle's official opposition. Neurath launched a fierce attack on Popper, pointing out several major flaws in his critique. He scoffed at the idea that scientific theories were abandoned after one "falsification." Negative results can shake our confidence in a theory "but does not reduce it automatically to zero."[5] After all, you would not abandon a theory unless you had a better one to replace it with.

Neurath aside, however, the rest of the Circle saw Popper, in Feigl's words, as making a "valuable and helpful"[6] contribution. Popper's very first academic article appeared in the Circle's periodical *Erkenntnis*. Even

Schlick, who could not abide Popper personally, came to value him as a thinker. Popper's *Logik der Forschung* appeared in the Circle's Writings on the Scientific World Conception series, and the decision to publish (once Popper had agreed to shorten the tome from its original length) was supported by Schlick and particularly by Carnap. Several Circle members, including Carnap, reviewed it generously. This reflected the fact that, Popper's protestations to the contrary, he and the Vienna Circle operated in the same philosophical arena, struggled over similar questions, and were animated by similar concerns. Popper's intellectual heroes—especially Bertrand Russell—were equally the heroes of the Circle. Some of his intellectual villains—especially Martin Heidegger—were also the villains of the Circle. His interests and writings about the philosophy of science were a response to those in the Circle, not apart from or parallel to them. In that sense, he owed his entire philosophical career to the Circle, and it was a continued irritation to them that he overemphasized their differences. He would fiercely resist the characterization, but he must be considered a Circle thinker, despite being excluded from their meetings. It was only his furious dogmatism—or to put it more generously, his refusal to accept the authority of others—that set him apart.

Then there were the personal links. Popper had many friends and associates who were Circle members, and with whom he engaged in intense discussions. They included Carnap, Feigl, Kaufmann, Kraft, Menger, Neurath, Rand, Waismann, and Zisel. With Feigl, he struck up a particularly close bond. Their first meeting, says Popper, "became decisive for my whole life."[7] So absorbed in conversation about the philosophy of science did they become that they stayed up all night and Feigl urged Popper to publish a book. Feigl thought Popper an outstanding mind. As for Menger, Popper knew him well enough to be invited to his mathematical colloquium. With Carnap, Popper jousted on and off for decades. Popper reserved probably his greatest admiration for the Circle associate, Polish logician Alfred Tarski. When Tarski visited Austria in 1935 he and Popper sat on a bench for twenty minutes ("an unforgotten bench"[8]) while Tarski expounded on his theory of truth. "No words can describe how much I learned from all this. . . .

Although Tarski was only a little older than I, and although we were, in those days, on terms of considerable intimacy, I looked upon him as the one man whom I could truly regard as my teacher in philosophy."[9]

————

Of all his perceived victories, his self-proclaimed triumph over the Vienna Circle was the one that meant most to him. He was always eager to stress his originality, though in recent years some scholars have traced the provenance of some of his key thoughts to others, notably Karl Bühler.[10] In any case, it is worth noting that while the Circle took Popper's ideas seriously, they did not seem to Circle members to have shattered their *Weltanschauung* (worldview). In a letter from Schlick to Carnap in November 1934, Schlick wrote that Popper "is completely of our persuasion."[11]

Popper's use of language when he raised his rhetorical question— Who killed logical positivism?—was unfortunate. Because there was a literal killing; a murder that did much to finish off what was left of the Circle.

15

Now, You Damn Bastard

I can easily imagine, e.g., witnessing the funeral of my own body.

—MORITZ SCHLICK[1]

IN VIENNA on Monday 22 June 1936, at around eight in the morning, Johann Nelböck left his apartment carrying a small automatic pistol. We know many of the details of what followed over the next seventy-five minutes, culminating in his shooting Moritz Schlick to death. Nelböck's motive is less clear-cut. Later, after the Anschluss, he would alter his story. He had believed his victim to be Jewish, he would claim, and his actions were driven solely by ideology. But that was not the explanation he gave at the trial, nor was it the first time he had revised his account.

Whatever drove Nelböck, the murder of Moritz Schlick can be understood only in its political context. For, apart from anything else, the Austrian newspapers reacted to it in a highly politicized fashion.

Nelböck had known Schlick for almost a decade. In 1925, when he was a twenty-two-year-old undergraduate at the university, he had enrolled in Schlick's class. He was a decent student, going on to earn a doctorate. Sometime in 1928 he came to know, and develop an infatuation for, another student of Schlick's, Sylvia Borowicka. Nelböck confessed his attachment to her but was rebuffed. Worse, in 1930 she told him that she had "a certain interest" in Professor Schlick.

Borowicka claimed that her feelings were reciprocated, but there is no independent evidence for this. Schlick was certainly typical of married men in the Circle in being routinely unfaithful to his wife. In any case, Nelböck became convinced that Schlick and Borowicka were in a sexual relationship, and his thoughts toward Schlick became both vengeful and obsessive. Sometime in 1931, Nelböck warned Borowicka that he would shoot Schlick and then kill himself. She found the threat sufficiently credible to pass it on to Schlick, and he found it sufficiently worrisome that he notified the authorities. After an investigation, Nelböck was diagnosed with schizoid psychopathy and committed to Am Steinhof, a psychiatric hospital in Vienna. Borowicka also came under suspicion and was assessed by the same psychiatrist, Professor Dr. Otto Pötzl, who described her as "a nervous girl of slightly eccentric character."[2] After she had stayed in Dr. Pötzl's clinic, he wrote to the rector of the university recommending that she be given a chance to finish her studies.

Schlick must have hoped that this would be the end of the matter. But after three months Nelböck was released. With his doctorate, teaching was an obvious career path, and he studied for and passed a teaching examination. We do not know how often he and Schlick bumped into one another, but in 1932 there was another fierce confrontation, which again resulted in Nelböck being detained, this time for only nine days. The police would sometimes deploy a bodyguard to protect the professor, but then nothing would happen and the security would be withdrawn. Schlick noted, "I fear they begin to think that it is I who is mad."[3]

In 1934 Nelböck delivered a lecture entitled "A Critique of Positivism" at an adult education center. Was his hostility to logical empiricism a product of his animus toward Schlick? Quite possibly. In any case, now he was (barely) earning his keep by tutoring students preparing for their doctoral exams. In the summer of 1935 he was due to begin teaching a course in adult education, which promised a more stable income. Since the 1934 coup, power within the adult education center had shifted from left to right. But in January 1935, just a few months earlier, he received notice that the job offer had been withdrawn. The explanation given was that logical empiricism was so out of fashion that a lecture series on the topic would not go down well with students.

The real reason for the change of mind was Nelböck's history of mental instability. How the center found out about this was and is a matter of dispute. Nelböck claimed that behind his back Schlick had objected to his appointment (and recommended Waismann give the course in his place) and that another letter to the center, probably from

Waismann, carried details of his (Nelböck's) mental health history. The center's secretary general denied this version of events, insisting that he discovered about Nelböck's problems independently.

Deprived of his teaching course and worrying that his period in the asylum would dog him for the rest of his life, Nelböck fell into depression. A few months later, his head once more full of murderous thoughts, he managed to purchase a Singer pistol and ammunition. First kill Schlick, then take his own life, that was the plan. But he had a change of heart and disposed of the ammunition in the Danube, while retaining the pistol.

In the summer of 1935, Herbert Feigl, now based in the United States, joined Schlick while he was on holiday in Bolzano, in South Tyrol. He found Schlick in a gloomy mood, weighed down by recent disagreements with Otto Neurath and with the young, cantankerous Karl Popper, and more seriously, by some menacing letters from Nelböck. Repeating his threats, Nelböck had also plagued him with calls at home. Just as unsettling, the younger man had developed the habit of sitting in on Schlick's lectures. He attended one lecture, on immortality, in early 1936. For the logical empiricists there was a puzzle about whether claims to immortality were meaningless. The lecture stoked the Catholic Nelböck into a state of extreme agitation.

He acquired ten more bullets.

———

Schlick was not supposed to have been in Vienna on 22 June 1936. The Second International Congress for the Unity of Science began on 21 June in Copenhagen, and he was to present a paper there. The star of the gathering was the Danish physicist Niels Bohr. Officially, the theme for the Congress was causality in biology and physics, and it would address the philosophical implications of some of Bohr's discoveries.

It is not clear why Schlick did not attend—one letter to Neurath earlier in the month suggests that he was overworked, but it's also possible that his travel permit did not arrive in time. Instead, he would deliver his last lecture of the summer term. That same morning, shortly after he left his apartment, Nelböck seems to have reached a fatal decision, one that had been plaguing him all night. He returned to his residence to pick up his gun, loading it before tucking it in his jacket. Then he walked to the university and positioned himself close to the steps leading up to the School of Philosophy.

Meanwhile, just before 9:00 a.m., Schlick left his own apartment in Prinz Eugen Strasse. His habit before heading off to deliver a lecture was to prepare himself mentally by walking around the breakfast table. As usual, after leaving his apartment, the professor took Tram D, down the slope past the Belvedere gardens and park—bathed in sunlight—toward the center of Vienna. The trams were described in a contemporaneous account as "highly efficient but suicidal looking."[4] This particular route was short and direct. Schlick arrived around 9:15 a.m.; students in Room 41 were already awaiting him. We can assume that, as usual, the lecture room would have been packed.

Schlick walked up the grand staircase at the main university entrance, through the iron gate, down the hall, and turned right up the stairs to his destination. There, he walked past Nelböck; it is hard to imagine that he did not notice him. Nelböck rushed ahead of Schlick, turned round, and fired straight at him from barely a meter or two away. A witness heard him shout, "Now, you damned bastard, there you have it!" The university administrator, Heinrich Drimmel, called the police on hearing the shots, but it was too late.

The founder of the Vienna Circle was dead. The court documents reveal that he was hit by four bullets; two had gone straight through the heart.

Nelböck waited placidly for his arrest.

———

The dramatic news from Vienna was deemed of sufficient consequence to merit coverage in the foreign press, though the United States newspaper of record, the *New York Times*, accorded it only one paragraph, buried at the bottom of the page below a much larger space devoted to an advertisement for women's tennis clothing including a knitted headband for only 95 cents (this was the eve of the Wimbledon Tennis Championship, in which the British sensation Fred Perry was competing to win his third successive single's title). Schlick's murder was summed up with typical *Times* economy: "Professor Moritz Schlick, 54 years old, a distinguished faculty member of Vienna University, was shot and killed as he entered a classroom today. Police say the slayer was a mentally deranged graduate of Professor Schlick's course in philosophy."

That was it. There was, to be fair, a lot going on in the world. In the US, the Democratic National Convention, at which Franklin D. Roosevelt would be renominated for a second term in the White House, was about to open in Philadelphia. With the US economy still in the doldrums from a deep and prolonged depression, Roosevelt would tell the delegates in his acceptance speech that Americans had "a rendezvous with destiny." Internationally, there were many stories to occupy the *Times*, though it was a fringe one from Germany that attracted the attention of their correspondent. The Nazi propaganda minister, Josef Goebbels, was considering banning a recently released movie entitled *The Country Doctor*. This sentimental comedy, about an unlicensed Canadian doctor in a remote lumber town, starred the famous Dionne quintuplets, the first quintuplets known to have survived infancy. Although there was no official explanation as to what lay behind Nazi disapproval of this apparently innocuous film, the *Times* pointed out that the scriptwriter was Sonya Levien, and speculated that this may have led Berlin to consider it non-Aryan.

Some British papers also covered Schlick's murder, including the *Daily Mail*, which provided the added (and fictional) detail that Schlick had been in conversation with a female student when the bullets were fired. But British papers too had other preoccupations. In the week of Schlick's murder, the British parliament was debating the Italian invasion of Abyssinia and the lifting of sanctions. Meanwhile, another colonial adventure was costing British lives. Palestine—including Jerusalem—had come under British control in 1922, under a League of Nations mandate and following the collapse of the Ottoman Empire. Ever since, there had been an ongoing guerrilla war against the British troops, waged by first Palestinian Arabs and later by Jews as well. The Jews, mostly newly arrived, were pursuing Herzl's Viennese dream. The week of Schlick's murder there was a rare British "success" story. After an Arab attack on a train, the British had used warplanes to track and kill the fleeing Palestinian "terrorists" at a cave near Nablus.

In the papers too were reports of Viennese opera, theater, and cinema performances being disrupted by Nazis throwing stink bombs. This tactic was used to interrupt Richard Wagner's *Tristan und Isolde*, conducted by Bruno Walter, a Jew. Despite the simmering unrest in Austria—or perhaps because of, and to counter it—the Austrian State Travel Bureau took out a big advertisement in *The Daily Telegraph* to lure British tourists to Austria: "For a Perfect *Gemütlich* Holiday."[5]

———

With Schlick's murder, Austria lost one of its most renowned thinkers. Although German-born, Schlick had chosen to spend the most productive years of his academic career at the University of Vienna. He had gathered together a group of talented, like-minded mathematicians, logicians, and philosophers and overseen a movement that had shaken the world of philosophy. He had made Vienna a beacon of critical thought about science and knowledge.

Tributes, in Austria at least, were naturally to be expected. In fact, though several Austrian papers such as the Catholic daily *Die Reichspost* covered the news, Nelböck was seen as the more compelling character in this bloody episode. So far as Schlick was mentioned, several editors judged that what their readers wanted to hear about were allegations that he had been involved in some sort of ménage à trois. Little was published about Schlick's achievements apart from, as one would have anticipated, a shocked response in the house organ of the Circle, *Erkenntnis*, where friends such as Philipp Frank and Hans Reichenbach paid their respects. "How is it possible that Schlick was killed by a human being?"[6] wrote the distraught and bewildered Reichenbach. More surprising was the generous homage from *Der christliche Ständestaat*, a journal associated with the Austrofascist government. Professor

Dietrich Hildebrand, a theologian, described Schlick as noble and amiable, and expressed "deep pain over the loss," while acknowledging that "his philosophical orientation was not ours."[7] There was also a glowing homage in *Die Neue Freie Presse* from author Hilde Spiel, an ex-student of Schlick's. In a later book, she described how she heard the news.

> On June 22, 1936, I travelled to town on the number 71 streetcar, and by chance glimpsed the headline of a newspaper over my neighbour's shoulder: "The philosopher Moritz Schlick shot dead." Even today I sense how my knees became weak, my head dizzy. Involuntarily my tears coursed down, there in the overcrowded streetcar. I got off and leaned for a long time against a house wall. It was the deepest of sorrows that I had yet experienced, not to be compared with the earlier pains of love.[8]

But elsewhere the reaction was different. The lead was taken by the German daily, the *Berliner Tageblatt*. On 23 June it ran an article about Guatemala, where Jews and Negroes had been forbidden to open businesses, and nearly adjacent it had news of Schlick's murder. There were some details of Schlick's academic background, what he wrote about, when he had received his habilitation, when he had arrived in Vienna, and in passing readers were informed—or rather misinformed—that Schlick was Jewish.

This set the tone. Back in Austria, on 10 July, the *Linzer Volksblatt* ran an article condemning Schlick for corrupting "the fine porcelain of the national character."[9] Students had been forced to drink from positivism's poisonous vial. Then, two days later, in the intellectual weekly paper *Schönere Zukunft* (*Better Future*) came this: "The Jew is a born anti-metaphysician and loves logicality, mathematicality, formalism, and positivism in philosophy—in other words, all the characteristics that Schlick embodied to the highest degree. We would like to point out, however, that we are Christians living in a Christian German state, and that it is up to us to determine which philosophy is good and appropriate."

This was one paragraph in a lengthy article whose author was too cowardly to reveal his true identity. He used a pseudonym, Prof.

Ernst Mach

Source: Christoph Limbeck-Lilienau and Friedrich Stadler, *Der Wiener Kreis* (LIT Verlag, 2015). Reprinted courtesy of the Vienna Circle Society / Wiener Kreis Gesellschaft.

Olga Hahn

Source: Christoph Limbeck-Lilienau and Friedrich Stadler, *Der Wiener Kreis* (LIT Verlag, 2015). Reprinted courtesy of the Vienna Circle Society / Wiener Kreis Gesellschaft.

Philipp Frank
Source: Christoph Limbeck-Lilienau and
Friedrich Stadler, *Der Wiener Kreis* (LIT Verlag,
2015). Reprinted courtesy of the Vienna Circle
Society / Wiener Kreis Gesellschaft.

Rose Rand
Source: Christoph Limbeck-Lilienau and
Friedrich Stadler, *Der Wiener Kreis* (LIT Verlag,
2015). Reprinted courtesy of the Vienna Circle
Society / Wiener Kreis Gesellschaft.

Otto Neurath
Reprinted courtesy of the University of Pittsburgh
Library System, Archives of Scientific Philosophy.

Moritz Schlick

Source: Christoph Limbeck-Lilienau and Friedrich Stadler, *Der Wiener Kreis* (LIT Verlag, 2015). Reprinted courtesy of the Vienna Circle Society / Wiener Kreis Gesellschaft.

Edgar Zilsel
Source: Christoph Limbeck-Lilienau and Friedrich Stadler,
Der Wiener Kreis (LIT Verlag, 2015). Reprinted courtesy of
the Vienna Circle Society / Wiener Kreis Gesellschaft.

Friedrich Waismann
Source: Christoph Limbeck-Lilienau and Friedrich Stadler,
Der Wiener Kreis (LIT Verlag, 2015). Reprinted courtesy of the
Vienna Circle Society / Wiener Kreis Gesellschaft.

Herbert Feigl

Source: Christoph Limbeck-Lilienau and Friedrich Stadler, *Der Wiener Kreis* (LIT Verlag, 2015). Reprinted courtesy of the Vienna Circle Society / Wiener Kreis Gesellschaft

Hans Hahn

Source: Christoph Limbeck-Lilienau and Friedrich Stadler,
Der Wiener Kreis (LIT Verlag, 2015). Reprinted courtesy of the
Vienna Circle Society / Wiener Kreis Gesellschaft.

Gustav Bergmann
Source: Christoph Limbeck-
Lilienau and Friedrich Stadler,
Der Wiener Kreis (LIT Verlag,
2015). Reprinted courtesy of
the Vienna Circle Society /
Wiener Kreis Gesellschaft

Karl Menger
University Archives and
Special Collections,
Chicago, IL, Paul V.
Galvin Library, Illinois
Institute of Technology.

Viktor Kraft
Source: Christoph Limbeck-Lilienau and Friedrich Stadler, *Der Wiener Kreis* (LIT Verlag, 2015). Reprinted courtesy of the Vienna Circle Society / Wiener Kreis Gesellschaft.

Otto Neurath chatting to Alfred Tarski
Source: Christoph Limbeck-Lilienau and Friedrich Stadler, *Der Wiener Kreis* (LIT Verlag, 2015). Reprinted courtesy of the Vienna Circle Society / Wiener Kreis Gesellschaft.

Kurt Gödel
Photographer unknown. From the Kurt Gödel Papers, Princeton,
NJ, the Shelby White and Leon Levy Archives Center, Institute
for Advanced Study, on deposit at Princeton University

Willard Van Orman Quine
With thanks to Douglas B.
Quine, PhD, on behalf of the
W. V. Quine Literary Estate.

Rudolf Carnap
Photograph by Francis
Schmidt, 1935.

Karl Popper
Reproduced courtesy of the Karl Popper Foundation.

Frank Ramsey

Ludwig Wittgenstein
Reproduction by permission of the Ludwig Wittgenstein Trust, Cambridge, UK.

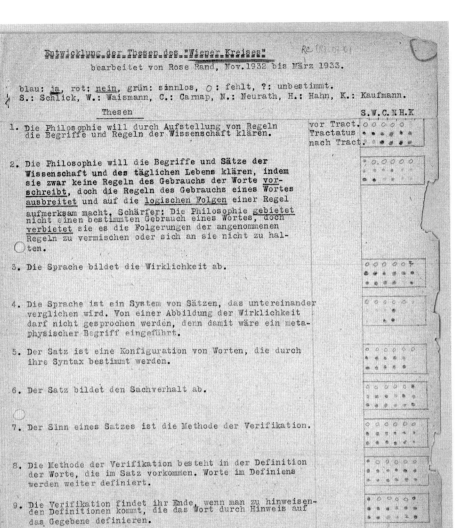

Rose Rand's color-coded spreadsheet
Rose Rand Papers, 1903–81, Pittsburgh, University of Pittsburgh Library System, Archives of Scientific Philosophy, Archives and Special Collections, asp.1990.01

Dr. Austriacus, and there was much more in a similar vein from Austriacus: Nelböck had been turned into a psychopath by Schlick's radically destructive philosophy. This loathsome philosophy was antireligious and antimetaphysical. The bullet that had killed Schlick was "not guided by the logic of some lunatic looking for a victim, but rather by the logic of a soul, deprived of its meaning of life."

The Vienna Circle, the article continued, had come to be seen abroad as representing Austrian philosophy, "much to the disadvantage of Austria's reputation as a Christian state." Schlick had not pursued his philosophical project alone, of course. Among his collaborators was his "close friend," the communist Otto Neurath.

Nowhere in the article did it state that Schlick was of Jewish ethnicity (he was not). But the assumption (or allegation) was plain. If not a Jew, Schlick was at the very least a friend of the Jews, and he represented a Jewish strain of thought. Among other charges directed at Schlick in the article was the claim that he had Jewish research assistants (Waismann and two Jewish women). The article concluded with the wish that some good come from the killing:

> Let the Jews have their Jewish philosophers at their Cultural Institute! But the philosophical chairs at the University of Vienna in Christian-German Austria should be held by Christian philosophers! It has been declared on numerous occasions recently that a peaceful solution of the Jewish question in Austria is also in the interest of the Jews themselves, since a violent solution of that question would be unavoidable otherwise. It is to be hoped that the terrible murder at the University of Vienna will quicken efforts to find a truly satisfactory solution of the Jewish Question.

Prof. Dr. Austriacus was Johann Sauter, a philosopher at the University of Vienna, a Kantian and a Nazi and an ally of Othmar Spann, the ultranationalist sociologist and economist who maintained that society represents a higher degree of reality than the individuals within it. Sauter would publicly come to Nelböck's defense only later. But the vehemence of his onslaught against Schlick prompted one principled professor at the university, Dr. Richard Meister, to object.

He wrote first to Schlick's son Albert, for a comment on the Austriacus article.

Albert was understandably defensive, but his response does not reflect well on him. He chose not to point out that the racial origins of his father's assistants were irrelevant, and instead disputed the facts: it was not true that his father employed two female Jewish assistants. And Waismann was merely a librarian, not "a regular research assistant." Nor was it true, wrote Albert, that his father was an atheist. He was a devout Protestant. And then, in the desperate attempt to salvage his father's name, he delivered a spiteful attack on Neurath. "Neurath was not my father's friend (he never ever visited us at home, for example), but rather was in opposition to him. I remember occasional remarks of my father which clearly indicated that he did not think very highly of Neurath." He also claimed that his father was not the clubbable kind, had accepted the chairmanship of the Ernst Mach Society only out of a sense of duty, and had had little to do with its activities. As to another claim made by Austriacus that his father had become a member of the Fatherland Front purely to protect himself, this was ridiculous; it was out of genuine conviction.

These remarks were forwarded by Meister to the university authorities. Meister felt that, out of loyalty to their murdered colleague, the university's Academic Senate had an obligation to respond to the personal attacks on Schlick. That body duly met on 28 November 1936 and passed on their objections to the Austriacus piece to the Federal Ministry of Education. It was a small but honorable act. The vain hope was that the ministry would offer an official defense of Schlick. They did not.

Nelböck's trial began on 24 May 1937. Schuschnigg had introduced the death penalty, and for murder this would be the expected punishment. Nelböck was not a stupid man. He clearly understood that his best prospects for a lenient sentence rested on stressing an ideological as well as a personal aspect to his motivation. Schlick had promoted a treacherous Jewish philosophy, he argued. Nonetheless, after three days he was found guilty; no other verdict would have made any sense. Still, the judge was sympathetic. The guilty man was sentenced to ten years, with his conditions to be aggravated four times a year by having to sleep on a hard bed.

In July 1936, an article appeared in the prestigious journal *Philosophical Review* about the principle of verification. Verifiability meant the *possibility* of verification, it explained. In theory it was possible to verify statements about what it was like on the other side of the moon, even if in practice it was not feasible to fly to the moon. Then the article moved on to statements about immortality. *After my death I will continue to exist.* Such statements were not meaningless either, it argued. After all, the author could imagine witnessing the funeral of his own body. *I will survive the death of my body* was a statement that in principle was verifiable.[10] This article was published posthumously, and its author was Moritz Schlick—grappling with verificationism until the very end.

16

❧◦❧

The Inner Circle

All the evil and the tragedy to come to Vienna was foreshadowed when in June 1936 Moritz Schlick was murdered. . . . After this anything could happen. And almost everything did.

—HILDE SPIEL

LIKE THE SHOW, the congress must go on. The second Unity of Science congress had gathered in Copenhagen. The event opened on a wonderfully sunny day on Sunday, 21 June, and ran to 26 June. The United States was only slowly emerging from depression, and another trip to Europe was too costly for some Americans. Still, there were between eighty and one hundred participants there. The reception was held at the home of Niels Bohr; it was he who had proposed Copenhagen as the location, and he was the central figure, delivering the first paper. He was a terrible lecturer, difficult to hear because he ignored the microphone, swallowed his words, and spent half the time scribbling on the blackboard with his back to his admiring but exasperated audience.

In theory the conference had a specific focus (though some speakers chose to address the attendees on completely separate topics): how were we to understand "causation" in physics and biology? New puzzles had emerged with quantum mechanics. Bohr, for example, had proposed the complementarity principle. Take light: depending on the experiment, it exhibits either wave or particle behavior. To understand light completely you have to acknowledge both these aspects of light, but they cannot be measured simultaneously. Heisenberg had discovered that it was impossible to measure the position and the speed of a particle at the same time. The world, at least at the quantum level,

180

appears to be indeterminate—there are some things about it one cannot know or predict. So how does causation fit into this picture? The idea that physical stuff operated according to causal laws was basic to Newton's laws of motion and classical mechanics, whereas the new science introduced a degree of subjectivity into science—the measurer became inextricably intertwined with the measurement. Popper, a conference attendee, was a realist; there was an underlying reality out there that existed independently of human minds. During the conference, Popper befriended Bohr and could be seen in intense discussion, the two men standing on the stairs, with Bohr sucking on his unlit pipe looking down at Popper.

The paper Schlick had been due to read at the congress, had he been granted the right to travel, was called "Quantum Theory and the Knowableness of Nature" ("Quantentheorie und die Erkennbarkeit der Natur"), and was read by Philipp Frank. It was Frank who informed the delegates of Schlick's murder. They had been on a bus outing to the quaint city of Helsingør, home of Kronborg Castle, the setting used by Shakespeare for Hamlet. Frank received the news just before they sat down for dinner. There does not seem to have been any proposal to call off proceedings, though Frank said a few words and a telegram of condolence was organized and sent to Blanche, Schlick's wife. The remainder of the congress was naturally subdued—the only minidrama being a typical Popper explosion, in response to Neurath criticizing his friend Tarski.

———

It may not have stopped the conference, but Schlick's murder concentrated minds. Austrian-born author Hilde Spiel wrote that the death of her beloved teacher heightened her sense of insecurity and hastened her departure out of the country. She was not alone. For Kaufmann, the assassination of Schlick was a horror story that he could never forget.[1] Schlick had always been a vital support to Waismann, whose situation had become desperate. He had already lost his poorly paid job, and there was another mouth to feed after his wife, heavily pregnant at the time of the murder, gave birth to a boy, Thomas, in September. He raised some money by giving a private seminar on the *Tractatus*, but it was not enough. He now began to look at options abroad.

Popper too wanted out, as did Karl Menger, who ceased attending Circle meetings. In normal times, he was the obvious candidate to succeed Schlick, but the appointments commission determined that henceforth philosophical studies were to focus on the history of philosophy, and so the chair, graced by both Schlick and Mach, was to be abolished. Menger also had a growing family to provide for. He had married a student, Hilda Axamit, in 1935, and the first of their four children was born in 1936. In 1937 he became a visiting professor at the University of Notre Dame in Indiana.

The murder had still more serious consequences for Gödel, precipitating a possible suicide attempt, a mental breakdown, and a lengthy spell in a sanatorium. In Prague, Carnap, who was not Jewish but was left-wing, was increasingly nervous about the rise of the Right in Europe. After four years in Czechoslovakia, he moved to the US, and with the support of Charles Morris landed a job at the University of Chicago in 1936. Eleven days before Schlick's death he had written to Neurath, "Over here the anti-Semitism is pretty bad too, particularly in the universities—for example I have heard that no non-Aryan has even the remotest chance of obtaining the position in Princeton that I've turned down."[2]

Wittgenstein was in Ireland when he heard the news of Schlick and wrote to Waismann. "Schlick's death is really a great misfortune. You and I too have lost a great deal with him. I do not know how to express the sorrow that I—as you know—really feel to his wife and children."[3] He asked Waismann to do him a great favor and visit Mrs. Schlick or one of the children, to tell them "that I think of them warmly, but that I do not know what to write to them."[4]

Waismann visited Wittgenstein's eldest sister, Hermine, to see if she would help persuade her brother to return to Vienna—the idea seems to have been that he would replace Schlick. Hermine passed on the news to Ludwig, reporting that in "friendly" terms she had told him that the family "would never let ourselves be used like that and if we ever did, that you would strike us dead and that if you didn't strike us dead, then you would never consider it anyway."[5]

Nonetheless, Waismann was determined that Circle discussions continue—and so they did for another two years. Sometimes they were convened by Waismann, at other times by Josef Schächter, now a trained rabbi, having completed his dissertation under Schlick in 1931. Edgar Zilsel also attempted to keep the Circle spirit alive by often inviting a group to his apartment.

———

Beyond the seminars, other Vienna Circle projects limped on. A year after Copenhagen, in 1937, Paris played host to the third Unity of Science Congress. For the fourth congress, in July 1938, the strong links forged between Vienna and Cambridge were cemented in the decision to select the English university town, with the focus on the language of science. G. E. Moore delivered a talk, but Wittgenstein was absent. Surprisingly, despite his hostility to the Circle's manifesto in particular and his discomfort in formal gatherings in general, Wittgenstein had initially contemplated attending. With just a few days to go he decided against it, writing to his friend Rush Rhees that even Rhees's presence could not compensate for the "nastiness" of having to sit there "among logical positivists."[6] In addition to G. E. Moore, Neurath, Frank, Waismann, and Zilsel all spoke.

Publication of *Erkenntnis* persisted for a time, as did plans for the International Encyclopedia of Unified Science series, published by the University of Chicago Press and masterminded by Neurath, who had been in The Hague since 1934. There had been no flagging of his energy. Home was an upper maisonette in Obrechtstraat not far from the center of town. On the first floor was a study area and a bedroom where Otto and his wife, Olga, slept, while Marie Reidemeister, his long-term collaborator at the Museum of Society and Economy, occupied a bedroom on the top floor. Their chief picture designer, Gerd Arntz, had also fled to The Hague, and together they established the International Foundation for Visual Education. It was in The Hague that Marie Reidemeister came up with a name for their pictorials—the International System of Typographic Picture Education, or ISOTYPE.

Neurath worked on his contribution for the Encyclopedia series, for which he doubled up as coeditor with Carnap and Charles Morris. He also joined the Dutch Peace Movement, which had its own building, including a library, where he delivered lectures. As always, he acted as a magnet for talent: leading scholars sought him out. He became particularly friendly with economist Jan Tinbergen, who in 1969 would win the first Nobel Prize in economics. Like Neurath, Tinbergen believed in technocratic socialism, and the power of planning.

Starting all over again in an alien place was bound to be tough, in this case exacerbated by serious money worries, the principal reason for which was the failure by Moscow to honor their contract; a letter from the Soviet authorities claimed that it somehow violated Russian law. Neurath was owed $6,000, but even he acknowledged that he would not win a fight with the Soviet state.

Still, after adjusting to his exile, Neurath quickly returned to his default psychological state—exuberance. Here, in the Netherlands, it was "like being on holiday every day,"[7] he wrote in a letter back to Vienna. He brushed aside their penury. "We eat sugar snap peas when the cucumber is too expensive and apple sauce when the jam is too expensive."[8] Eventually they began to win some commissions. The National Tuberculosis Association in New York wanted them to produce charts on infection with advice on how people could protect themselves. A traveling exhibition crisscrossed the country, educating people about the disease. Then they received an invitation to lecture in Mexico for six weeks. They also started to win jobs in the Netherlands itself, including from the Department of Health.

———

The irony was that while the Vienna Circle was winding down in Austria, its reputation abroad was growing. The international congresses were helping to spread the word, as were some of the Circle's prominent foreign visitors. Quine delivered a series of lectures at Harvard in 1934 on Carnap, and campaigned, successfully, for him to be awarded an honorary degree, which Carnap received in 1936. At the ceremony Quine claimed that the philosophy represented by the Vienna Circle "must be recognized as one of the decisive movements of modern times."[9] In Britain, the movement had several champions. Crucial among them was a self-effacing woman whose role usually goes unacknowledged. London-based logician Susan Stebbing first met Schlick in 1930 at an Oxford conference and was struck by his talk on the role of philosophy. She endorsed the idea that philosophy was about logical clarification. In 1933, she became the first female philosophy professor in Britain and cofounded the journal *Analysis*, which established itself as *the* place to publish analytic philosophy (and still exists today). That same year she was at the British Academy to deliver what may have been the first lecture in the UK specifically on logical positivism. She invited Carnap to lecture at the University of London in the fall of 1934. Although sympathetic to logical empiricism, she was by no means uncritical. Still, she invited several figures linked to the Circle to lecture in the UK, including Carnap and Popper, and at the Paris Conference in 1935 she was asked and agreed to join the organizing committee for the International Congress for the Unity of Science. It helped that she spoke German. It was she who organized the Cambridge gathering at Girton College in 1938 and gave an opening address.

She, however, is not the British academic popularly associated with the Circle.

A. J. Ayer was considerably more assertive than Stebbing. When he returned to Oxford in 1933, still full of Vienna, he wrote a paper for the journal *Mind*. Isaiah Berlin suggested he lengthen it into a book and persuaded publisher Victor Gollancz that it would be the most significant philosophy book since the *Tractatus*. Ayer gave it the title *Language, Truth, and Logic*, borrowing from Waismann's unpublished *Logik, Sprache, Philosophie*. It took him eighteen months to complete, during which he wrote to Neurath, "At Oxford, where I work, metaphysics still predominates. I feel very isolated here."[10] The book's self-assurance, bordering on arrogance, alienated many scholars. When some Oxford students suggested it be taken up by a philosophy discussion group, the

Master of Balliol, A. D. Lindsay, dropped the book from the window and proposed a different, more suitable topic.[11] Ayer's dismissal of moral statements as pseudo-concepts antagonized many, who regarded him as not just wrong but wicked. Yet the book's clarity and combative and swaggering nature were also qualities that readers found so appealing and refreshingly different from the stuffiness of traditional Oxford philosophy.

———

The regular Thursday-evening gatherings were no more, but the Circle was still meeting sporadically, when it could. One Saturday, in early 1938, Gödel was invited to address those members still in Vienna. The meeting took place at the apartment of Edgar Zilsel. It is thought to be the last gathering before Austria lost its independence.

17

<small>◄○►</small>

Escape

One blood demands one Reich.

—ADOLF HITLER, *MEIN KAMPF*

ITALY HAD PROVIDED some reassurance to Austria that it might be able to retain its independence. But with its ally now moving politically closer to Germany, Austria was squeezed. In July 1936, a month after Schlick's murder, Austrian Chancellor Kurt Schuschnigg secured a deal with Germany that in theory guaranteed Austrian independence. It was a typically cynical maneuver by Hitler. In fact, encouraged by Berlin, the Austrian Nazis escalated their campaign of terror; violence on the street became commonplace, demonstrations routine. As relations between Austria and Germany deteriorated, Schuschnigg made a number of concessions, including the appointment in February 1938 of a Nazi, Arthur Seyss-Inquart, as minister of security. But, after another menacing speech by Hitler later that month, Schuschnigg finally snapped. He announced on 9 March that there would be a national plebiscite on the issue of Austrian independence.

Hitler's reaction was instant and furious. Threatening military intervention, he demanded that the plebiscite be canceled, Schuschnigg resign, and Seyss-Inquart be appointed his successor. On the evening of Friday, 11 March 1938, much of Austria tuned in to the radio to listen to a speech from Schuschnigg. To avoid bloodshed, Schuschnigg said, he had surrendered Austria to Hitler's Germany. He ended his speech with an appeal for divine protection: "God protect Austria" ("*Gott schütze Österreich*").

———

After Schuschnigg's resignation, events evolved rapidly. Austrians did not need to await the arrival of German tanks, which were already rolling toward the border. As bystanders jeered, Jewish businesses were ransacked, synagogues smashed, *Jude* and *Juden* scrawled on Jewish-owned shops. Jews were seized from their homes, kicked, punched and spat at, forced on their hands and knees to scrub pavements. "Work for the Jews at last," chanted the mob.

German troops entered Austria on Saturday, 12 March. Austria was incorporated into Germany on Sunday, 13 March: every non-Jewish Austrian was now a German citizen. Hitler arrived on Monday: reflecting the mood of the masses, there was glorious spring sunshine. Ecstatic crowds waved flags adorned with swastikas as he drove around the Ringstrasse: people struggled to get a better view, branches of trees doubled up as dress-circle seats. The bells of Austria rang out, courtesy of Cardinal Innitzer, or "Heil-Hitler Innitzer" as Neurath called him.[1] "To say that the crowds which greeted him along the *Ringstrasse* were delirious with joy," wrote one British journalist, "is an understatement."[2] On Tuesday morning, Hitler spoke to a vast throng, estimated to be a quarter of a million, from the balcony of the Habsburg Imperial Palace. "I can in this hour report before history the conclusion of the greatest aim in my life: the entry of my homeland into the German Reich."

For several weeks the violence against Jews continued, the ferocity of it taking even the Germans by surprise. No Jew was safe. Bourgeois Jews were to discover that money, status, and assimilation were illusory shields. The doctor and the peddler, the lawyer and the artisan, the lecturer and the rabbi were indistinguishable to the rabble. Prof. Dr. Freud's sign was removed from his Berggasse apartment—now hanging across the door was a swastika flag.

For students of psychology interested in the limits of human depravity, 1938 in Vienna was the time and place to be. The organs of the state initially gave free rein to primeval hate and the craving to humiliate. There was a lustful merriment in the cruelty. Jews were compelled to goose-step, the beards of the pious were clipped, demeaning placards were strung around necks, professors pushed to the floor and made to clean toilets with tefillin straps, Jewish children were forced to abuse their parents. Ex-diplomat-turned-MP Harold Nicolson was in Vienna and saw men stripped naked and made to "walk on all fours on the grass."[3] Old women were ordered to climb into trees and chirp like birds.

The pogrom continued unabated for several weeks. Between March and April, 160 Jews killed themselves. Although at first they did not intervene, some high-ranking German Nazis had reservations about the sadism the Anschluss had unleashed. They preferred organized to chaotic destruction. They preferred their plunder to be pseudo-legal rather than ad hoc. Order was eventually restored. Meanwhile, the first few thousand non-Nazi political activists, criminals, and Jews were despatched to Dachau, outside Munich, the Nazis' first concentration camp.

The Nazis arranged their own plebiscite for 10 April. Austrians were asked whether they acknowledged Hitler as their Führer and endorsed the Anschluss. Jews were ineligible to participate. The Austrian bishops released a statement appealing for the faithful to approve the union. Some Austrians were silently aghast at events, and historians dispute what the result would have been had there been a free press in the run-up to the vote and had proceedings been genuinely free of intimidation. But, given the euphoria with which the German arrival was greeted, the discomforting truth is that, even so, the result would almost certainly have gone Hitler's way—though not with the 99.75 percent yes vote the Nazis declared.

The University of Vienna had been closed since the Anschluss. On 25 April it was reopened under new conditions. Henceforth Jews could constitute a maximum of 2 percent of the university students and faculty, and Jewish students could only enter the university with a permit. Most of the medical faculty were dismissed.

A petition was sent in for clemency for Schlick's murderer, Johann Nelböck, on the grounds that Schlick had been an unsuitable educator of young people. It was rejected, but in July, Johann Sauter, the academic who had published the pseudonymous poison on Schlick after his killing, submitted another appeal that added yet more calumnies. In philosophy, Schlick had been an exponent of Jewry, the appeal said. Nelböck, whom Sauter had known for several years, and who came from humble rural origins, was "a man of strong national motives and explicit anti-Semitism." His actions were driven by ideological and political necessity.

In October, Nelböck received a conditional release.

Meanwhile, over the summer of 1938, Austria's legal system was absorbed within Germany's. Numerous regulations took effect to dehumanize the Jews further. Jews were forbidden to enter parks, sit on benches, go to the theater. Jewish professionals—lawyers, teachers, orchestral musicians—lost their jobs. In May, the German 1935 Nuremberg Laws, which declared that only those of German blood could be Reich citizens and forbade intermarriage between Jews and Germans, were extended to the new Austrian province of Greater Germany. On 17 August, a German law prohibited Jews from taking "Aryan names": Jewish men had to adopt the name "Israel" and Jewish women "Sarah." All Jews were required, henceforth, to carry identification cards. In early October, there was a new decree: all Jewish passports had to be stamped with a J.

On a parallel track, Jewish wealth was systematically plundered. All Jews had to declare their material assets. It was the job of the "asset transfer office" (*Vermögensverkehrsstelle*) to reassign Jewish property to non-Jews. Those apartments which had not been confiscated now had to house several Jewish families.

———

Then, on 9 November 1938, came *Kristallnacht*, the "night of broken glass." That week a young Jew shot dead a German diplomat in protest at the expulsion from Germany of his Polish Jewish family. The response was a wave of state-sanctioned anti-Jewish violence; cemeteries and synagogues were desecrated and burnt, Jewish-owned businesses smashed, thugs kicked in the doors of Jewish homes, beat up the occupants, and threw them out of windows or down stairs. Thousands of Jewish men were carried off to concentration camps for "protective custody." The rampage was nationwide, but once again Austrians out-competed their German brethren in viciousness. In Vienna alone, ninety-five synagogues were set alight.

Before the rubble was cleaned away, new measures were introduced to ban Jews from concerts and cinemas. Hermann Goering, responsible for a large part of the economy, declared that German insurance companies need not compensate Jews for damage to their property on Kristallnacht; instead, he announced, Jews must pay for it themselves. What was more, they would also fund the cost of clearing up the mess. A third of the bill was levied on Austrian Jews. As further punishment for the murder of the German diplomat, it was later announced that Jews were prohibited from driving cars.

Kristallnacht was the final proof that for Jews life in the German Reich was untenable. Some had already left, but the rush to flee now became a stampede. Meanwhile, an Office for Jewish Emigration had been set up with the power to grant Jews permission to leave the country. It was run by Adolf Eichmann, who used it to develop a career-enhancing reputation for efficiency and for his knowledge of Jewish affairs. This was the period in which official policy was not yet to exterminate the Jews but rather to legalize the expropriation of their property, goods, and money. In exchange for almost everything they owned, Jews were allowed to go. It was an indication of life in post-Anschluss Vienna that, for most Jews, escape at the cost of almost all their savings was self-evidently the only option.

But go where? In July 1938 Franklin D. Roosevelt convened an international conference, in Évian-les-Bains in northern France, to discuss the Jewish refugee crisis. When Hitler heard about it, he offered to help. "I can only hope and expect that the other world, which has such deep sympathy for these criminals, will at least be generous enough to convert this sympathy into practical aid. We, on our part, are ready to put all these criminals at the disposal of these countries, for all I care, even on luxury ships."

In fact, the Évian conference, attended by representatives from more than thirty countries, made no progress; there was no loosening of immigration controls. Politicians feared increasing Jewish immigration would be hugely unpopular; four in five Americans were opposed to allowing in a large number of refugees.[4] A poll shortly before the conference in the United States revealed that a majority of Americans believed that the Jews bore at least some responsibility for their persecution. The Australian delegate at the conference summed up his government's attitude and probably the attitude of others. "It will no doubt be appreciated that as we have no racial problem, we are not desirous of importing one."[5]

An indirect consequence of failure at Évian was that the Nazis came to believe that, if foreign states would not take their Jews, they would have to find another solution to the Jewish problem. For the Jews left in Austria and Germany these were traumatic times. They had the right to leave—with virtually nothing—but no automatic right to arrive.

———

There was a strict quota system in the US: the minimum requirement to gain a visa was a demonstration of "adequate means of support." That privileged the well-to-do, the well-connected, and the in-demand. For the rest, letters were sent to distant relatives asking for the necessary financial guarantees. There were lengthy queues at the US embassy in Vienna.

There were long queues too at the UK embassy, for the UK was the other attractive option. Those queueing were frequently targets of verbal and physical harassment from Nazi sympathizers. Post-Anschluss, the situation was exacerbated by the downgrading of the UK embassy to a consulate, with the result that the diplomatic bag from London reached Vienna only every fortnight.

Fearing an influx of refugees, Britain initially tightened the rules. Unemployment in the UK had remained stubbornly high throughout the 1930s and there was no appetite to absorb outsiders. A work permit could be obtained only if it could be demonstrated that no British worker would be harmed by the foreigner's arrival. But after the November pogrom, public opinion became more compassionate and Britain, while shutting the door to Palestine (governed under a League of

Nations mandate), eased its procedures at home. In a private letter, Prime Minister Neville Chamberlain wrote, "No doubt Jews aren't a lovable people; I don't care about them myself; but that is not sufficient to explain the pogrom."[6] By September 1939 there were up to seventy thousand refugees in the UK from Nazi Germany, most on temporary transit visas. All had had to demonstrate they would not be a burden on the state.

There were various routes in. One was through applying to work in domestic service, for the British middle and upper classes were struggling to find suitable staff to run their homes. In Vienna, Jewish men tried to boost their credentials by taking a class for prospective butlers or on cocktail mixing. Jewish women, like Rose Rand, signed up for cooking and cleaning lessons. For industrialists and professors this felt demeaning, likewise for those once-comfortably-off women, more accustomed to employing staff to wash, dust, and scrub than to doing it themselves, let alone for others. Some Jews coarsened their hands before meeting with British embassy officials, in an attempt to convince them that were not strangers to manual labor. The category "domestic servants," most of them women, would, in the end, constitute a third of all refugees who came to Britain in the 1930s.

The *Kindertransport*, in which Britain accepted ten thousand unaccompanied Jewish children, began in December 1938. The departure point from Vienna was West Station, the first train leaving at 11:45 p.m. on Friday, 10 December. Each child had one suitcase and a number around their neck. Anxious parents waved goodbye with their handkerchiefs as the trains set off: most would never see their children again.

Even before the post-Kristallnacht loosening of regulations, Britain had made an exception for eminent scholars, artists, and industrialists. Yet there were still endless bureaucratic obstacles to overcome. Sigmund Freud, who had a love-hate relationship with his hometown, had been reluctant to leave. Now his decision was taken, he was told to sign a document stating he had not been ill treated. Freud scrawled a remark on the papers, "I can heartily recommend the Gestapo to everyone."[7] Fortunately for him, the comment appears to have been taken at face value, irony being yet another victim of Nazi rule. On the day of his departure, 2 June 1938, he dedicated one of his books, *The Future of an Illusion*, to Wittgenstein's sister. He seems, to use a Freudian phrase, to have been in denial. "Mrs. Margaret Stonborough on the occasion of my temporary departure." One item the Nazis did not appropriate was the world's most famous couch: that was shipped to London too.

———

Béla Juhos and Viktor Kraft were to remain in Vienna. Juhos was not Jewish. Kraft's wife, Johanna, had converted to Christianity but was of Jewish origin. Kraft lost his job, becoming an inner exile. Exactly why Johanna was not picked up by the Nazis is a mystery, but it may have been because the Krafts' daughter Eva was married to Walter Frodl, who held a prominent position under National Socialism in the museum and art world.

One by one, other Circle members managed to get out. Menger was already in the United States, on a sabbatical. On 23 March, he fired off a telegram to the Ministry of Education announcing that he was quitting his Viennese position at the university and remaining in the United States. His resignation was recorded on 24 March, the date the telegram arrived. A so-called *Sippenforscher*, or genealogist, would later make inquiries about Menger's family background. Kaufmann fled to New York via Paris and ten days in London. In New York he became an assistant professor at the New School for Social Research. Gustav Bergmann sent his wife and daughter ahead of him to England and followed them in October. He had applied for an immigration permit to the US with the support of an academic friend at Princeton. On 9 August 1938, the *Israelitische Kultusgemeinde*, long recognized by the state as the official representative of Vienna's Jewish population, and now compelled to do the Nazis' bidding, declared that he was a pure Jew. Like other Jews, he would have had to pay hefty "taxes" to leave. Bergmann travelled via The Hague, so that he could meet Neurath. "Don't worry," Neurath reassured him, when Bergmann bewailed the state of the world, "in 200 years' time Hitler will be just another mad dictator who lived at the time of Freud."[8] Neurath, who had barely any savings of his own, offered

Bergmann sufficient financial support to pay for the family's passage from the UK to the US. No, he did not want repayment—at least not in money. Instead, he asked Bergmann to write down his recollections of the Circle. This Bergmann did on shipboard during the voyage to New York.

In New York he deployed his mathematical skills to scrape a living as a bookkeeper, but with Feigl's support and through an organization called the Committee in Aid of Displaced Scholars, he landed a job at the University of Iowa, where he would remain. The Rockefeller Foundation had established the Committee in Aid of Displaced Scholars and offered grants for any university taking on refugees.

The adjustment for the Kaufmanns was even more marked. Although he had worked barely four hours a day at the Anglo-Iranian Oil Company (devoting the rest of his time to scholarship), Felix Kaufmann had become a rich man. Now, though there was an income from the New School in New York to keep them going, the family's wealth was gone. Kaufmann adapted his book on the methodology of the social sciences for the English-speaking market and took solace in smoking: his policy of increasing his habit by one cigarette after the publication of each book had earned him a daily diet of eight cigarettes.

———

Some escape details are unclear, including the dates for Zilsel's departure from Austria. But he had been in London for some time when he wrote to Neurath from there in January 1939. His son, Paul, began attending an English school and stayed in the UK to finish his studies when Zilsel took a boat to the US on 26 March. In New York he managed to pick up some work as a private tutor to an émigré he met on the journey over. In June 1939 he was awarded a Rockefeller fellowship to research early modern science, giving him a degree of security for at least a year.

Meanwhile, the Anschluss forced the Wittgensteins to confront an uncomfortable fact. They had little to no Jewish identity; their lives had barely overlapped with the Viennese Jewish community. Insofar as they had a religious affiliation, it was to Christianity. But if, as was the case, three of their grandparents were ethnically Jewish, they themselves would be classified as Jews. Family members tried to reassure each other that they, the Wittgensteins, were safe. Surely they were too respected, too influential to be targeted? Privately they were nervous.

Ludwig Wittgenstein, now living in Cambridge, submitted his (successful) application to succeed to G. E. Moore's chair in philosophy and began the process of acquiring British citizenship. With the help of a solicitor recommended by John Maynard Keynes, he became a subject of the crown on 14 April 1939. His two elder sisters, Hermine and Helene, were stubbornly determined to remain in Vienna. With the security of his new passport, Ludwig became personally involved in complex and protracted negotiations with the Nazi authorities to have one of his grandparents reclassified as a gentile, thus earning his sisters "mixed-race" (*Mischlinge*) status. The tactic would cause a permanent breach among his siblings. Paul thought his sisters should leave and felt emotionally blackmailed into going along. Success in the negotiations hinged less on genealogical evidence and more on the price the Wittgensteins were in a position to pay. Eventually, the equivalent of 1.7 tonnes of gold was transferred to the Reichsbank.[9] If ever there was a morally ambiguous transaction, this was it. Hermine and Helene lived out the war years untouched, while their money was enough to make a real difference to the Nazi war effort.

The Wittgensteins were used to operating according to their own rules. But deals were not an option for other figures associated with the Circle. Fortunately, as we shall see, there was a specific organization in London to which a few of them could turn for help.

———

On 30 September 1938, the British prime minister Neville Chamberlain returned to London after negotiating the Munich Agreement with Hitler. This allowed Germany to occupy a western part of Czechoslovakia, known as the Sudetenland, and declared that in future all differences would be resolved through peaceful means. Upon landing on British soil, Chamberlain proclaimed that he had secured "peace for our time." In March 1939, the German army rolled into the remainder of Czechoslovakia.

Even before the invasion, the Czechoslovak Nazis had been gaining in influence. In Prague, Philipp Frank had come under pressure, which he resisted, to apply Nazi race laws to the appointment of staff and the admission of students. In October 1938 (as Germany took possession of the Sudetenland), Frank began a lecture tour in the US, speaking at a score of universities. In the fall of 1939 he was offered a job in Harvard as a research associate in physics and philosophy, which two years later would be converted into a part-time job as lecturer in physics and mathematics. It was hardly the status he had had in Prague—Harvard was absorbing other refugees from Europe and claimed they could not be more generous. Conscription during World War II cut student enrolment, putting additional pressure on universities. Still, though Frank would struggle financially, he was safe.

––––––

The case of Kurt Gödel was always a bit different. He was not Jewish, so there was not the urgency to get out, nor had he been active in left-wing politics. Indeed, he was almost preternaturally indifferent to the political convulsions tearing Central Europe apart. Gustav Bergmann recalled meeting Gödel for lunch not long after he had arrived in the United States in October 1938. "And what brings you to America, Herr Bergmann?" Gödel innocently inquired![10]

Gödel had been at the Institute for Advanced Study and only returned to Austria after the spring semester of 1939. Even at the time this seemed to others a peculiar decision, and in hindsight it seems even odder. But Gödel was planning to return to Princeton in the fall and foresaw no complications. In Vienna, however, he was asked to go for a physical examination to determine whether he was strong enough for military service. Gödel was convinced that he would be declared unfit and that, in his words, "he would be sent back for good by the military authorities."[11] Two developments complicated matters. The first was that the examination was delayed several times until after war broke out. The second, far more remarkable, was that Gödel passed.

According to a Gödel biographer, John Dawson, "It was a rude surprise. Yet if the German authorities had refused to believe that Gödel's heart had been damaged by his childhood bout with rheumatic fever, it was most fortunate that they had also overlooked his episodes of mental instability. Had they taken notice of them he might indeed have been 'sent back for good'—perhaps to a concentration camp for "mental defectives."[12]

In any case, now it would be tricky to gain permission to travel to the US. Meanwhile, his license to teach—*Lehrbefugniss*—had run out in April 1938. Clearly his position was deeply unsettling, though not life-threatening. He applied for a particular position—*Dozent neuer Ordnung*—that, unlike the Privatdozent, came with a fee. This required an investigation by Nazi authorities. A report sent to the university concluded that Gödel could be recommended scientifically but pointed out that "the Jewish Professor Hahn" had overseen his habilitation. It was noted that Gödel had "always travelled in liberal-Jewish circles" but, to be fair, he could not entirely be blamed for this since mathematics had been strongly "Jewified."[13] Since there was no evidence of Gödel's being anti-Nazi, the report reached a noncommittal verdict. It could not explicitly approve his application, nor give solid grounds for rejecting it.

For the time being, Gödel was in limbo. And Greater Germany was at war.

18

<o>

Miss Simpson's Children

Hitler is my best friend. He shakes the tree and I collect the apples.

—WALTER COOK, PRESIDENT OF THE INSTITUTE OF
FINE ARTS, NEW YORK UNIVERSITY[1]

HER NAME WAS Miss Simpson to strangers, Esther Simpson to colleagues, Tess to her friends. The history books have been miserly in granting her the coverage her heroic efforts deserve. Something similar could also be said of the organization for which she worked, the Academic Assistance Council (AAC). She, and it, offered a life-saving opportunity to many refugee academics, sixteen of whom went on to win the Nobel Prize. Among those helped by Tess Simpson and the AAC were several members of the Circle.

———

Parentage of the AAC is contested. Credit must partly go to Leo Szilard, a dynamic Hungarian physicist who had left his Berlin university position when Hitler came to power. Among multiple accomplishments, he conceived the idea of a nuclear chain reaction and later pushed for setting up the Manhattan Project, which built the atomic bomb. It was Szilard who first recognized the need for an organization to help threatened academics, mentioning the concept to Englishman William Beveridge. But many years on—due, no doubt, to nothing more sinister than a faulty memory—Beveridge gave a different account, erasing Szilard's role. He explained that the idea came to him as he was sitting in a Viennese coffeehouse in 1933, with fellow economist Ludwig von Mises, brother of Richard. The Nazis had been in power across the border for only a matter of weeks. Von Mises, wrote Beveridge, read out the names, published in the evening paper, of a dozen Jewish academics sacked under the new German government.[2]

Beveridge, who would transform Britain and its welfare system through the recommendations of his 1942 Beveridge Report, was a man with straightforward and usually unerring moral antennae. He was far from alone in being quick to identify the evils of Nazism. But he was rare in combining his powerfully felt judgments with a talent for mobilization and organization.

As soon as he was back in the United Kingdom, Beveridge set to work. He raised some money by appealing to faculty members at the London School of Economics, many of whom donated generously. He also contacted other prominent academics at other universities. On 22 May 1933, a letter signed by some of the university sector's great-and-good was published in the establishment's newspaper, *The Times*. It announced the launch of the AAC, stating that its objective was "to raise a fund, to be used primarily, though not exclusively, in providing maintenance for displaced teachers and investigators, and finding them work in universities and scientific institutions."[3] One of the signatories, and also one of the first to write a check in support, was John Maynard Keynes. Another was New Zealand–born physicist and Nobel Prize winner Ernest Rutherford, who, after some cajoling by Beveridge, became the AAC's president. Jewish figures were deliberately excluded from the executive committee, out of concern that they might put off potential supporters. On 3 October, Einstein helped raise more funds when he addressed a packed Albert Hall on the subject of "Science and Civilisation," urging the crowd to resist the powers that threatened intellectual and individual freedom.

Beveridge was in no position to run the AAC on a day-to-day basis, though he evangelized for its mission in many talks delivered up and down the country. Instead, two full-time officials were appointed. One was the secretary, Walter Adams, a historian who would go on to become director of the London School of Economics (1967–74). The second held the lowly status of assistant secretary, but for the AAC it was

to prove an inspired appointment, "of lasting and growing importance,"[4] wrote Beveridge.

Welcome aboard, Miss Simpson.

Tess Simpson grew up in Leeds, in northern England, and won a scholarship to study modern languages at Leeds University, gaining a First Class degree, before moving to Europe to practice her languages. She spent a period in Germany working as a governess for a rich but tedious family, then had a spell in Paris before accepting a job in 1928 at the International Fellowship of Reconciliation in Vienna, a body promoting reconciliation between former warring countries. She was in the Austrian capital until 1933—in her own words, she had "a marvellous few years."[5] She enjoyed walking in the woods, going to the theater and museums (her favourite was Otto Neurath's) but mostly she indulged her lifelong passion, music. In Vienna, she would later recall, playing chamber music was taken so much for granted that it was "like cleaning your teeth."[6] She was a gifted violinist and regularly joined in chamber music ensembles. She played in one quartet with an uncle of Karl Popper's. Hanna Schiff, Popper's cousin, painted her portrait. To Neurath she would write, "Vienna I happen to know better than any other city in the world."[7]

Simpson had recently moved to Geneva and taken a job at the World Alliance of YMCAs, when she was offered a new position as assistant secretary of the Academic Assistance Council. The AAC initially operated out of two small rooms in the attic of a large house in Piccadilly, in central London. In Switzerland she was hardly well remunerated; nonetheless, the AAC post, at two pounds ten shillings a week, represented a massive pay cut. But it would prove a life's calling.

Simpson had that rare talent of being able to persuade people to do what she asked. She also had the most astounding reserves of energy, resilience, and patience. She worked "preposterously hard,"[8] according to a colleague. In those days, she routinely finished at 10:00 p.m., when the gates out to the street were locked—otherwise she would have stayed later. After the Anschluss she took no holiday for thirteen years. While trying to patch back together the lives of those undone by

Nazism, she had to deal with the mostly benign, but frustratingly slug-gish and often idiotic, British bureaucracy.

Although the AAC was always short of money, it had a little pot of funds to disburse—giving annual grants of £182 for single academics, £250 for married ones. But the more important function was to act as a conduit between displaced academics and the university sector, finding out which scholars had been replaced, what their expertise was, and whether there was a university with a matching department and a pos-sible vacancy. The AAC's small sums of money could then leverage and lubricate a deal—providing the refugee academic the support to keep them going until a living wage came their way.

In 1936, the organization was renamed the Society for the Protection of Science and Learning (SPSL). It was becoming transparent that for German-Jewish academics this was not a temporary crisis. The priority for the SPSL was to save threatened academics and to help resuscitate their careers; it was not the enrichment of British intellectual life (though that was a happy side effect). To this end, Adams and Simpson began to improve their links with American universities. Sometimes they would provide a grant to subsidize a lecture tour in the US. For some of the less prestigious academic institutions in the States, here was a chance to nab a thinker who might in normal circumstances be out of their league. After finishing their lecture tour, Simpson remembered, they invariably "came back with a job in their pocket."[9]

Karl Popper had met Simpson while it was still the AAC. Invited to England to lecture by Susan Stebbing, he had chosen as his topic Tar-ski's theories about truth. He used these talks to improve his heavily accented and still faulty English. He arrived in late 1935, returned to Vienna for Christmas, and then spent the first half of 1936 back in London. Ayer looked after him "as a hen looks after a chick."[10] At the London School of Economics he met Friedrich von Hayek, a fellow Viennese who had been lecturing in the UK since 1931. The patrician Viennese and the uppity bourgeois Viennese established an unlikely rapport.

During that first trip, Popper was based in west London, in cramped, shoddy lodgings; in one letter he complained that he lacked the space

even to open his suitcase. His financial position was precarious. It was Hayek who told Popper about the AAC, which was just the sort of body that might help the young academic, but there were two complications. First, Popper was still a teacher, and the rules of the charity stated that it could only help academics who had been forced out of work. Second, Popper had yet to acquire an international reputation: at thirty-four, he was a relatively young man. The SPSL had to check his credentials.

The primary problem was resolved by Popper's resigning from his job. This decision had been building for a while. He had moved schools and his duties now included teaching handicrafts and singing, cutting into time he wanted to devote to his research. In a letter to Professor Austin Duncan-Jones, who had invited him to Birmingham to lecture as part of his 1935–36 UK tour, he explained how his position was becoming untenable, while sensitive enough not to equate the noxious atmosphere in Vienna with the even more toxic environment across the border in Germany. "I don't feel myself able any longer to listen day by day to allusions and affronts concerning my Jewish origin equally made by nearly all of or my colleagues and—under their influence—even by some pupils."[11]

Giving up his livelihood was, of course, a risk. But Popper had been emboldened by Felix Kaufmann. One of the wealthier members of the Circle, Kaufmann was in London at the end of 1936 and while there entered into negotiations on Popper's behalf—receiving word that, once jobless, Popper would be in a strong position to access AAC support. As a Jew, Kaufmann might have been expected to focus his energies on securing his own future. But he was unusual within the Circle in having chosen to work partially outside the world of teaching and research. As the general manager of the Anglo-Iranian Oil Company, he had won a lucrative contract to supply oil to the Austrian Federal Railways: his pay and status appears to have lulled him into the complacent belief that he would be fine. Kaufmann was only five years older than Popper, but Popper sent him an effusive letter to thank him for his role as middleman. "It is nothing new to me that you take care of me as only rarely a father does of his son. . . . I shall never forget what you have done for me, and the way you did it."[12] (Naturally, being Popper, he did in fact forget.)

Popper's tactic in confronting the second concern was to gather a list of glittering references. Indeed, so starry were the names he put down that the AAC/SPLC could have been forgiven for assuming it was some kind of elaborate hoax. Popper's supporters included Einstein, Bertrand Russell, G. E. Moore, and Niels Bohr, who wrote that Popper's "unusual power of tackling general scientific problems with his thorough knowledge of the fundamental concepts of physics, justifies the greatest expectations as regards his future scientific and pedagogic activity in this field."[13] A letter to the AAC said there were half a dozen people who would be willing to contribute to a fund to help Popper if he were left destitute after leaving Austria.

With these backers, it is not surprising that the AAC decided to offer him a one-year grant, although the archive reveals that there were some reservations. After taking soundings, Duncan-Jones had reported that not everyone was convinced that the young man had exceptional talent. In any case, once the grant was on the table, the next step was to identify an appropriate institutional base. The plan was for Popper to lecture in Cambridge. And, after much to-and-fro, and some anxious moments when paperwork went missing, the official invitation from Cambridge duly arrived. Popper was to give eight lectures in all, beginning in 1937.

The news came as a tremendous relief. Popper had secured an escape from the drudgery of high school teaching and, more critically, from rising right-wing extremism.

In the end, however, he chose a different route. He had also applied for a job in Christchurch, New Zealand. When an offer eventually came through, he decided to take it: a permanent job in a less prestigious university was preferable to a temporary one in Cambridge. Perhaps he also thought that New Zealand was likely to be safer than Europe. He wrote to the SPSL, "It [New Zealand] is not quite the moon. But after the moon it is the furthest place on earth."[14]

———

Popper's moonward move had welcome repercussions for Friedrich Waismann, still very much on earth, in Vienna. The grant that Popper had been planning to take up could now be allocated elsewhere. And the lectures that Popper was due to give in Cambridge could now be delivered by someone else. Popper had the unemployed Waismann in mind. Felix Kaufmann, who had lobbied successfully for Popper, now stepped in to campaign for Waismann, writing to the SPSL. But, as Tess Simpson explained to Kaufmann in February 1937, the transfer of a grant from Popper to Waismann was far from automatic. Waismann was a tougher case than Popper, because he "is not known in this country as well as Dr. Popper was, nor has he lectured here."[15]

There was the standard SPSL form to fill out. Waismann had to declare his income (6,720 schillings in the years 1932–33, of which 6,000 derived from private lessons and courses). Stating where in the world he would be prepared to go for work, he exhibited little flexibility: next to "Tropical Countries" he scrawled "no . . . on account of the climate."[16] And of course he had to supply referees prepared to vouch for his intellectual distinction.

These included three Vienna Circle stalwarts, Carnap, Feigl, and Menger. Carnap described him as "one of the most excellent and promising students I ever had."[17] The fact that he had not published much, wrote Carnap, was in part because he had always had to struggle to make a living. As well as being a first-rate philosopher, he was a first-rate teacher too, said Carnap: "it is deplorable that the anti-Semitism of the University of Vienna made his teaching there impossible, after the assassination of Professor Schlick."[18] Susan Stebbing also assured the SPSL that Waismann was "a brilliant philosopher."[19] There is no Wittgenstein reference in the file, an augury of their relationship to come.

Still there were hiccups. G. E. Moore was concerned that Waismann's English might not be up to scratch, and Simpson promised to look into this. When she established that it was—and Waismann's letters are written in flawless English—a deal was brokered on much the same terms as had been agreed with Popper. Moore sent an official invitation from Cambridge, and the SPSL authorized a grant for a term at the rate of £182 a year.

While Popper instinctively understood that the situation in Austria was capable of further deterioration, the apolitical Waismann still hesitated. He pleaded for a postponement of the lectures until October 1937, to give him time to finish the book that he had begun many years earlier with Wittgenstein. He finally arrived in the UK on 21 October 1937. As usual, Tess Simpson had quietly and efficiently sorted out the mundane but essential details, booking a room for him to stay in London before he moved on to Cambridge, identifying someone who could help cash his checks until he had his own bank account, and so on.

His lectures began in November 1937. A month later the SPSL informed him that he would get a short extension on his grant but urged him to seek a more stable academic position. He was a gloomy presence in Cambridge. Philosophers Moore and C. D. Broad professed not to want him to go, but there was no permanent vacancy in Cambridge itself. Having gotten to know him, they were happy to provide glowing testimonials. Moore wrote that Waismann was exceptionally well qualified to occupy a chair of philosophy. Broad added, "We should all be very sorry, on selfish grounds, to lose Dr. Waismann. But it is impossible in Cambridge, with our limited resources and the small number of students taking the subject, to provide any adequate permanent appointment for him. Therefore we would be delighted if he were to be appointed to a permanent post worthy of his very great abilities."[20]

Waismann had arrived in the UK alone, leaving his wife, Hermine, and baby son, Thomas. They were being supported financially by Felix Kaufmann. But after the Anschluss Waismann became desperate to get them out. He visited the SPSL several times to discuss their fate. Richard Braithwaite, another member of the Cambridge faculty (who was sympathetic to logical empiricism), came to the rescue. Braithwaite was married to Margaret Masterman, a clever, eccentric, imposing young woman and an expert in computational linguistics. They had just had their first child, a boy. The Braithwaites offered Waismann's wife a place to stay and a small wage in exchange for child care and help in the house, thus taking advantage of the relatively lax regulations for bringing in foreigners to work as domestic servants.

There were still many hurdles to overcome. Mrs. Waismann had to have her passport stamped at the British consulate in Vienna. That was easier said than done. She went there every day, queuing for hours, but was repeatedly told that there was no information about her case. The SPSL offered to pay the expense of cabling the consul, a proposal that was accepted by the government, even though *its* officials were to blame for the failure of communication. After the cable had been sent, the Foreign Office pursued the bill (5s/od), demanding "a crossed cheque or a crossed postal order for that sum"![21] Perhaps during a time of heightened international upheaval, this penny-pinching should be regarded as fiscally prudent. An alternative term is callous.

Meanwhile, Waismann received a reassuring note from the Cambridge philosophy faculty on 23 May 1938. It stated that they could pay him a small sum, £75, for the next academic year, if he failed to obtain work elsewhere. This was a vital source of money, but hardly enough to survive. A condition of Waismann's visa was that he not undertake any other paid work besides his Cambridge lecture duties. But an approach was made to the Home Office to ask whether he could receive a gratuity of £25 for extra informal teaching, and the Home Office raised no objection.

Finally, his wife and child arrived in Dover on 9 June 1938. Waismann's permit to remain in the UK was extended first until 30 June 1939 and later to 20 June 1940.

———

Even with the family safe, it was not a happy time for the Waismanns. Hermine was not cut out for child care. As for her husband, on the teaching front he told Simpson that he felt overshadowed by Wittgenstein, who had made a generous offer to lecture for nothing, allowing funds to be released for Waismann. In the end money was found for them both. But for the most part Wittgenstein's presence was a personal disaster for his former disciple. Whatever their intellectual differences, they operated on roughly the same scholarly terrain, and it was excessive to have two people teaching similar topics: for that reason, faculty members were opposed to offering Waismann a permanent position. To make matters worse, Wittgenstein actively discouraged students from attending Waismann's seminars and lectures. Waismann grumbled that

Wittgenstein ignored him in the street. The two men had once contemplated writing a joint book; for Waismann, the snubbing of his former philosophical guide and inspiration must have been acutely painful.

Socially, Waismann found it tough to settle in. Simpson tried to encourage academics in her Cambridge network to make the Waismanns feel welcome, but their landlord, Braithwaite, was not overflowing with sympathy for his refugee. It was largely Waismann's own fault, he wrote. "He knows lots of people but does not take much initiative in arranging to meet them."[22]

Meanwhile, Gilbert Ryle and Isaiah Berlin were pushing his cause in Oxford, and when a vacancy came up at Magdalen College, Waismann immediately took it, even though it meant temporarily leaving his family. He was not offered a full salary, but his miserly Magdalen earnings were soon supplemented by a stipend from All Souls College, and when the SPSL lent him some more money, he was able to transport his family and possessions from Cambridge.

But by then, war had broken out.

19

◄○►

War

I faced one or two anxious moments last week. One naturally has
something to worry about when one has a family of six hundred.

— TESS SIMPSON

I want to look like a lady, not like a factory worker.

— ROSE RAND

IN 1937, in The Hague, Otto Neurath's wife, Olga, died of complications
from a kidney operation, and for a while he was inconsolable. It was the
only time his assistant—and mistress—Marie had seen him cry. Meanwhile, any hopes he had of returning to Vienna were vanishing. After
the Anschluss, his son, Paul, who had remained in Austria, was arrested
and sent to first Dachau and then Buchenwald concentration camps.
Released in 1939, Paul managed to escape to Sweden. His father had had
two close escapes in his life, fortunate to be released from a Bavarian
prison cell in 1919, and to be out of the country when the Austrofascists
came hunting for him in 1934. He was under no illusion about the likeli-
hood of a third escape were he to be seized by the Nazis.

When the Germans invaded Poland on 1 September 1939, followed
two days later by the British and French declarations of war, Neurath
was in Harvard, attending the Fifth International Congress for the Unity
of Science. It was there that he would argue with his distant relative
Horace Kallen about whether the project to unify the sciences was
driven by a fascistic impulse. Against advice, Neurath decided to return
to The Hague, and he quickly gathered letters of recommendation to
ease his passage through the British blockade back to Europe. He remained in the Netherlands until May the following year.

On the evening of 9 May 1940, Otto and Marie were reading history books in the Royal Library in The Hague. They did not leave until closing time, 10:00 p.m. The next morning the German air force, the *Luftwaffe*, without warning or official declaration of hostilities, launched an attack on the Netherlands (and Belgium and Luxembourg). On Tuesday, 14 May, at around lunchtime, Nazi bombers flattened the beautiful port city of Rotterdam, just twenty miles from The Hague. Late that afternoon, fearing that other cities would suffer the same fate, the Dutch announced their surrender.

During those four days, Otto and Marie spent much of their time indoors, listening to the radio and playing chess. They felt the ground shake from the carpet bombing of Rotterdam. They packed a small suitcase and gathered up what money they possessed. When news of surrender was announced, Otto put on his coat and said, "Let's go." He left the draft of his book for the Encyclopedia series in his apartment. Another casualty was the collected papers of the Harvard conference—just about to go to press.

With ammunition dumps exploding and oil dumps in flames, he and Marie made their way through the black smoke to The Hague's fishing port and beach resort, Scheveningen. It was a half-hour walk. "If we do not find a boat I'm going on a piece of wood,"[1] Otto said. The beach was teeming with desperate people, mostly Jews, willing to hand over money, gold, jewelry, whatever was required to secure a passage out.

Otto and Marie spotted a motorized lifeboat, *Zeemanshoop* (*Seaman's Hope*), already full, including a Jewish couple they knew from Berlin. They jumped on, the last passengers aboard bar one who was hauled in from the sea.

The *Zeemanshoop* had been commandeered by four Delft University students, who had used a bayonet to break the padlock. They were desperate to escape the Netherlands to continue the fight against the Nazis. One marine engineering student, Harry Hack, had considerable sailing experience and was confident he could steer the boat to England. What he had not expected was the company of forty-two other passengers. They had no suitcases or bags, just the clothes they were wearing, though someone had bought a few bottles of rum and a few had poison to take in the event of capture. Many of the men were formally dressed, with hats, ironed white shirts, ties, and raincoats, as if they were heading for a night at the opera. One woman was pregnant. Most of the women sat on the side bench seats: the men stood, steadying themselves by holding on to the rail. Otto and Marie were at the back.

The dangerously overweight vessel lurched away from the Dutch shores at dusk. We know the names of all those on board through the survival of a list compiled at sea, scrawled on the back of a chart of the Dutch coast. A little bracket was put around the names of Neurath and Reidemeister to indicate that though unmarried they were together. The weather was calm, but the engine struggled, and at least twice during the night there was a heated discussion among the passengers about whether they should turn back, with some arguing that it was too risky to continue. Otto may not have believed his chances of survival on the boat were high, but a return to the Netherlands meant certain death. They sailed all night. Otto asked the students what the price of the fare was, and was told it was free. He later wrote to Carnap claiming that he had begun to plan his future activities in the UK while on the boat.[2]

Meanwhile, HMS *Venomous*, a destroyer that had sailed from Dover, in the south of England, was operating between the British and Dutch coasts, escorting mine-sweeping ships. At dawn the ship's lookouts saw the packed *Zeemanshoop* with its raised Dutch flag and passengers making frantic distress signals. All forty-six of them were hauled on board and given a mug of tea and bread and butter. A slightly more congested HMS *Venomous* docked at Dover that evening.

The Dutch students were free to go.

But if the Greater German nationals—including Otto and Marie—were expecting a warm welcome, they were in for a cruel surprise. On British soil they immediately fell into the category of enemy aliens.

———

In the period before the outbreak of World War II, Jewish refugees in Britain had begun the slow process of rebuilding their lives. They had lost almost all their wealth and possessions, they were in a strange environment, and they had to adapt to a new language. In many cases, their professional qualifications were unrecognized. There was the non-stop worry about family members who still had not escaped. It was best not to talk about events on the continental mainland. Most British people could not really envisage them, and when they were told, they did not believe it. It was best just to get on with life.

The German occupation of Poland changed things, of course, but not markedly. For the time being there was little military activity in Britain, and the prevailing atmosphere was one of uneasy calm. There were around seventy thousand German-speaking émigrés in the country, who were now declared "enemy aliens," obliged to register with the police, and prohibited from living in areas of military significance. None-theless, at least initially, the government took a relatively relaxed approach to these foreigners. Tribunals were set up to classify them into three categories, depending upon how much of a threat they were deemed to pose. Category A were considered sufficiently threatening to be detained. Category B had some restrictions placed on their movements. Category C were exempt from restrictions. Less than 1 percent were placed in Category A, while the vast majority—over 64,000—were Category C.

The so-called phony war lasted until the early summer of 1940. With the German invasion and occupation of the Low Countries and then France in May 1940, the public mood immediately turned ugly. The press began to whip up fears of the "enemy within." "Act! Act! Act!" demanded *The Daily Mail* of the government. One of their leading commentators, Nazi sympathizer George Ward Price, had this advice for Jewish immigrants. "They should be careful not to arouse the same resentment here as they have stirred up in so many countries."[3] A British diplomat warned that "the paltriest kitchen maid not only can be, but generally is, a menace to the safety of the country."[4] Thousands of cooks and housemaids were dismissed. This all added to refugee anxiety. Stefan Zweig was living in Bath in the west of England when he heard the news that German troops were storming toward Paris. Britain, no doubt, would be Hitler's next target. "I have already prepared a certain phial,"[5] Zweig wrote in his diary.

Now the authorities reviewed its list of aliens to determine which among them were too dangerous to be at large. In the end, around twenty-seven thousand were arrested and dispatched to various detention centers—most destined for the Isle of Man, off Britain's west coast. They had not proved difficult to locate; their address details, after all, had all been registered with the police. But people joked that the most effective means to trawl for refugees was to carry out sweeps through the public libraries of northwest London.

———

That was not where Otto Neurath and Marie Reidemeister were arrested. When they landed in darkness at Dover on 15 May 1940, the passengers of the *Zeemanshoop* were separated, causing some of them to become hysterical. They were medically examined and in a crash course on British cuisine fed an almost inedible meal of boiled potatoes and corned beef with sharp English mustard. Otto was bound for Pentonville Prison and later to a racecourse, Kempton Park, where he slept on a mattress on the stone floor. Marie was removed to a Fulham Institute she later described as a Dickensian poorhouse, where she slept on the floor. "There was a woman walking with high heels, clack, clack, clack. I didn't sleep that night."[6] From there she was sent to Holloway Prison. There were minor humiliations aplenty: they had to keep the door open when they went to the toilet.

From their respective London cells, Otto and Marie were dispatched to separate camps on the Isle of Man—Neurath near the capital, Douglas, Marie to a camp in the southwest. The detainee population was mixed. Not all the "enemy aliens" were Jewish or political refugees: a few were German citizens who for one reason or another were in the UK at the war's onset; some were Hitler supporters. The British made no distinction between Jew and Nazi: the "enemy aliens" found themselves in the same detention center. For the Jewish inmates, that brought anguish. As one internee wrote in October 1941, this unfortunate setup "creates a continual strain of nerves, hearing of fascist songs, exchange of fascist salutes. . . . [Y]ou will easily imagine what I feel when I see people smiling when the radio announces the executions in France and other countries under the fascist yoke."[7] Some of the Jews had been in Dachau, so it was not their first time behind barbed wire. In a few camps, Aryan German groups were formed. Among the Jews there were a number of suicides (including one man who had escaped alongside Otto on the *Zeemanshoop*.)

Still, for all the traumas of detention, this was a relatively benign experience compared to what most detainees had been through before arriving in the UK. Otto received books, new shoes and pajamas, and occasionally cakes. Marie said later that having escaped the Gestapo, "even in prison I felt safe."[8] The present author's great-grandfather kept a diary during his internship, recording the petty bureaucracy, the deprivations, the shortage of toilet paper, the depression and suicides, but also the vibrancy, the concerts, the lectures (one about the problem of infinity, by a colleague of Einstein's), the "businesses"—the best shoe polisher was Viennese and attracted clients with "his good jokes." There were daily football games ("Wake up Germany," shouted the spectators in a Germany versus Austria match). During a game among Austrian prisoners an English sentry with a gun twice kicked back a ball that had landed behind the goalposts. This small act of decency made an enormous impression on a man who had experienced anti-Semitism Viennese-style.[9]

————

Wittgenstein had acquired British citizenship in April 1939 and so was exempt from the new measures. Not so Waismann. On 3 July 1940, the Society for the Protection of Science and Learning was sent a letter from Hermine Waismann. "I should like to inform you that my husband, F. Waismann, has been interned as an enemy alien a week ago."[10] It is hard to imagine anybody who posed less of a threat to the British state than this apolitical, introverted, mildly depressive forty-four-year-old Jewish philosopher. On 22 July the SPSL secretary, Walter Adams, commented with reference to the Waismann case: "The treatment of alien refugees in this country has been incredibly stupid and the SPSL has had to devote a great deal of its energy lately to trying to correct some of the grosser stupidities."[11] Hermine wrote to Tess Simpson in August that she was "deeply depressed" to be separated from her husband.[12]

At the Isle of Man, inmates made the best of their predicament, establishing an informal university. Classes were offered in a variety of subjects, from languages, math, and business to bacteriology and Chinese theater. There were, of course, philosophy lectures, including at least one delivered by Neurath in January 1941. We know from the camp newspapers that this was attended by more than two hundred people, though the content remains a mystery (the German title roughly translates as "How Do You Make a Tennis Court Durable?"). Besides academic lectures, there were rich cultural offerings too—concerts, an art exhibition. Business ventures mushroomed—shoe polishers and hairdressers—some asking for money, others bartering their services for razor blades or cigarettes.

At its peak, in late summer of 1940, there were 14,000 detainees in the Isle of Man, including Walter Hollitscher, the young communist with a special interest in Freud. But once the hysteria about the enemy aliens had died down, saner voices began to make themselves heard. The bishop of Chichester, George Bell, in a speech to the House of Lords, pointed out the absurdity of paying to incarcerate people who were desperate to support the war effort against the Nazis. He had visited the Isle of Man and "was astounded at the quantity as well as the quality of material available—doctors, professors, scientists, inventors, chemists, industrialists, manufacturers, humanists—they all want to work for Britain, freedom, and justice."[13]

But what really swung public opinion was news in July 1940 of the sinking of *Arandora Star* by a German U-boat. As well as interning people in Britain, the authorities had forcibly exiled thousands of others, who were shipped off to Canada and Australia, perilous journeys through contested seas. The *Arandora Star* was bound for Canada and was full of Italians. Many were chefs and waiters, who had worked in the restaurant business in the UK for years and had little or no interest in politics. Nearly seven hundred people died. Now the media changed tack, with several of the leading papers publishing scathing articles about the treatment of refugees.

In the camps there was some relaxation of the rules. On 26 July 1940, husbands and wives were allowed to meet to discuss whether they would be willing to travel abroad together, and thus Marie and Otto, though still not officially married, saw each other for the first time since they had been separated upon arrival in England. Such meetings became more regular: the rule was that a couple had to be married or engaged. "Then," as Marie put it, "everyone was engaged."[14] Neurath's love letters to Marie during internment are all signed off with variations of his elephant theme. Images did not count toward the strict word limitation imposed on letters.

————

After arriving in the UK, Marie and Otto had been permitted to make a phone call, and in this way were able to inform Susan Stebbing of their circumstances. Stebbing, another largely forgotten and unacknowledged heroine in this story, found a solicitor to act on their behalf. Otto's case was brought to the attention of the SPSL.

At the SPSL, Tess Simpson now had a new cause. Of those detained, 560 were academics, almost all of whom she had helped to settle in the UK. She opened a file on each and every one of them and began to prepare the documentation to petition for their release. A turning point came when the government announced that those who posed no danger and had a vital contribution to make to the nation were free to go, and, just as important, when a concession was wrung from the home secretary that this included contributions to science and learning.

The process was protracted. Simpson needed references to vouch for each detainee. For Neurath, biologist Julian Huxley was obliging. "He is most definitely anti-Nazi. I am sure that he could be very usefully employed by the Ministry of Information or other similar body on propaganda and information work."[15] Others, like writer H. G. Wells, were less helpful. Wells saw "no reason why Dr. Neurath should be made the subject of a special campaign for preferential treatment."[16]

Neurath did not help his cause. Patience was never one of his virtues, and at the same time as Simpson was plodding through the formal process, he was directly appealing to the Aliens Department. He explained that, if released, he would not be a burden on the state, since both he and Marie would receive a salary from the American branch of his Isotype Institute. His Isotype work could also "render some useful service to this country"[17] by addressing various topical issues, such as public health.

These overlapping appeals confused matters. However, on 20 September 1940, a letter of support for Neurath arrived from Princeton, and from an individual that even the British establishment could not ignore. "Neurath," Einstein wrote, "is very well known to me through his scientific work and through common friends who know him well personally. On the basis of my reliable information I am gladly taking every responsibility for the political reliability of Professor Neurath. His release from internment would, in my opinion, by fully justified."[18] Neurath's case was dragging on, but Tess Simpson was upbeat. "The word of Professor Einstein will count a good deal; Professor Einstein has appealed only on behalf of a very few internees so that this appeal should carry weight."[19] Oxford University sent an invitation to Neurath to deliver a series of lectures on logical empiricism and the social sciences.

Finally, on 6 December 1940, both Otto and Marie were allocated a January date to review their case in front of a tribunal. On 7 February 1941, Otto was told he was to be released. The following morning, he gathered his belongings and picked up a voucher to cover travel to his destination. The gates opened at 7:00 a.m. From the harbor he embarked on a boat to Liverpool or Fleetwood, before taking an onward train, destination Oxford. A fortnight later, he and Marie were married.

As an unusual expression of gratitude, he sent Tess Simpson his next scholarly article, "Universal Jargon and Terminology." It may not have been everyone's notion of the ideal present, but somehow, amid her ongoing campaign to have others released, she found time to read it. "I see that you mention Karl Popper in your paper; we knew him before he went to New Zealand."[20] As for the article, "It is good to know that you are receiving the recognition in this country which you deserve, and I hope that it will help to make up for the disagreeable experience which you shared with almost all the refugees."[21]

In November 1941 he again wrote to Simpson. The irrepressible Neurath was already upbeat about the future. "We are highly pleased by the atmosphere in England. We really have not the feeling to be in a foreign country."[22] He himself did not live a life of moderation, but he had witnessed enough extremism to appreciate the orderly culture in Britain and its mostly moderate politics. "It is impressive to listen to plain people here, how they avoid boasting and over-statements in daily matters."[23] He had once described how he spoke "broken English fluently"[24] but now he began to collect English expressions. He particularly approved of the way fire-watch leaders explained that during air raid attacks people should stay calm and behave with the "usual common-sense." "I like this type of habit much more than the continental one, with 'highest duty', 'national community', 'self- sacrifice', 'obedience', 'subordination', etc./ 'eternal ideals.'"[25]

They had a nice home with a giant bath—this particularly pleased Otto—and began to rebuild their library. With the help of Susan Stebbing (and just before Stebbing was diagnosed with the cancer that would kill her), Otto and Marie set up an Isotype Institute in Oxford (in 1942), and soon had work commissioned. A distinguished documentary filmmaker, Paul Rotha, became an important client. Among Rotha's films was one about blood transfusion, in which he needed to explain blood groups. Then there was his Ministry of Information film, *A Few Ounces a Day*, to encourage British citizens to salvage items—tins, bulbs, boxes, wrappers, newspapers—which could be reused as raw material to rebuild ships. The film used an unbroken series of Isotype images: a few ounces saved and collected from each household were transformed into a new ship, which then replaced a ship sunk by a torpedo.

Neurath kept an ongoing correspondence with his old Circle colleagues. There was a terrible falling-out with Carnap. Neurath objected to Carnap's 1942 book, *Introduction to Semantics*, which Carnap had sent him as a gift. Full of metaphysics, he carped ungratefully. Then, in 1943,

Carnap, who coedited the Encylopedia series with Charles Morris, insisted on having a disclaimer inserted into Neurath's book for the Foundations of the Social Sciences series—saying he, Carnap, had not had time to edit it. This was true. To appease the publisher, the book's publication had been accelerated, and when he eventually read it, Carnap thought it slapdash. Indeed, he told Neurath that in places it was so unclear that "I would not know whether I agree with you or not."[26] Understandably Neurath felt humiliated. There were recriminations and long rambling letters. Carnap called him "Neurath the Volcanic"[27]— their friendship never fully recovered. It reinforced Neurath's suspicion that his Circle colleagues rated his organization skills above his philosophical.

The rolling Encyclopedia series Neurath regarded as a war effort (as we shall see, a phrase that would also be used by Popper). The publisher had received only nine of the twenty volumes promised, and, with printing costs rising, they threatened to break off the series. Neurath was unhappy. "[T]he war is going on very well and victory comes nearer every day. It would be like defeatism to suspend now anything."[28] He would find another publisher unless they relented, he said. Naturally they did.

―――――

Only one member of the Circle left his escape until after the war had begun. Even after the Anschluss Gödel had naïvely returned to Vienna from Princeton. Now he approached the US consul about applying for a visa. This too was problematic. The easiest type of visa to get was for academics teaching in US colleges. Gödel was not, strictly speaking, "teaching," so the head of the Institute for Advanced Study, Frank Aydelotte, wrote a supporting letter that flirted with the truth. "The instruction here is on a very advanced level and is consequently less formal than in the ordinary university or graduate school."[29]

The visa process was protracted, and Gödel came to terms with the possibility that he would, in fact, have to remain in Austria. Then he suddenly became desperate to leave. His biographer, Dawson, traces this to an episode that also involved Gödel's wife. While walking with Adele one day in the vicinity of the university, Kurt was assaulted by a band of young Nazi rowdies. "For whatever reason—whether he was mistaken for a Jew, recognized as one who had fraternized with Jewish colleagues, or was simply targeted as an intellectual—the youths seized him, struck him, and knocked off his glasses before Adele managed to drive them off with blows from her umbrella."[30]

Aydelotte wrote to the German embassy in Washington. Gödel was an Aryan, he pointed out. He was also exceptionally brilliant, so his case could be treated as an exception. Surely, he pleaded, Germany would acknowledge that the most important thing was that Gödel be permitted to continue his work rather than, say, go into the military.

The visa arrived in January 1940. The war was now four months old. The way out was through Lithuania, Latvia, Russia, and then by the trans-Siberian railway to Manchuria and Japan. From there it was a boat trip to San Francisco—then a long train trip to New York, and finally, a short one to Princeton, NJ. All in all the journey took about two grueling months.

Gödel had married Adele Nimbursky in 1938, despite vehement family disapproval—she was older than Kurt, a divorcée, and from a lower social rung. On the boat to America, Gödel and Adele—along with all the other passengers—were required to respond to a list of questions before disembarking on US territory. One asked whether they—the passenger—had ever been a patient in a mental institution. Both Gödels answered no. This was not the time for total candor.

They reached Princeton by March. There Gödel soon made one firm friend—Albert Einstein—and the two men developed a routine. Each morning Gödel would stop off at Einstein's house, sometime between ten and eleven, and each afternoon they would walk home together. Einstein joked, "I go to my office just to have the privilege of being able to walk home with Kurt Gödel."[31] Bertrand Russell visited Princeton in 1943, and he, Einstein, Gödel, and physicist Wolfgang Pauli (Viennese-born and a godson of Ernst Mach, who in 1945 would win the Nobel Prize for his contributions to quantum mechanics) met weekly. It was an *Übermenschen* discussion group that nonetheless left Russell dissatisfied. "Although all three of them were Jews and exiles, and, in intention, cosmopolitan, I found they all had a German bias toward metaphysics." Gödel was not of course Jewish, but he was an immigrant Austrian academic—it was statistically reasonable to assume that he was.

———

Carnap too had discussions with Russell during the war. In 1939, after three years in Chicago, Carnap moved to Harvard for two years. In 1940, Russell was invited to Harvard to deliver the William James lectures. This came just a few months after the shameful New York Supreme Court ruling in which Russell was pronounced unfit to teach. He had been appointed to a chair of philosophy by New York's Board of Higher Education, prompting a public outcry led by New York's Episcopalian bishop, William Manning. The judge, John E. McGeehan, reached his ruling after reading several of Russell's books, including *What I Believe* and *Marriage and Morals*, and concluding that they were, among many other flaws, erotomaniac and atheistic. Russell's Harvard lectures were later published in *An Inquiry into Meaning and Truth*, allowing Russell to add one more qualification to his bulging curriculum vitae: "Judicially pronounced unworthy to be Professor of Philosophy at the College of the City of New York." After the legal circus in New York, the refined atmosphere of Cambridge, MA, was a welcome contrast. As well as Russell and Carnap, there were Quine and von Mises, Tarski and Feigl. Feigl was there on a Rockefeller Foundation grant—he would take up a chair at the University of Minnesota in 1940. Carnap suggested they meet regularly—which they did, usually at 6:30 p.m. on Thursdays. Echoes of Vienna past.

———

One Circle member did not survive the war—Edgar Zilsel. After arriving in the US in 1939 he had sought work and funding with the help of the transmigrated Frankfurt School. A Rockefeller Fellowship—to research the origins of modern science—helped support him for two years, and when the money ran out in 1941 he accepted a part-time teaching post at the all-female Hunter College in New York, and then, in 1943, a job at another all-female institution, Mills College in Oakland, California. His mentally unstable wife had had several breakdowns and did not want to move with him to California, and his son by this time had gone to study in Wisconsin. While the other academics went home at night, he lived on campus, and dined in the hall with the young female students. He felt humiliated and lonely.

The best day for him was the regular gathering of academics at the History of Science Dinner Club. It was the sort of forum he was used to, a reminder of his Vienna days, with a group of like-minded thinkers congregating for intellectual stimulation. The club valued his contributions to debate. Still, these meetings were only monthly; providing insufficient social sustenance. On the night of 11 March 1944, six years to the day after Chancellor Kurt von Schuschnigg announced the end of Austria as a sovereign state, Zilsel sat in his office and wrote three notes; one to the president of Mills, one to his son, and the third he left on his desk:

> No fuss, please!
> Just inform Dr. French, don't tell anybody else, please. Keep silent, please!
> Nobody must know of the suicide, everybody must be told that I died through a traffic accident.
> No students must see the body.
> Please, please, don't try to wake me up again.
> I am sorry to have inconvenienced you.
> Thank You.

He had left some money with the note, which went on, "If the janitor finds me, he may keep the $10 bill as compensation for the shock."[32]

The *Oakland Tribune* ignored his pleas to keep the suicide a secret. The following day, in the Sunday edition, the paper carried news of his death. Having written the note, they said, Zilsel "fashioned a pillow from excelsior [wood shavings] and his jacket, took poison and then reclined on the floor awaiting death—his hands in his pockets."[33] Zilsel was found by Dr. French, the dean of the faculty.

———

None of the Circle or those associated with it saw action in World War II. Mostly too old, they nonetheless tried to do their bit. Wittgenstein volunteered to be a hospital orderly in Guy's Hospital, London, transferring drugs from the pharmacy to the wards. He then took a post as a laboratory assistant in the Royal Victoria Infirmary in Newcastle upon Tyne.

Rose Rand also worked, but reluctantly. She had left her escape from Austria till desperately late, and the exact details of how she managed it are murky—it was almost certainly with the aid of Susan Stebbing in London. She arrived in the UK on 11 June 1939. One might have expected her principal emotion after escaping Austria to have been one of relief. But in a letter from Stebbing's address sent that same week, she described her misery: she was, she said, wholly unhappy.

She always had a tendency to see the world through soot-tinted glasses, though her circumstances hardly merited a happy disposition. Poor in Vienna, she arrived in London poorer still, and had to earn her keep. The first work she found was in a home for hundreds of mentally handicapped children. She lasted only three months; she found it exhausting and was disdainful of her fellow nurses, "simple peasant-women."[34]

She tried her hand at several other jobs, hated them all, and complained none offered remuneration adequate for her needs. She was not shy in requesting help, but the well-meaning organizations she approached—the SPSL and the British Federation of University Women (BFUW)—found her infuriating: immature, grasping, unreliable, proud, and exhaustingly persistent—this latter trait accounting for the fat files on her that now sit in the archives.

The central problem for Rand was that while she cared about only one thing—the pursuit of her studies in logic—she could not land a university job. She applied for a grant from the SPSL, and filled out the usual form, demonstrating more flexibility than Waismann. Where would she be prepared to go for work? "Anywhere."[35] How much longer could the means at her disposal be expected to last? "I have no means."[36] She had references from Circle colleagues Carnap, Zilsel, Kaufmann, and Kraft, who said that she was "one of the best among the students of Prof. Schlick."[37] The head of the Pötzl clinic, Professor Pötzl himself, rated her "extraordinarily expert and well trained in matters of psychology."[38]

Nonetheless, the SPSL determined that she was not a sufficiently worthy case to merit support. They reached the same verdict many times when repeated requests from Rand over the next few years forced them to review her situation. The BFUW regarded her as "a very difficult, if not hopeless, case."[39] She's "definitely in need of psychological treatment, has no insight into her own problems and is extremely difficult to handle."[40] In February 1940, when Rand wrote to the SPSL for help in finding academic work, Simpson sent back an unusually tough reply. "There is no chance whatever of an academic position. . . . I am afraid I can only advise you to register with the Labour Exchange."[41]

An irritant she may have been, and yet the relief organizations did what they could for her, sending her small grants and loans, with no expectation that these would be repaid. Unknown to Rand, this money had a surprising provenance. Between 1941 and 1943 Rand was in Cambridge, where the status of "distinguished foreigner" enabled her to attend classes and lectures. These included Wittgenstein's, before he went to London. To sustain herself, Rand took a job as an inspector in a lathe factory, measuring small machinery parts: Wittgenstein advised her not to give it up, though she detested it: the job did not pay much, the fumes made her sick, and it entailed long hours, including night shifts. In a comment Simpson related to Wittgenstein, Rand moaned, "I want to look like a lady, not like a factory worker."[42] Here she and Wittgenstein had a fundamentally different outlook. He urged her to make use of her manual skills and not to think of working with her hands as shameful.

In fact, Wittgenstein was the source of the money sent to Rand by the SPSL. Rand's relationship with Wittgenstein reveals a compassionate facet of his character that runs contrary to his self-absorbed and austere image. The SPSL archive holds a file of correspondence with him, running across a five-year period from 1942. Although he too was unconvinced of Rand's intellectual merit, telling Simpson "she wasn't any good as a philosopher,"[43] he shows a long-running concern for her well-being.

His financial assistance began in the summer of 1941. Since both Simpson and Rand had relocated from London to Cambridge, Rand was able to stop in occasionally at the SPSL office. Her visits were not always announced, and sometimes resented, though they allowed Simpson to keep Wittgenstein abreast of Rand's life and mood. Rand was depressed, Simpson explained in June 1942: Wittgenstein had earlier raised the idea of using the SPSL to channel funds to Rand, and he now began to give small donations, a practice which continued for several years. But, he stressed, his name must be kept out of the arrangement. It was "very important that she shouldn't know"[44] that he was involved.

Simpson's normal tolerance was tested to the limit by Rand, and she did little to encourage Wittgenstein's generosity. Indeed, she found Rand's continual supplications for money vexing and some of her spending decisions inexcusable, given her precarious financial position and constant complaints. In particular, Simpson was appalled when Rand bought a tailor-made coat for three pounds. "I myself would not think of paying three pounds for the making of a coat, at the present time," [45] she complained indignantly to Wittgenstein on 18 January 1943. And now Rand was asking for still more money. "Of course I have to tell you of Miss Rand's request, but honestly I can't support it."[46] Wittgenstein wrote back on 9 February from Guy's Hospital: he agreed that "it would be quite wrong for me to pay Miss Rand's tailor's bills. On the other hand I'd like you to have some money from me for other purposes, so, as soon as I can, I'll send 5 pounds."[47]

Simpson and Wittgenstein had developed an unlikely friendship. They discussed classical music together, particularly Brahms; Wittgenstein once queued for an hour in Cambridge to buy her a bun. In October 1943 Simpson sent a long letter to Wittgenstein, who was now in Newcastle, informing him that Rand had recently been committed to a psychiatric hospital, after threatening to kill herself. Simpson entered negotiations for her release. As she told Wittgenstein, "there's a good distance between being queer, which Miss Rand certainly is, and insane, which I felt sure she was not."[48] Two years later, Wittgenstein reluctantly agreed to serve as her reference for a job she had applied for. His response to her request is interesting, not least because it shows the brutal truth-teller was on occasion prepared to withhold the truth. "Whether there is any chance of your being any good as a lab assistant I don't know. In fact, I doubt it; though I wouldn't tell them."[49] Rand annoyed him by sending him books and chocolates as gifts, and he warned her not to do it again. "I will send any present back, however much trouble this may give me; so, please, stop sending me things."[50]

––––––

When the Unity of Science Congress took place in Harvard, Karl Popper was already ensconced in New Zealand. In Popper's archive there is a revealing letter from Hempel's wife, Eva. She tells him about the Harvard Unity of Science Congress in September 1939 and how it was such a success and everyone was there, Feigl, Zilsel, Carnap, etc., adding, "in fact almost all the remaining members of the Vienna Circle, except Waismann and you (if I dare include you under that heading)."[51]

Popper may have regarded himself as a thinker apart: they saw him as one of them. Meanwhile, he was hard at work. His most significant piece to emerge from the war years was *The Open Society and Its Enemies.* The book was a monumental effort, which traveled through multiple drafts, diligently typed up by his loyal and long-suffering wife, Hennie. All his life Popper worked incredibly hard. He rarely took days off, weekends and holidays included. His self-imposed regime often made him ill, bringing him to the edge of physical and mental collapse. But at no period did he exert himself more than when in New Zealand. *The Open Society* nearly killed him, and so one should not deride his description of it as his "war effort." His circumstances were made more trying by his remoteness. He felt cut off from debate; the university library held fewer books than his father's.

Although it was written during the hottest period of conflict, in which millions were being slaughtered, the book would come to be seen as a cold war text, in particular directed at the totalitarian regimes within the Soviet sphere of influence. Popper took aim at several philosophical colossi, Plato, Hegel, and Karl Marx. He attacked the notion that there was an inevitability to the unfolding of history as Marx claimed—that history had, as it were, a direction. The belief that human society was governed by inexorable laws was pernicious, encouraging intolerance and the imposition of large-scale damaging "solutions" on society.

Drawing on his work in the philosophy of science, he proclaimed the benefits of an open society. The real way for society to progress was through trial and error and piecemeal social engineering. Not every policy worked. Just as scientific theories could be falsified, so too state policies should be exposed when they fail. An open society was a prerequisite for social and economic progress. And there needed to be a legitimate, peaceful means of getting rid of unsuccessful governments. The issue of who gets to govern was secondary to how the government could be removed.

Now regarded as a classic of political theory, written with rare passion and clarity, a phenomenal struggle was needed for *The Open Society* to secure a publisher—the wartime cost of paper did not help, and *The Open Society* was not a short book. Despite Popper's boast about his independence from, and slaying of, the Vienna Circle, it is worth mentioning that in a biographical note to publishers, and presumably believing it would boost his credentials, he claimed to have been a Circle member. With the assistance of friends, Popper's book eventually found a publishing home with Unwin and appeared in 1945. Popper was handed a copy when he stepped off the boat from New Zealand on 6 January 1946. He was in the UK to take up a job—for which Waismann had also competed—as reader in logic and scientific method at the London School of Economics.

20

❮◦❯

Exile

Do have another piece of cake, please do, in remembrance of our journey through the Old and the New World.

—GEORGE CLARE[1]

ALMOST ALL the Jews still in Austria when World War II broke out—men, women, children—perished in the Holocaust. In all, 65,500—a third—of the prewar Jewish population was murdered. Some were shot after being transferred to the ghettos of cities the Nazis occupied in the Soviet Union, like Riga and Vilnius. Others ended up in the camps whose names have become grimly familiar, Auschwitz, Buchenwald, Dachau, Mauthausen, Sobibor, Theresienstadt.

The few Austrian Jews who survived the camps and returned were met with a frosty welcome. "There were no kind words; [only] the typical explanation . . . 'you people always come back.' "[2] Unlike Germany, Austria opted not to engage in a wide-ranging and honest reckoning with its past. Instead, the people who embraced the Anschluss settled on the comforting narrative—and originally the formulation of the victorious Allies—that they had been the Nazis' first victim.

Remarkably, not a single member of the Circle was a direct victim of the genocide. Three non-Jewish philosophers, Viktor Kraft, Béla Juhos, and Heinrich Neider, stayed in Austria and survived the war. By the time World War II broke out, with the exception of Gödel, who left in early 1940, all the others had gone.

Whatever magic formula had transformed Vienna into a hub of intellectual and creative activity in the first half of the twentieth century vanished too. Postwar, Vienna seemed much more provincial—a medium-size capital of a minor country on a battered continent. Vienna would eventually regain its wealth, but never its energy.

Postwar attempts to revive the fortunes of the Circle floundered, and antipositivist feeling remained. Kraft became a full professor only in 1950, retiring two years later. He established the Kraft circle, which met for a few years before his retirement. It made little impact, although it was attended by one brilliant student, Viennese-born Paul Feyerabend, who would become an influential philosopher of science. Kraft wrote a book about the Vienna Circle in which he foolishly called Schlick's murderer, the paranoid psychopath Johann Nelböck, a paranoid psychopath. Nelböck sued him, and Kraft, all too aware of what Nelböck was capable, settled out of court. On 3 February 1954, Nelböck died peacefully in Vienna.

———

To be in exile is typically to dream of going home. But not where the wrench has been so painful and humiliating as to make a return almost unimaginable. Walter Hollitscher was the only one to go back. A few others, like Menger, did ponder a postwar career in Vienna. But for most, Austria was associated with memories they were eager to forget. They had been stripped of their nationality and livelihood, their friends and family members had perished. Living in Vienna would necessarily entail coexistence with neighbors and colleagues who had held Nazi sympathies.

"Would you ever consider returning to Vienna?" asked Carnap of Popper shortly after the end of World War II. He received an emphatic response: "No, never!"[3] Popper had lost sixteen relatives in the Holocaust. His aunt Hennie, for example, had been deported to Theresienstadt on 25 May 1943 from an old-age home. Even Gödel, who had fewer grievances than the others, wrote in a letter just after the war, "I feel very well in this country and would also not return to Vienna if some offer were made to me. Leaving aside all personal connections, I find this country and the people here ten times more congenial than our own."[4]

The real question they faced was less whether they should go back permanently—and more whether they should go back at all. Menger wrote that it took until the early 1960s before he overcame his aversion to visiting Austria. One of Bergmann's students recalled a conversation at the University of Iowa between Bergmann and a colleague who happened to mention he was flying to Vienna, "and Gustav said, 'when you get there and get off the plane, kiss the ground for me, and then spit on it.'"[5]

Inevitably, the unforgiving attitude flummoxed many citizens of their adopted countries. Partly this was grounded in a failure of imagination. Even in Britain, the target of German war planes, where thousands of buildings lay in rubble, the wider population could not, or did not want to, grasp the nature of what refugees had been through. In *Last Waltz in Vienna*, novelist George Clare, who had been in Vienna in the Anschluss, and later witnessed Kristallnacht, recalled describing events to his kind British friends. "'It must have been quite, quite terrible for you', they said. 'Do have another piece of cake, George, please do.'"[6]

In any case, a new chapter had begun and these immigrants were keen to settle down. Nowadays we are used to first-generation immigrants retaining their mother tongue. Indeed, it would seem bizarre for a recently arrived Mexican couple in Texas, or a newly arrived Bengali family in East London, to communicate in English in the privacy of their homes. A remarkable aspect of the post-Austrian lives of the Circle was how swiftly they accommodated themselves to English—exemplifying a general pattern among refugees from the Nazi era. They were soon speaking English at home and to each other. As early as 1942, Popper and Carnap were writing to each other in English. They retained thick accents, and had trouble enunciating various English-language sounds. But with only a few exceptions (Rose Rand was one) they mastered the grammar quickly, and most of them developed an elegant, idiomatic writing style. Some even grew to love it, with the zeal of the convert: "no German reader minds polysyllables," Popper wrote. "In English, one has to learn to be repelled by them."[7] Bergmann declined even to speak German. Hempel told his daughter that his dreams were in English.

The embrace of the language was partly dictated by their situation. They moved into English-speaking academic environments; failing to learn English was not an option. But there were deeper reasons. They felt considerable societal pressure to integrate; that was the spirit of the times (and during the war speaking German in public was frowned upon). They also felt immense gratitude to the country that had provided them with sanctuary, and adopting the language was a powerful illustration of their commitment to their new home. Perhaps most important, communicating in English represented a psychological break with the past, a way of marking a fresh start.

So assimilation was the norm, and the aim was to integrate as rapidly and wholeheartedly as possible. Old identities were discarded. Carl Hempel spent his formative decades in Germany, yet his daughter would say, "my father did not feel German. He considered himself an American without qualification."[8] They were Americans of a particular type, of course, combining a strong sense of patriotism with an international outlook, a cosmopolitan sensibility.

There were prosaic reasons for laying down roots. Postwar, the United States had emerged as the unrivaled leader of the democratic world, affluent and eager to snap up academics as the university sector expanded. Many Circle members and associates were carving out stellar careers. They acquired citizenship in their new home—be it the US or the UK—as soon as they were eligible. Popper became a naturalized Briton in the year he took up his London School of Economics post, 1946. The most surreal episode, about which it is a scandal that no play has yet been written, involved Kurt Gödel. There was a US citizenship test to be taken, for which Gödel studied. Being Gödel, he was alive to internal constitutional inconsistencies and he became especially agitated by one putative problem, which he claimed left the back door wide open to dictatorship. Fearing that Gödel would air his concern and complicate matters, his closest friends, Oskar Morgenstern and Albert Einstein, decided it would be wise to accompany him: Einstein had already been through the same process with the same presiding judge. On the car journey down, the physicist and mathematician tried to persuade the logician not to mention the flaw and then distracted him with stories. The plan failed. When questions about the Constitution began, Gödel could not restrain himself. It may have been Einstein's presence that prompted the judge to interrupt. "You needn't go into that."[9] Gödel became a not incomplete American.

————

Naturally there were aspects of the old country that the immigrants missed, including the desserts, the *Sachertorte*, *Kaiserschmarren*, and *Apfelstrudel*. They missed the vibrancy and intimacy of the coffeehouses. Philipp Frank was not alone in trying to re-create the atmosphere of the Viennese coffeehouse. He would often limp over to a particular corner—some called it Frank's Corner—of the Hayes-Bickford Cafeteria in Harvard Square, where he would read the newspaper and welcome any colleague or student who wished to join him. Several Circle figures set up Circle-style discussion groups. Menger formed a mathematical colloquium. Carnap, with Charles Morris, ran the Chicago Circle, which met on Saturdays.

There were also alien features of their new culture to which he and some others could never reconcile themselves. In Vienna professors had been gods. The informality of American culture, in particular, felt uncomfortable, even objectionable. In German the *Du* and *Sie* form was just one way of identifying dear friends, while keeping acquaintances and strangers at a suitable distance. Bergmann hated how he was routinely addressed by his first name by those he did not consider to be close. Nor did he ever quite manage the shift from central European restraint to American hyperbole. Bergmann's highest praise was to declare someone "not completely stupid."[10] Ina Carnap complained that her husband did not receive sufficient respect and that some "quite young boys . . . in the department . . . deem themselves a bit too equal for my taste."[11]

The land of the free fell short of utopia in more serious ways too. Olga Taussky moved from the UK to the US after World War II and ended up teaching at the California Institute of Technology (Caltech), but attitudes toward women were no more progressive than in Austria, and this held back her career. Furthermore, neither the United States nor Britain were strangers to anti-Semitism. When Feigl applied for his job in Iowa, a question was raised as to whether or not he was a Jew. Many of the elite colleges operated a quota system to control the intake of Jewish students: it was deemed undesirable to have "too many." Still, polling in Britain showed that anti-Semitism existed throughout the class system; it was common for clubs and societies to have a policy of excluding Jews. At university High Table you did not need to listen too attentively to hear sotto voce racist asides. On the whole, however, the degree of anti-Semitism was not such as to arouse grumbles from the refugees. If anything they were thankful that it was so restrained. As one Jewish British-born historian put it: "Of course, they had seen the real thing and knew how to differentiate between that and golf-club snobbery."[12] In the US too there was no comparison between the minor bigotry refugees encountered and the full-blown Austrian variety. In response to the question about Feigl's Jewishness a future colleague responded, "I am sure I don't know, but if he is, there is nothing disturbing about it."[13] There were enough employers who took the same stance. Nonetheless, it was to be expected that the Jews would retain a degree of wariness, sometimes bordering on paranoia. "I am *Konfessionslos* (without religious faith)," said Bergmann, "but when they come to round up the Jews, I will be a Jew."[14]

Jewish or not Jewish, they were foreigners. In the US, with the onset of the cold war, anticommunism became a far more potent force than anti-Semitism (although anti-Semitism was one of the anticommunist ingredients). A combination of a foreign accent and vaguely left-leaning politics were sufficient in postwar America to arouse the interest of the FBI. The leftists who came under suspicion included Philipp Frank. Somehow, the crime-fighting organization had caught on to some entirely bogus claim that he had come to the US to organize "high-level Communist Party activities."[15] This was passed up to the director of the FBI, J. Edgar Hoover, in August 1952. Further investigations revealed the damning evidence that Frank's biography of his friend Einstein—which he had written in the US to supplement his low salary—had received a glowing review in the *Daily Worker*, a communist newspaper, and that he knew one or two communist sympathizers. The FBI was told by one informant that Frank was a "muddle-headed" intellectual who could be a communist because "he is Jewish and the Jews have a penchant for Communism."[16] At some stage two FBI men visited him at his home. To show that he was no Russian spy, Frank went to his bookshelf, took out a copy of Lenin's *Materialism and Empirio-Criticism*, and showed them the passage in which he was personally attacked: "the two FBI men practically saluted him, and left speedily and satisfied."[17]

Frank was not unique among Circle figures in drawing the attention of the FBI. Others mentioned in FBI notes included Carnap and Tarski. As early as 1935, when Carnap was about to travel to the US for a lecture tour, Ernest Nagel had passed on a warning from philosopher Sidney Hook. "Tell Carnap that Universities throughout the US are becoming politically more reactionary daily, and to exclude from his prospectus anything which some dumb conservative—who 'feel' these things—might regard as cultural Bolshevism."[18] Carnap never attempted to disguise his leftist leanings. In the 1950s he declined a visiting professorship in California as well as invitations to lecture there, in protest at the state's demand that academics sign an oath of loyalty. He supported the civil rights movement and openly called for clemency toward Julius and Ethel Rosenberg, who were executed in 1953 after being convicted of spying for the USSR. He also trumpeted various international causes. Behind his back, the FBI sought out friends and colleagues. They discovered nothing that was sufficiently incriminating to take the investigation further—in the main because there was nothing to discover.

In this febrile atmosphere, the question of whether science, the scientific philosophy of positivism, and politics were linked was bound to be revisited. Perhaps self-preservation motivated the stress that some placed on drawing a sharp distinction between the two. Feigl wrote that science cannot, "by its very nature, provide a reason for our fundamental obligations or for the supreme goals of life."[19] "Scientific truth is ethically neutral,"[20] and criticizing a genuinely scientific outlook in philosophy for these limitations "would be like reproaching a weaving loom for its incapacity to produce music."[21]

———

So much for the general themes that bound their experiences together: what of their individual stories?

V-E (Victory in Europe) Day was 8 May 1945. Half a year later, Neurath was dead, though in that short period he had been typically Stakhanovite. An enticing job offer had turned up from an unexpected place. The small town of Bilston (population 31,000), in the county of Staffordshire, intended to demolish its slums, containing thousands of houses, and replace them with modern homes. Neurath was approached to help shape the project, to advise on what would work for people, and to educate the residents, with his famous Isotypes, about healthy living in their new accommodations. Among other concerns, council officials were worried that those who had no experience of inside bathrooms might use them to store coal. From Vienna Neurath was familiar with these condescending bureaucratic anxieties. He assured the local officials that if people put coal in their bath it would only be for a rational reason; perhaps there was nowhere else to stockpile fuel. Take away the rationale and the vast majority of people would behave hygienically and socially.

It was the first appointment of its kind in the country. Neurath was heralded in the local press as a "sociologist of happiness." Already he was fizzing with ideas. He wanted mixed housing; it was vital, he thought, that families and single people, as well as rich and poor, were accommodated in the same areas. He also wanted to ensure that elderly people were not hived off to one part of town, but integrated with everyone else—although in ground-floor flats. That would keep them active and in touch with their families and the community: it would prevent them from feeling depressed and isolated.

Some of Neurath's creative proposals now seem prosaic. Others never took off. Neurath wanted to create "silence rooms" close to bus stops and shopping venues, where those who wished to do so could sit or rest. He recommended "room libraries," a room on each street to house books, which would be cheap to run because they were to be operated by volunteers. He did not think many books would be stolen, and if a few were, replacing them would be only a fraction of the cost of salaried assistants. Another proposal required an initial outlay, but he thought it would pay off in the long term—a free vacuum cleaner for each household.

Neurath visited Bilston several times. A contemporary press article about his involvement explains that Neurath's plans were driven by the belief that "people, if given the chance, will exhibit the good in the ordinary man and not the bad, or as this cheerful Viennese doctor puts it, 'You cannot organise kindness, but you can organise the conditions for it.'"[22] Lessons learned in the Austrian capital were now being applied to a small town in Staffordshire. Neurath delivered a talk on the BBC Overseas Service (now the BBC World Service), entitled "Vienna Comes to Bilston."

On 13 December 1945, Neurath celebrated his sixty-third birthday. Just over a week later, on 22 December, he and Marie spent a pleasant morning in Oxford, browsing in Blackwells, the city's landmark bookshop, and, in the afternoon, meeting Tscha Hung, the Chinese philosopher who had attended Circle meetings for several years in the 1930s: they discussed coauthoring a book about Moritz Schlick. Then there was supper with friends and a walk up the steep slope home. Sometime after, Neurath retired to his office, to write and read about Goethe. He showed his wife some letters he had written that humorously mimicked Goethe. The next time she looked up, Neurath had his head on his desk. A Goethe volume was to his side.

Of all the people to have lived through the tumultuous first half of the twentieth century, Neurath was about the least likely to have died peacefully in his home. That, at least, represented some achievement.

———

The general rule was that those Circle figures who struggled in Vienna were also the ones who found difficulty adapting to exile. Waismann and Rand, both of whom found refuge in the UK, were cases in point.

Waismann's Oxford appointment was in the philosophy of mathematics and science. He did not draw big, or indeed medium-sized, lecture crowds. One of those who saw him in action was Anthony Kenny, who himself became a distinguished philosopher. "He was rather a pathetic figure: there were very few of us in attendance, four or five, I would say and we kept on going as the term progressed not because we found his classes interesting or useful, but because we felt it would be horrible for him if we all left and he had no audience."[23] He was not regarded as approachable. With his waistcoat and moustache, he resembled an old English gentleman, although, despite his decent English, he retained a thick accent (about which he was acutely self-conscious) and appeared "as Austrian as one could possibly be."[24] English idiom baffled him and he would always have on him a notebook to write down new examples he encountered. The students would sometimes retire to the pub after his class, but Waismann never joined them. It was not the University of Vienna way: it certainly was not Waismann's way.

Around town Waismann cut a forlorn figure. He at least had an income and status, being attached to first New College, Oxford, then to Wadham. Nonetheless he felt underappreciated, convinced that his salary was lower than that paid to British-born colleagues, whom he contrasted, unfavorably, with his former Viennese colleagues. Oxford was not immune from the austerity of the postwar years afflicting the rest of the country. Waismann found the city cold and damp and grim and the social niceties of High Table impossible to navigate. He made few friends. He wrote to Popper one January to say that he had been suffering from Christmas depression. "I wished only that I were dead."[25]

His personal life was beset by tragedy. His wife gassed herself in 1943. His son, Thomas, took his life in the same way, when he was a sixteen-year-old schoolboy in 1956; the relationship between father and son had been fraught.

Throughout, Waismann toiled away on the work that he had begun years earlier in Vienna. In lectures, Wittgenstein was barely mentioned by name. Waismann came to believe that Wittgenstein was "the greatest disappointment of his life."[26] One philosopher observed that when Wittgenstein died in 1951 it was as though Waismann was released from a tyrant. He began to find his own, unique philosophical voice. His wonderfully lucid *Principles of Linguistic Philosophy* appeared only posthumously (and with the original Schlick introduction, stressing its debt to Wittgenstein). The book accomplished the near-impossible: elucidating ideas inspired by Wittgenstein but in a way that could be easily understood.

Waismann himself died in 1959. Gilbert Ryle delivered the graveside address and celebrated Waismann's seriousness. "He cut himself loose from the comfortable half-truths in which our minds love to repose."[27]

———

Rose Rand's story was no less wretched. She was still in Britain at the war's end, still living hand-to-mouth, the constant shortage of money being a consuming leitmotif of her life. She drew for support on her network of old Viennese colleagues. They, to varying degrees, sympathized with her and tried to help, although they had reservations about both her character and her talent. One of the branches of the newly formed United Nations, UNESCO, was seeking translators and Rand decided to apply. Popper was happy to provide a reference and on 1 March 1947 he wrote to Carnap for his endorsement too. The damning reply, two months later, from the well-meaning and normally obliging German reflected the ambiguity many felt about Rand.

> The case of Miss Rand is really a difficult one. I have tried for years to help her and have written to various organizations and persons about her. However, in the present case, I did not think that I could recommend her with a good conscience. . . . I think that the people needed by UNESCO are those which have administrative and organization abilities or are good as translators for various languages, or at least are skilful typists. It is clear that Miss Rand does not fill any of these requirements. Although she knows several languages she cannot even now after years in England, write a simple letter in correct English. Her real abilities are as you know in the field of philosophy; but even here I do not estimate her capabilities as high as she does herself.[28]

The job did not materialize. But in September 1947, Rand applied for and was offered another job, giving evening courses in psychology and German at Luton Technical College, to the north of London. Popper continued to look out for her, helping to secure a small grant and, in 1950, to get her Recognized Student status from Oxford University and the right to attend lectures. He implored her to live as economically as possible.

Much to their irritation, Rand's appeals to hard-up refugee organizations persisted. A letter about her in the British Federation of University Women archive from 8 March 1949 summed up their attitude. Rand is described as "one of our black sheep, utterly unable to adapt herself to anything and anybody, and possessed by her very specialised subject, some kind of mathematical philosophy. Besides, her personality is objectionable. We have only helped her because we felt sorry for her, and gave it up at the end, as she would have been on our hands for ever."[29]

Rand had, for years, been contemplating a move to the US, where most of the Circle had settled, and where she thought there might be more academic opportunities. In 1948, Gustav Bergmann, now in Iowa, promised he could provide her with the affidavit demanded by the US immigration authorities, though in the end this fell through when it became clear that Rand was presuming that Bergmann would also put her up. Eventually, however, she obtained a visa and crossed the Atlantic in 1954. She was to survive by teaching elementary math and logic and taking research associate positions at various universities, including the University of Chicago and the University of Notre Dame. She would eventually make Princeton her home, eking out a living with small grants for translating the work of Polish logicians. She contemplated writing a book on the Circle, but it never materialized. Over the years, her old Viennese colleagues, Carnap, Feigl, Frank, Hempel, and others, continued to assist her financially though normally found excuses not to put her up. "Because of my continued illness your visit would be inconvenient,"[30] wrote Carnap on 13 May 1960. Rand died on 28 July 1980, as poor and unfulfilled as ever.

———

Carnap had mixed feelings about his adopted home. He arrived in the US with a starry reputation—logical empiricism's most prominent proponent. He was delighted that modern logic—unlike, say, in Germany—was regarded as something worthy of philosophical development and examination. But he never felt fully at ease. During the course of his career he had moved from Germany to Vienna to Prague to Chicago, and each step had taken him further from the culture in which he had been raised. What is more, at the University of Chicago there were a few metaphysicians—such as Mortimer Adler—who were scornful of logical empiricism and with whom he had to battle (Carnap was particularly scathing of one lecture delivered by Adler in which he claimed he could show that man was not descended from subhuman animals, purely through metaphysical principles, ignoring any scientific evidence). There were also health problems. He suffered terrible back pain and had bouts of depression, as did his wife, "ina," who killed herself in 1964.

A decade earlier, in 1954, Carnap left the University of Chicago to join the philosophy department at UCLA, taking over from Hans Reichenbach. Age sixty-three, he was now a grand old man of philosophy. In the US, he devoted much of his intellectual energy to issues around probability, confirmation, and so-called inductive logic. His ambition was to create a logic that mapped the relationship between statements and evidence. The underlying point was to provide a mathematical account of the reliability of a scientific theory—so that the claim, backed by confirming evidence, that water boiled at 100 degrees centigrade could be compared and expressed in mathematical/logical terms to the claim that it boiled at 90 degrees. These were statements, as Carnap would put it, not within science but "of science."[31] That is, they were analytic statements about the logic and methodology of science.

There was also a second major project. Before moving to the West Coast, Carnap had been approached by P. A. Schilpp, who edited a series called the Library of Living Philosophers about some of the world's most important philosophers. Schilpp asked Carnap whether he would be willing to feature in the series and Carnap agreed. It required Carnap to produce an intellectual biography (a component of each book in the

Schilpp series) and to respond to various critical essays about his work written by contemporary philosophers.

The process of commissioning and responding to the essays proved to be protracted. Carnap hated working on it because it distracted him from thinking about induction. "For heaven's sake," he wrote in a letter to Hempel and Feigl, "a logician should not be asked to write a history or an autobiography, unless he is a genius like Russell."[32] After several years, when the manuscript was finally complete, Schilpp informed Carnap that there would be a further delay, because it was in a queue and they first had to publish another volume in the series (on Cambridge philosopher C. D. Broad). Carnap had come to see his volume as the last major endeavor of his life and he became embroiled in an uncharacteristic and bitter row. On 27 February 1959 he typed a furious letter to Schilpp: "if this is to be the library of Living Philosophers, then let's have the volume while I am still alive."[33] Schilpp responded in wounded tones a week later. "I must confess—after my own patience with you over a period of between 4 and 5 years (!)—your last letter surprised me more than it hurt me."[34]

―――

Gödel had had his first major mental collapse in 1931 and in Austria began to develop paranoid fantasies that people were out to poison him. These were given fuller expression in the United States, when for periods he ceased to eat altogether. Chronic digestive problems emerged in 1946. He was hospitalized in 1951 with an ulcer, and was extremely sick again in 1954, and again in 1974. In 1951, J. Robert Oppenheimer, now director of the Institute for Advanced Study, telephoned Gödel's doctor to inform him that he had in his charge "the greatest logician since the days of Aristotle!"[35]

Gödel did not seek out doctors of his own accord: they too, he believed, were out to get him. (He took his own temperature several times a day.) Theoretical physicist Freeman Dyson remembered once having to open a boxed present for him, because "he was scared it contained poison gas."[36] Toward the end of his life he refused to let nurses into his home. His health was not helped by the fact that he rarely took exercise. As his condition deteriorated, he cut back on travel—in 1964 he refused an offer from Popper to attend a British Philosophy of Science conference because the trip was too daunting.

Meanwhile he labored away on his own work, publishing a few articles. However, his most original days were behind him in Vienna. There he had been an obscure young mathematician. As so often, fame and status were slow to fasten on to accomplishment—but in the US he received the recognition he deserved. He was promoted to professor in 1953, given the newly endowed Einstein award, and awarded honorary doctorates from Yale and Harvard.

Einstein's death in 1955 was a severe blow to Gödel and it was followed a year later by the passing of another Institute for Advanced Study titan, John von Neumann. Gödel became more and more reclusive, preferring to interact with people, if at all, by phone. He had terrible nightmares of being trapped in Vienna. He still had Adele for support, but like Popper's wife, Hennie, she never accommodated herself to exile. Poorly educated, she felt out of sorts in Princeton, the subject of snobbish contempt from fellow "Mitteleuropean" academics who viewed her as coarse and mocked her taste in furniture. She must have felt like Einstein's wife, who told Philipp Frank, "When he [Einstein] commits a breach of etiquette, it is said that he does so because he is a man of genius. In my case, however, it is attributed to a lack of culture."[37]

In late 1977, when Adele returned home in an ambulance after herself being in hospital for an operation, she found her husband almost wasted away and even more paranoid. He was taken to hospital but could not be saved. He died on 14 January, the death certificate giving the cause as "malnutrition and inanition, caused by personality disturbance."[38]

————

Gödel, Rand, and Waismann were unhappy but unrepresentative tales. On the whole, the ledger of happiness over suffering for Circle figures came out in the black. They arrived with a reputation in the philosophical world for being brash, evangelical, and not consumed by self-doubt.

It was a pleasant surprise when they turned out to be in most cases kindly and supportive. Feigl was particularly popular. "I suppose I half-expected Herbert to be a fire-breathing atheistic rebel,"[39] wrote one of his younger colleagues, who confesses to have initially been in awe of him. But Feigl, it transpired, was very approachable, "Herbert" to everyone. Toward the end of his career he could be seen each day walking across from the philosophy department to the faculty club, where he would take a midday nap.

Menger was another beloved figure. In researching this book, I put out appeals for memories of the Circle from former students. Menger's students from the Illinois Institute of Technology responded in large numbers. He clearly aroused tremendous respect and affection. "A great teacher," "inspiring," "a true gentleman," "without question the professor I'll remember as long as I live."[40] His appeal lay in his ability to demystify complex mathematical formulas and render them accessible. In his courses on curve theory or calculus, he operated on multiple sliding blackboards, furiously covering them one by one with chalk, talking enthusiastically and loudly all the while in his thick accent. Slightly tubby, with a wild tuft of white hair, Menger wore dark, double-breasted suits, but still appeared disheveled, sometimes inadvertently leaving his fly undone. From his Vienna days there are no references to Menger being scatterbrained, but many American students fondly recalled his absentmindedness: the time he kept walking back and forth over his jacket, which had slipped off the back of the chair; the time he opened the desk to discover a long-lost raincoat; the chaos of his office, piled high with correspondence and journals, though Menger himself could always draw a map with coordinates to locate a much-needed article.

———

Carl Hempel moved from the University of Chicago to New York, to Yale, to Princeton, to Pittsburgh, and back to Princeton. His wife, Eva, died in 1944, shortly after childbirth, leaving him with a baby son. He later married again (Diane Perlow). Hempel drummed home to his students the message that they were to pose two key questions in the face of statements put before them. First, what do you mean? Second, how do you know? Although kind and gentle and with a reputation as a lover of truth, perfectly willing to change his mind, he shocked writer and philosopher Rebecca Goldstein, "because HE SAID THINGS, IN THE SERVICE OF SIMPLICITY, THAT WEREN'T, STRICTLY SPEAKING, TRUE AND THAT I KNEW FOR A FACT HE DIDN'T BELIEVE. That, by the way, is how I experienced it, in capital letters."[41] When she confronted him about this, he explained that when students were first introduced to difficult ideas, it was best not to confuse them with subtleties. On the hundredth anniversary of Carl Hempel's birth, the city where he had been born, Oranienburg, named a street—Carl Gustav Hempel Strasse—in his honor. His son found out about this only by chance. "I like to think my father would have been pleased, but it's hard to be sure."[42]

———

Gustav Bergmann also prospered, though he divided opinion. Rude, arrogant, insecure, and argumentative, Bergmann was acutely sensitive about status and thought his talents received insufficient recognition. His insecurities once led him to turn down a blown-up signed photo of Einstein, offered by the physicist himself, a decision he would come to regret. (He was proud, however, of having a signed and original copy of Gödel's incompleteness paper.) He was a memorable professor and an eccentric showman. In seminars he was known to lie down on a central table, with a cigar in his mouth, spin around, and blow smoke at the person whose turn it was to speak. That would force students to participate: because he was so intimidating, those who were not his favorites were disinclined to volunteer questions. But he was a dedicated teacher, perhaps a bit too dedicated for some, who became accustomed to his ringing them up late at night when an idea grabbed him.

———

Karl Popper carried on working prodigiously hard. He chose places to live that were out of London, and a deterrent to visitors, operating, in the words of one biographer, in "legendary seclusion."[43] Of the figures linked to the Circle, no reputational stock rose higher and more rapidly than Popper's. He had been only on the fringes of academic life in Austria. Now he was celebrated. This did not make him any less complex to deal with. Herbert Feigl was one of those who made the journey to visit him in his small Buckinghamshire village, thirty miles west of London. Feigl reported back to Carnap, Frank, Hempel, and others that Popper was "more autistic than ever" and "megalomaniac."[44] Carl Hempel met him in London but preferred to read his work rather than talk to him about it. "On the whole I had a sense that it was difficult to discuss with him, that he was too easily hurt and felt this was somehow a personal attack if one took a critical view."[45]

Hennie missed Vienna and suffered from depression. But Popper finally had security and status. He was appointed to a full professor at the London School of Economics in 1949 and remained there until his retirement. At the LSE Popper ran a seminar that he believed was an open forum for debate but which one American observer likened to the House of Un-American Activities Committee at the height of the anti-communist witch hunts. He would belittle students and colleagues alike, demand that those who had the temerity to argue with him admit their error and concede defeat. He remained, throughout his life, "marvellously argumentative."[46]

An early notorious episode occurred in October 1946. Popper had only recently arrived in the UK, but *The Open Society* had already gained a heavyweight reputation and he was invited to address the Moral Sciences Club, the Cambridge University philosophy society then dominated by his nemesis Wittgenstein. He had still never met Wittgenstein, despite their shared Viennese background, but he nursed a deep animus toward him. Wittgenstein's latest ideas were not yet in book form (they would be published posthumously), but they had circulated in notes taken by his student disciples. The centrality of language to philosophy— and the notion that philosophical confusion could be dissolved by attending more closely to the varieties of ordinary linguistic usage—were nostrums with which Popper had no patience. Popper was asked by the club secretary to bring up a "philosophical puzzle." Wittgenstein's approach clearly lay behind the wording. Popper believed there were philosophical problems, not, as he saw it, petty linguistic squabbles.

The situation was complicated by the presence too of Bertrand Russell, whom Popper revered and wished to impress. Popper began his talk, which he titled "Are There Philosophical Problems?" What happened next is open to dispute and subject of a "brilliant and epic book."[47] Popper offered various examples of philosophical problems, to which Wittgenstein kept objecting. At some stage Wittgenstein, now extremely agitated, picked up a fireside poker and demanded an example of a moral rule. Popper replied, "Not to threaten visiting lecturers with pokers," whereupon Wittgenstein threw down the poker and stormed out of the room, leaving Popper victorious on the field of battle. At least that is how Popper related the episode, although one witness accused him of lying, and it seems probable that, in his desire to show how he had bested his opponent, he misremembered the sequence of events.

There were to be numerous other illustrations of Popper's lust for battle. He continued to snipe at Carnap about his inductive logic project. Carnap wrote to Popper in 1959 in a none-too-subtle appeal for debate to be conducted on civil terms. "I am now advanced in years, and I think it best from now on to . . . avoid as far as possible any polemic with opponents."[48] It did no good. Popper took on Carnap in a London symposium on logic in 1965. Quine was also present and witnessed two of Popper's leading disciples soften up their opponent in the early sessions. "I sensed that he was deploying his henchmen, Imre Lakatos and John Watkins, with military precision as the three of them undertook preliminary skirmishes."[49] Carnap remained cool in the face of Popper's ferocity.

Vienna had been the start of the conversation, not its end. The fundamental issue of which questions were to count as being subject to empirical inquiry continued to preoccupy Popper and the old Circle members. Criteria were fought over and refined. Meanwhile, Popper was harvesting academic garlands. In 1949–50 he delivered the prestigious William James lectures in Harvard, then gave another lecture at Princeton attended by Bohr and Einstein, who stayed afterward for hours to discuss its content. Feigl arranged for Popper to spend time at his center in Minnesota, although Popper haggled so hard about the pay and conditions that the exasperated Feigl may have regretted his original offer.

Popper's accolades included many honorary doctorates. He was admired by world leaders from German chancellors Helmut Schmidt and Helmut Kohl to the Dalai Lama and the Japanese emperor. In the Soviet Union and Eastern Europe, his championing of the Open Society made him something of an intellectual pinup: he was particularly venerated by dissident Vaclav Havel, who would become president of Czechoslovakia. It was said, too, that he was one of Margaret Thatcher's favorite philosophers—her other favorite being his Viennese friend Friedrich von Hayek. In 1965 Karl Popper became Sir Karl. Like Carnap (and later, Ayer), Popper had bestowed on him the tribute of a volume in the Library of Living Philosophers.

———

Popper, Carnap, Feigl, Gödel, and Menger would all receive honorary degrees. There was to be no honorary doctorate for Ludwig Wittgenstein: the idea of preening around in a ceremonial gown would have appalled him. He continued teaching in Cambridge until 1947, his ideas and thoughts pouring out. Students would attend his intense, austere seminars watching the professor struggle, the perfect manifestation of the agony of genius. Many students became disciples—who, like Waismann in Vienna, subconsciously came to mimic his mannerisms.

With two sisters still living in Vienna, Wittgenstein did return to visit. He spent four months there from December 1949 to March 1950, but he was already seriously ill from the pancreatic cancer from which he died in 1951, a few days after his sixty-second birthday. "Tell them I've had a wonderful life,"[50] were his final words. His disciples had already fanned some of his ideas into the wider philosophical atmosphere. But only after his death did the Wittgenstein industry really begin to flourish—all the philosophy books that bear his name, bar the *Tractatus*, emerged posthumously. The *Philosophical Investigations*, arguably the greatest work of philosophy of the twentieth century, was published in 1953. Along with many others, such as *Zettel* and *Remarks on the Foundation of Mathematics* and *On Certainty*, it has spawned a vast secondary literature. In death, Wittgenstein achieved what no other Circle figure managed: cult status well beyond the confines of academic philosophy, becoming the subject of novels, poetry, plays, painting, music, sculpture, and films.

———

Popper was to survive Wittgenstein by another four decades. Waismann died in 1959, Frank in 1966, Carnap in 1970, Béla Juhos in 1971, Kraft in 1975, Gödel in 1978, Rand in 1980, Tarski in 1983, Menger in 1985, Bergmann in 1987, Feigl in 1988, Ayer in 1989, Taussky in 1995, and Hempel in 1997.

Many of the Circle remained in contact until the end—though as they were scattered across the United States and the UK, it was impossible to reproduce the intimate conditions which had made debate in Vienna so fertile. But their network remained useful. They could help each other with their careers, support each other on grant applications. There were conferences and reunions, at some of which grudges could be sustained and hostilities renewed. Carnap still refused to talk philosophy in the evening: for him it was like a heavy meal, which if consumed too late would inhibit sleep.

The correspondence between Circle figures is conspicuous for its absence of nostalgia. There are few repeated anecdotes of the good old days in Vienna. There is, nonetheless, something touching about their interactions: long-standing comrades aging together. We hear about their divorces and their children, their holidays and seminars, their articles and books. Inevitably, with the passage of time, there are reports about physical decline. As well as Carnap's back pain, Feigl developed a painful muscular problem and grumbled about his Swiss-cheese memory. Popper had so many complaints it was a wonder he was able to function at all.

With time, attitudes to Vienna began to mellow. Austria began to reclaim the intellectual and cultural *haut monde* of its heritage. Popper was a case in point. The City of Vienna awarded Popper a prize in 1965, there were events to mark his eightieth birthday in 1982, and in 1986 he received the Grand Decoration of Honor in Gold for Services to the Republic of Austria. Popper considered returning to live in Austria after his retirement from the LSE in 1969, but told Hayek that he and Hennie had decided against it because of anti-Semitism. When he died his cremated ashes, as per his instructions, were placed in an urn in Hennie's Viennese grave.

The city from which the Circle members fled has been reclaiming it. There's a Kurt Gödel Research Center and most important, a Vienna Circle Institute, which was founded in 1991 to document and develop the Circle's work. Popper's bust is now in the courtyard of the University of Vienna. There's a Karl Popper Strasse and a Dr. Otto Neurath Gasse.

Tram D, on which Schlick commuted to the university, still follows the same route. The beginning and end of his journey on 22 June 1936 are marked by plaques: one on the outside of 68 Prinz Eugen Strasse, the other at the spot at which he was shot.

21

◄○►

Legacy

I suppose the greatest defect [of logical positivism] is that nearly all of it was false.

—A. J. AYER

THE INSTITUTIONAL branches of the Circle did not prosper abroad. *Erkenntnis* ceased publication after the Nazi invasion of the Low Countries in 1940 (although it was resurrected in the mid-1970s and continues to this day). The Encylopedia project stuttered on. The University of Chicago Press had been promised twenty books; the last one reached them in 1970. Neurath's original ambition to produce another hundred volumes never materialized.

Two years after the 1939 International Congress for the Unity of Science at Harvard, another gathering, the sixth of its kind, was held at the University of Chicago (institutional home of Carnap and Morris). It would be the last: in the midst of war there were other priorities, and in the absence of Neurath there was no one with the energy to keep the enterprise afloat. The Institute for the Unity of Science was resurrected in Boston with some short-term funding from the Rockefeller Foundation and with Philipp Frank as president, but it never took root and the grant money dried up. In fact, with Circle members now dispersed around the country, several hubs in the philosophy of science emerged. As well as Harvard/Boston, there was the University of Pittsburgh and clusters of expertise in New York and Chicago. Perhaps the most important successor to the Circle was the Minnesota Center for the Philosophy of Science, which Feigl founded. Carnap, Hempel, and other important philosophers of science would gather there for discussions two or three times a year.

The Vienna Circle no longer had a presence in Vienna, yet, ironically, for a period its reputation in the English-speaking world continued to rise. That, despite the fact that some of the best-known Vienna texts were still unavailable in English: Carnap's *The Logical Structure of the World* was translated into English only in 1967, while Popper's *The Logic of Scientific Discovery* did not appear until 1959. The zeal of some of the new arrivals and their firmly held conviction that the Circle approach held the key to philosophy must have been persuasive. "Several of our group," wrote Feigl, "arrived in the United States in a spirit of 'conquest.'"[1] Born in Europe, logical empiricism became integrated into Anglo-American philosophy.

Undoubtedly the text that did most to popularize the Circle—a crude synthesis of its thinking—was A. J. Ayer's *Language, Truth and Logic*. Initially published in 1936, it was only in 1946, after a republication, that it became a surprise best seller. It is easy to see why. It was bold and brash and lucid, offering an escape hatch for knotty philosophical problems: "The traditional disputes of philosophers," it begins, "are, for the most part, as unwarranted as they are unfruitful."[2] But it horrified some of the stuffy old guard and Ayer was not offered a coveted Oxford job, having to settle for University College London instead. Elsewhere, disciples pushed a positivist agenda in some unlikely and far-flung places, such as Finland, Argentina, and through Dr. Tscha Hung in China (although he had to keep his empiricist head down during the Cultural Revolution).

———

Quite quickly, however, logical empiricism fell out of favor. One student who left philosophy in the late 1950s to do military service, returning to it only in 1960, described his shock at the change in the intellectual climate. "No one except undergraduates were still defending the verification theory of meaning. It was as if a Catholic had gone on an extended cruise and returned to find the Pope and the curia no longer believed in the Nicene Creed."[3]

One issue was that the Circle-in-exile no longer retained even the veneer of unity. Although there had always been splits and vehement disagreements within the Circle, to the outside world it had had the appearance of a movement with a more or less agreed approach to the problems of philosophy. The cracks in that façade were now visible to all. Physically separated, the Circle also grew philosophically apart.

Gödel was an example. He had sat in on Circle meetings silently disagreeing in particular with the claim that mathematics and logic should be understood as tautologies. Now he became more willing to let his opposition be known. He credited the Circle with his interest in the foundations of his subject, but in one letter in 1946 he commented on an article about Schlick, in which his name was absent: "You need not wonder that I am not considered in it. I was indeed not a specially active member of the Schlick Circle and in many respects even in direct opposition to its principal views."[4] In fact, there were few purists left. Bergmann became an apostate and even published a collection of critical essays, *The Metaphysics of Logical Positivism.* The book made the normally phlegmatic Carnap, a loyalist to the project, furious.

———

The flow of ideas from the philosopher who had done so much to inspire the Circle, Ludwig Wittgenstein, did not slacken until the onset of his illness. He would jot thoughts down, and then rearrange them in some sort of order, though not in any traditional way. He illuminated questions by approaching them from multiple angles, swooping over and around puzzles, examining them from one side, then another. As already described, many of Wittgenstein's earlier positions were inverted, including the notion that language and thought mirrored the world. The emphasis on the analysis of language now shifted. Natural language was in decent working order and we should stick with the surface and not try to seek hidden depths. We should remind ourselves how we use words. We erred when we used language in unfamiliar ways; language inveigled us, especially when it went "on holiday," when, as it were, we took it to places to which it did not belong. "Philosophy is a struggle against the bewitchment of our understanding by means of language."[5]

Acknowledging the variety of ways in which language is actually used led Wittgenstein to abandon the idea that words could have meaning only if there were necessary and sufficient conditions attached to their application. Take the concept of a game. The temptation is to assume that all games must have something in common, and that it is this common element that enables us to apply the term *game* ourselves and to understand the term when others use it. But upon reflection we realize that there is no one characteristic shared by each and every game. After all, some games use a racquet or bat, but not all. Some do not require any kind of ball. Some games involve teams, others are contests between individuals, still others are, or can be, played alone. Some games are played outdoors, others indoors. Some games are primarily tests of physicality, others test mental agility. And so on.[6]

Of course, there are overlapping similarities among games, but there are no necessary and sufficient conditions. Just pay attention to how the term *game* is used in ordinary language. Games are what Wittgenstein called "family resemblance" concepts. They are like families in which some members of the family have a snub nose, others a domed forehead, others frizzy blond hair; there is no single characteristic possessed by all members of the family.

The focus on ordinary language—with all its idiosyncrasies and inconsistencies—inspired a whole new school of philosophy, though in Oxford not Cambridge. In Oxford, Waismann, who had been so appallingly treated by Wittgenstein, spread a mixed gospel combining elements from traditional Viennese logical empiricism with ordinary language philosophy. A 1947 lecture was entitled "The Limits of Positivism." A former student remembers the first class he attended with Waismann, when the lecturer pulled out a tiny red notebook and announced, "In this book there are 50 philosophical problems which can be solved in two hours."[7] They seemed like major philosophical conundrums; in fact, they were mere linguistic confusions. He now scoffed at the claim that logical, formal languages could illuminate philosophy. Ayer said of Waismann, "He developed a penchant for the branch of linguistic philosophy which consisted in the study of ordinary English usage, undeterred by his own difficulties with the English language."[8] An important journal article, "Verifiability," published in 1945,[9] pointed out the difficulty of fixing definitions indefinitely. Since we cannot foresee every way in which ordinary expressions will be used in the future, definitions are bound to be open to change. This was an assault on the idea of analyticity to rival Wittgenstein's family-resemblance concepts.

W.V.O. Quine would seek to undermine the analytic-synthetic distinction from another direction. Nearly two decades after he visited the Circle, Quine published a hugely influential article. "Two Dogmas of Empiricism" (1951) challenged two basic premises of logical empiricism. One was that meaningful statements get their meaning by some sort of logical translation from immediate experience—in effect an attack on Schlick's (though not Neurath's) notion of protocol sentences. The other was a blow to an equally fundamental axiom of logical empiricism, the notion that there was a sharp and clear line separating the analytic from the synthetic. British philosopher Tim Crane illustrates the Quine objection with a question (and answer). "Do you know what an Umiak is? No? Well, it's a flat-bottomed Inuit canoe. So have I told you something about the word, or have I told you something about the world? I think you've learned something about both."[10]

Take another example. There are disputes that arise—sometimes for tax reasons—about which category a particular product belongs to. Famously, there was a legal dispute in Britain about whether a Jaffa Cake (a sponge structure topped by orange jelly and a cap of chocolate) was a cake or a biscuit. A Jaffa Cake has cake-like qualities and biscuit-like qualities. The ruling, that it was a cake, was not based solely on an investigation into the structure and ingredients of the product, nor solely on a conceptual analysis of "cake" and "biscuit": it required a combination of empirical and conceptual inquiry.

If there was no sharp difference between the analytic and the synthetic, then the logic of Quine's position was that in principle every statement could come to be rejected. Some statements were obviously more fragile than others, yet nothing was entirely safe. No single statement had rock-bottom certainty—an echo of Neurath's Boat.

For many years the Quinean blow against the analytic-synthetic distinction was held to have been decisive. More recently, attempts have been made to resuscitate it and to argue that Carnap has been misunder-stood. Carnap, it's said, never meant to claim that the analytic-synthetic distinction was cleanly applicable to natural languages like English. Rather, the distinction could operate in a formal, artificial language, where it was useful in clarifying disputes about contested concepts.

—————

By the 1960s logical empiricism had begun to be assailed on all sides—including, indeed especially, from Circle members and associates—so much so that many of its central tenets no longer seemed defensible. Then there is the principle of verification, which the Circle had strug-gled to make watertight. A satisfactory account of the principle—which excludes ethics, aesthetics, and metaphysical assertions but includes scientific theories about nonobservable entities—continues to prove elusive. All attempts to tighten the principle have let in either too little or too much. It is also self-undermining, for the principle itself seems neither analytically true nor verifiable.

Beyond the debates over the verification principle are debates over confirmation. If we accept the logical empiricist claim that for a state-ment to be cognitively meaningful it has to be verifiable or testable, there arises the further debate about whether it makes sense to talk of the degree to which a statement has been verified or confirmed. Can there be quantitative measures to ascertain the degree of certainty about a scientific claim? A scientific theory is tested by experimentation and by showing that it produces the predicted result. Intuitively it would seem as if a theory that had been tested a thousand times should surely be considered more robust than one that had been tested only once. But Carl Hempel spotted a puzzle. Take the hypothesis *All ravens are black*. If you look out the window and see a black raven it seems fair to con-sider that an observation notched up in favor of the theory—a bit of confirming evidence. But, logically, the statement *All ravens are black* is equivalent to the statement *Anything that is nonblack is not a raven*. Does that mean that when you look out of your window and see a red apple, or green grass, that you are providing confirmation for the hypothesis

All ravens are black? That does not smell right. All attempts to provide unassailable definitions of verification and confirmation inevitably seemed to throw up snags and paradoxes.

———

In the 1930s the Circle members would never have guessed that the philosopher in their area who would go on to become the most well known beyond the confines of philosophy would be Karl Popper. This was in part through Popper's outliving almost all of them—thus enabling him to press home the distortion, unchallenged, that he had slain the Circle. But even Popper's reputation has waxed and waned. His ideas in the philosophy of science found more support among scientists than among philosophers, where according to one leading philosopher of science, his standing has sunk to "rock-bottom."[11] His out-and-out skepticism—his claim that we have no reason to believe that an experiment repeated for the 1,000th time will produce the same result as the previous 999 times—is regarded as either banal or ludicrous. If the inductive method helps us to build bridges (that do not collapse), cure diseases, land humans on the moon, then why worry about it. And the idea that it is *never* rational to use induction seems crazy. "Nobody properly acquainted with the evidence doubts that cigarettes cause lung cancer, or that matter is made of atoms,"[12] writes philosopher David Papineau. The fact that smoking causes cancer is surely a fact, he says, not merely a provisional hypothesis awaiting possible falsification.

Just as the verification principle proved difficult to pin down, so the falsifiability criterion—aimed at distinguishing science from nonscience—turned out not to be as straightforward as it initially appeared. On its own, it does not tell us how to select between conflicting theories that have not yet been falsified—that matter has provoked a lively debate. Or take, for example, the old lady at the circus who peers into her crystal ball and foresees that you will have four children and an adventurous career in a foreign country. She is making testable predictions. But neither you nor she really believes that her trade has anything to do with science. And if the claim *All swans are white* is falsifiable (by the discovery of one black swan), what about the proposition *Some swans are black*? No number of sightings of white swans would falsify that. Popper tried to address some of the criticisms of the falsifiability criterion, as did some of his disciples, but he ran into the dilemma familiar to those who advanced the verification principle: either the simple and elegant falsifiability criterion had to be rejected, or else it had to be modified, thus compromising its simplicity and elegance.

Recall that Neurath back in the 1930s had pointed out that in practice scientific theories were not discarded after merely one "falsification." A similar thought was picked up by Thomas Kuhn, a new star of the philosophy of science. Kuhn is sometimes represented as having made a hand-brake U-turn in the philosophy of science, so it is worth noting, first, that Neurath had foreshadowed some of his intellectual moves and second, that Kuhn's famous book, *The Structure of Scientific Revolutions* (1962), appeared in the International Encyclopedia of Unified Science series—edited by Carnap and Morris. *The Structure of Scientific Revolutions* took a sociological approach to the evolution of science. The picture the logical empiricists painted of scientific practice and progress bore no relation to reality, Kuhn argued. Scientific knowledge did not advance gradually and in a linear way. And scientists did not ditch their theories when they seemed to be at odds with experimental results. Historically that is not how breakthroughs occur.

So how does science work? In normal times, according to Kuhn, if an experiment fails to satisfy a theory, the scientist will usually try to resolve the problem, to explain away the apparent anomaly. Sometimes, for example, a question mark might be raised not about the result but about the competence of the scientist or the conditions under which the experiment was held. The theory itself is not regarded as having been falsified. It is only when problem piles up on problem, anomaly upon anomaly, that the pressure builds, eventually engendering a violent intellectual spasm, a revolutionary change, in which the original scientific framework is overturned, replaced by a new framework that appears to resolve the tensions. Kuhn called these periods paradigm shifts. Then the cycle begins all over again. What once seemed revolutionary now becomes obvious orthodoxy.

With a paradigm shift, our assumptions, techniques, problems, even the meaning of fundamental concepts can undergo revision. Terms like *mass*, understood in one way during the Newtonian paradigm, come to be understood in a different way. What is more, since these paradigms operate with distinctive concepts and on different foundations, it is senseless to compare one paradigm with another—the same standards cannot be applied to adjudicate between different paradigms.

The Structure of Scientific Revolutions sold a million copies, and "paradigm shift" entered the vernacular, becoming familiar in the jargon of management consultants, advertising executives, civil servants, and other purveyors of policy and strategy. Kuhn supplanted Popper as the philosopher du jour—cited most often by both specialists and nonspecialists. His book retains its influence today, although heavily critiqued. The notion of a paradigm is vague, and Kuhn's project was charged with being postmodernist, detached from notions of immutable, objective truth, evidenced by his claim that some paradigms are incommensurable (that is to say, there is no common standard by which they can be judged). The incommensurability assertion infuriated Popper. If a new view could not be said to be an improvement, then, he thundered, we had sunk into an abyss of relativism.

But while Popper's philosophy of science has taken a battering, the standing of the *Open Society* has been more enduring. For some time, after the Berlin Wall came down and political commentators had proclaimed the end of history, his advocacy of the open society seemed an irrelevance, redundant. The only sentence I regret from a previous (co-authored) book *Wittgenstein's Poker* was in the final chapter, in which Popper's ideas on openness were described as "received wisdom."[13] That now looks naïve. The forces of intolerance have reemerged, not least in the form of strident nationalism and fundamentalist religion.

———

Facing division within and assault from outside, logical empiricism hit a reputational crisis. By 1963 a British philosopher felt justified in writing, "There are no more logical positivists left." In an *Encylopedia of*

Philosophy another philosopher pronounced logical positivism to be "dead, or as dead as a philosophical movement ever becomes."[14] A. J. Ayer was asked, in a television interview (1978), what he regarded as the main shortcomings of logical positivism. "I suppose the greatest defect is that nearly all of it was false,"[15] he replied. Many philosophers criticize logical empiricism for being anemic. The idea that logic and science can capture all that can be usefully or meaningfully articulated they regard as crude. It became standard to view the Vienna Circle as a long philosophical cul-de-sac. Or, to change the metaphor, an elaborate sandcastle, fleetingly impressive, but then leaving no trace after it is washed away.

The standard picture is unjust.

First, some of the work of individual members and associates has had important indirect impact. Gödel was never involved with designing computers, but his work in symbolic logic helped in the development of computers. The influence of Neurath's Isotype is disputed, but he has a parental claim to the everyday iconography that we now take for granted—the male/female symbols on toilet doors, the standardization of road signs internationally. Menger's mathematical treatment of ethics was a seed from which the former member of his mathematical colloquium, Oskar Morgenstern, developed game theory, now so central to a host of disciplines, especially economics.[16]

The standard picture also misrepresents the movement, whose disagreements in exile tend to be exaggerated. The philosophical glue between them became weaker but did not become entirely unstuck. Although their outlooks may have diverged, most of them continued to engage with the same subject matter—the essence and role of philosophy and the nature and foundations of science. In a cringe-inducing metaphor, Frank told his students that new scientific theories replaced old ones as a woman replaced a dress—wanting the new one to fit better and "particularly well over certain areas."[17] Even Quine, who became an important critic of the Circle, retained his empiricist instincts and his hostility to traditional metaphysics.

On the whole, their message to their students remained steady: that science was good and metaphysics was bad. As Neurath put it to Feigl in 1938, "what we have in common will remain; as products of their time, the differences will fade."[18] Nothing fortified old bonds more than mention of Heidegger's name. "One has to read Heidegger in the original to see what a swindler he was," said Popper. His philosophy was "empty verbiage put together in statements which are absolutely empty."[19] On this even Carnap—not Popper's biggest fan—concurred.

Carnap's agreement to participate in the Schilpp series had been conditional upon there not being a volume dedicated to Heidegger. "I appeal to the philosophers of all countries to unite and never again mention Heidegger or talk to another philosopher who defends Heidegger," said Popper. "This man was a devil. I mean, he behaved like a devil to his beloved teacher, and he has a devilish influence on Germany."[20] Bergmann's students learned not even to mention Heidegger, because of the vehemence of the outburst his name would provoke. Menger would put on a pompous voice and quote Heidegger with scorn; "It was clear that he regarded this as pretentious nonsense."[21]

The Circle and their descendants thus retained a broad unity about the purpose of philosophy and a clear vision of their targets. Although the logical empiricists were once forced out of Austria, they were later welcomed home. In 1991, the Vienna Circle Institute was founded as a society, and then in 2011 absorbed into the University of Vienna. It aims to document the Circle's work and, through books, conferences, exhibitions and seminars, to promote a continuation of the logical empiricist project.

In spite of running into intellectual hurdles and roadblocks, a more sympathetic and, I think, accurate interpretation of this project would credit it with being right in outlook, even if incorrect in detail. It is worth noting that after A. J. Ayer delivered his famous throwaway remark about nearly all of logical positivism being false—made, one suspects, principally for comic effect—he immediately qualified the statement by saying the thinking was "true in spirit."

Much of that spirit lives on. To this day logic remains an important tool in the philosopher's toolbox. Indeed, there is now a renewed interest among formal philosophers in Carnap, who is regarded as "something of a hero"[22]—though the distinguished philosopher David Chalmers says his general approach has been more influential than the details. There is still an ambition—perhaps expressed with more modesty—to place philosophy on a similar standing to science, acknowledging that philosophy is different but has a relationship with science. The direction of travel remains.

A precise meaning of "physicalism" has never been fixed, but a variation of physicalism or materialism is the dominant strand in today's philosophy. That is, most philosophers insist that all facts must ultimately be grounded in physical facts. In that sense, colors and consciousness, though they may not initially seem physical, can nonetheless be accounted for in physicalist terms. There is no difference between brain states and mind states. Beliefs and desires and emotions are all reducible in some way to brain states. After he arrived in the US, Feigl was instrumental in formulating this physicalist position on the mind. The philosophy of science has itself been established as a particular subgenre of philosophy, and one shaped by the Circle. New debates have emerged such as the focus on what is to count as a scientific explanation (inspired by the work in particular of Hempel). What, for example, counts as an explanation to the question *Why do some men go bald?*, or how does an explanation differ from, say, a description? What makes a scientific explanation distinct from another form of explanation? What is the link between an explanation and prediction? Can we provide logically necessary and sufficient conditions for a "scientific explanation" that do not stray into metaphysics?

Beyond this, there is the way the Circle shaped the practice of philosophy, particularly Anglo-American philosophy. It is easy to overstate the gap between analytic and continental philosophy, but by any reasonable understanding of analytic philosophy, the Circle is part of its DNA. Analytic philosophy has gone in various directions that the Circle would not approve. But the self-identifying merits of analytic philosophy are its meticulous attention to logic and language and the pursuit of clarity, the contempt for grandiosity, and the calling-out of nonsense. There is a suspicion of arguments that rely on "feel" or "intuition" over substance. The Circle was not unique in promoting these intellectual virtues, but they helped foster a climate in which they are now so much taken for granted that they are virtually invisible.

In that sense, success of the Circle ideas lies in their apparent absence.

DRAMATIS PERSONAE

ALFRED (A. J.) AYER (29 October 1910–27 June 1989). English philosopher who spent time in Vienna and whose polemical, best-selling book *Language, Truth and Logic* popularized the Circle's ideas in Britain. He once protected model Naomi Campbell from the unwanted attentions of world heavyweight boxing champion Mike Tyson.

GUSTAV BERGMANN (4 May 1906–21 April 1987). Member of the Vienna Circle who spent his postwar career at the University of Iowa, where he distanced himself from logical empiricism. He had a considerable gift for disagreement.

RUDOLF CARNAP (18 May 1891–14 September 1970). German born, a key Circle member, and perhaps the most technically gifted. He moved from Vienna to Prague to Chicago and finally to California.

ALBERT EINSTEIN (14 March 1879–18 April 1955). Hero of the logical empiricists, acquainted with several in the Circle, and himself well-disposed toward philosophy.

HERBERT FEIGL (14 December 1902–1 June 1988). Of Jewish origin; acknowledgment of how this affected his career prospects led to his being the first member of the Circle to emigrate. (Albert Blumberg, his coauthor for a 1931 paper, is credited with first using the expression *logical positivism*).

PHILIPP FRANK (20 March 1884–21 July 1966). Physicist; friend and biographer of Einstein. In his twenties he moved from Vienna to Prague, then immigrated to the United States.

KURT GÖDEL (28 April 1906–14 January 1978). Widely recognized as the most important logician of the twentieth century, famous above all for his two incompleteness theorems. From Vienna, he went to Princeton, where he would accompany his friend Einstein on a daily walk. Psychologically fragile, with a streak of paranoia, and convinced that his food was poisoned, he died of starvation.

HANS HAHN (27 September 1879–24 July 1934). Mathematician; played a crucial role in the Circle's formation, was instrumental in bringing Schlick to Vienna, and was a supervisor to several Circle members. His friends called him Hähnchen (Little Rooster).

OLGA HAHN-NEURATH (20 July 1882–20 July 1937). Mathematician and expert in Boolean algebra; blind since the age of twenty-two; smoked cigars. The sister of Hans Hahn and the second wife of Otto Neurath.

MARTIN HEIDEGGER (26 September 1889–26 May 1976). German philosopher. Anti-Semite. Genius or charlatan, depending on your point of view (to the Circle, he was the latter).

CARL (PETER) HEMPEL (8 January 1905–9 November 1997). Based in Berlin but spent time in the Austrian capital. Known, among other things, for a logical conundrum involving black ravens.

WALTER HOLLITSCHER (16 May 1911–6 July 1986). Born in Vienna, he studied philosophy, biology, and medicine at the University of Vienna (Schlick was his PhD supervisor). He was a communist/Marxist. After the war he returned to Vienna (the only member of the Circle to do so). Freud was a particular interest.

BÉLA JUHOS (22 November 1901–27 May 1971). Came from a noble Hungarian family and studied under Schlick. Along with Viktor Kraft he remained in Vienna during World War II.

FELIX KAUFMANN (4 July 1895–23 December 1949). Studied philosophy and jurisprudence at the University of Vienna and became a Privatdozent in 1922. He then moved into commerce. He helped several members of the Circle to leave Vienna and then himself escaped to the United States, where he taught at the New School in New York.

VIKTOR KRAFT (4 July 1880–3 January 1975). Lived in Austria during the war, despite having a Jewish wife. He restarted a circle in Vienna after the war—the Kraft Circle.

ERNST MACH (18 February 1838–19 February 1916). Physicist and philosopher, whose ideas profoundly influenced the Vienna Circle. The society that was the public face of the Circle was named after Mach.

KARL MENGER (13 January 1902–5 October 1985). Son of economist Carl Menger. Karl was a mathematician who participated in the Circle but also had his own mathematics circle. After Austria he went to Notre Dame, but spent most of his post-Austrian career at the Illinois Institute of Technology, where he was much beloved.

CHARLES MORRIS (23 May 1901–15 January 1979). American philosopher; taught at the University of Chicago for 27 years from 1931. He met the Vienna Circle on a sabbatical in 1934 and subsequently helped organize the Unity of Science Congress at Harvard. He encouraged several Circle members to emigrate to the United States. Along with Neurath and Carnap, he was the editor of the *Encyclopedia of Unified Science*.

OTTO NEURATH (10 December 1882–22 December 1945). Polymath, with a particular expertise in economics and sociology. Neurath was the driving force behind the Circle's organizational activities. An enormous man with an outsize personality, he signed his letters with a picture of an elephant.

KARL POPPER (28 July 1902–17 September 1994). Described as the "official opposition" to the Circle, a label he was proud to embrace. He spent World War II in New Zealand and his postwar career at the London School of Economics. Once called Margaret Thatcher's favorite philosopher for his championing of the open society. He preferred having disciples to being a disciple, though he revered Bertrand Russell.

WILLARD VAN ORMAN QUINE (25 June 1908–25 December 2000). American logician and philosopher, who spent a few months with the Circle. He later became a leading critic of some of its core ideas. He and Carnap were close friends and exchanged hundreds of letters.

FRANK RAMSEY (22 February 1903–19 January 1930). Precociously talented British philosopher; died at age twenty-six. He translated Wittgenstein's *Tractatus*. He traveled to Vienna in the 1920s to be psychoanalyzed after suffering mental anguish from a thwarted love affair. He is now recognized as having made seminal contributions in many areas, from math and logic to economics and probability.

ROSE RAND (14 June 1903—July 28 1980). Troubled, Polish-born mathematician and logician. For a period in the 1930s she took the minutes at Circle gatherings. She lived a life of struggle. Regarded by many of those who tried to help her as a "hopeless case."

HANS REICHENBACH (26 September 1891–9 April 1953). Founded the Society for Empirical Philosophy in Berlin—the sister organization to the Vienna Circle. He and Carnap became coeditors of *Erkenntnis*. Made important contributions to probability theory. When Hitler came to power, he took a teaching job in Istanbul, then immigrated to the United States to teach at the University of California, Los Angeles, in 1938.

KURT REIDEMEISTER (13 October 1893–8 July 1971). German-born mathematician; though in Vienna for only three years, he was important in persuading the Circle to focus on the *Tractatus Logico-Philosophicus*. Brother of Marie.

MARIE REIDEMEISTER (27 May 1898–10 October 1986). Worked on Otto Neurath's Isotype project. Kurt's sister, and Otto's mistress before becoming his third wife.

MORITZ SCHLICK (14 April 1882–22 June 1936). The unassuming leader of the Vienna Circle, a German-born physicist from a patrician background. He was murdered at the University of Vienna by a former student.

ESTHER SIMPSON (31 July 1903–19 November 1996). Initially, assistant secretary to the Academic Assistance Council, helping around 1,500 academics sacked by the Nazis flee from their homeland—16 of whom went on to win Nobel Prizes. She also secured the release of over 500 of them, after they were detained by the British authorities as "enemy aliens." A talented linguist and violinist. Wittgenstein bought her a bun.

SUSAN STEBBING (2 December 1885–11 September 1943). Played a major, if still largely unacknowledged, part in importing the ideas of the Vienna Circle into the UK. One of the cofounders of a respected philosophy journal, *Analysis*.

ALFRED TARSKI (14 January 1901–26 October 1983). Polish-born logician, mathematician, philanderer.

FRIEDRICH WAISMANN (21 March 1896–4 November 1959). Austrian philosopher (Russian father, German mother), disciple of Wittgenstein, and brilliant expositor of his work. Never quite fulfilled his potential, in part because he lacked self-confidence. Both his wife and son killed themselves. He died in Oxford, England.

LUDWIG WITTGENSTEIN (26 April 1889–29 April 1951). Architect, engineer, gardener, hospital porter, teacher—and, in the opinion of many philosophers, the greatest philosopher of the twentieth century. His book, the *Tractatus Logico-Philosophicus*, inspired the Vienna Circle. But the *Philosophical Investigations*, published posthumously in 1953, represents a repudiation of many of his early ideas.

EDGAR ZILSEL (11 August 1891–11 March 1944). One of the most left-wing members of the Circle, who advocated and supported adult education. He killed himself in the United States in 1944.

CHRONOLOGY

1895   Ernst Mach becomes the first professor of philosophy of the inductive sciences at the University of Vienna.

1901   Bertrand Russell discovers what has become known as Russell's Paradox.

1903   Publication of Bertrand Russell's *The Principles of Mathematics*.

1905   Publication in the journal *Mind* of Bertrand Russell's essay, "On Denoting."

1907–10   A prototype of the Vienna Circle: regular meetings between Frank, Hahn, Neurath, and, according to some (contested) reports, von Mises.

1908   Architect Adolf Loos publishes modernist book, *Ornament and Crime*.

1911   Hahn accepts job at the University of Czernowitz.

1914–18   World War I. Several future Circle members see action. Wittgenstein fights on Eastern Front, Carnap on the Western, Hahn shot and injured on the Italian Front.

1916   21 November: Emperor Franz Josef I dies.

1917   Publication of Schlick's *Space and Time in Contemporary Physics*.

          Hahn takes a job in Bonn.

1918   Completion of Wittgenstein's *Tractatus Logico-Philosophicus*.

          Publication of Schlick's *General Theory of Knowledge*.

          3 November: Wittgenstein taken prisoner of war.

          11 November: Six centuries of Habsburg rule come to an end.

1919   Neurath serves as minister in the brief socialist government of Bavaria. He's briefly imprisoned, then returns to Vienna.

          Socialists win election to take control of Vienna municipality.

1921   Hans Hahn, the mathematician, becomes a professor at the University of Vienna.

          January: Einstein delivers a public lecture in Vienna to a packed audience.

1922   Schlick takes up the chair in Vienna once occupied by Mach.

          Publication of Hugo Bettauer's book *The City without Jews*.

          Publication of English version of *Tractatus*.

          June: the krone already devalued, collapses from 52,000 to the pound to 125,000.

1923   Vienna Circle formed. Founding members, Frank, Hahn, Schlick.

September Ramsey visits Wittgenstein in Puchberg and passes through Vienna.

1924   Ramsey spends six months in Vienna.

Gödel matriculates from the University of Vienna.

1925–27   Vienna Circle discusses the *Tractatus Logico-Philosophicus.*

1925   1 January: opening of Neurath's Museum of Society and Economy in Vienna.

10 March: Hugo Bettauer, author of *The City without Jews,* is shot. He dies of his wounds two weeks later.

Autumn: Johann Nelböck enrolls in Moritz Schlick's class.

1926   3 May: Carnap arrives in Vienna as Privatdozent and joins the Vienna Circle.

Gödel joins Vienna Circle.

Tractatus read aloud sentence by sentence from 1925 to 1927.

1927   Wittgenstein meets Schlick and conversations begin with Waismann.

27 February: Berlin Society for Empirical Philosophy set up.

Heidegger publishes his great work, *Being and Time.*

17 June: Carnap meets Wittgenstein for the first time—at Schlick's home.

15 July: firing on demonstrators in Vienna results in over 80 dead.

Autumn: Menger arrives in Vienna and joins Circle.

1928   Carnap publishes *Der Logische Aufbau der Welt.*

10 March: Wittgenstein attends lecture by Dutch mathematician L.E.J. Brouwer.

Menger becomes associate professor in math and forms his Mathematical Colloquium.

November: public launch of the Ernst Mach Society, *Verein Ernst Mach.* Neurath, Carnap, Hahn, and Schlick all become officials.

1929   Wittgenstein returns to Cambridge.

Schlick offered a job in Bonn, which he turns down. He spends a brief time at Stanford. When he returns he is handed the Circle manifesto dedicated to him: *The Scientific Conception of the World.*

Feigl publishes his first book, *Theory and Experience in Physics.*

3–10 July: Feigl lectures at the Bauhaus.

24 July: Heidegger gives inaugural lecture, *What Is Metaphysics?,* as professor of philosophy at the University of Freiburg.

Hempel arrives in Vienna: leaves 1930.

13–15 September: Prague Conference on the Epistemology of the Exact Sciences: Manifesto gets public outing.

October: Wall Street crash.

1930   2 January: Wittgenstein mentions verification in conversation with Schlick and Waismann.

20 January: Ramsey dies of hepatitis.

February: Tarski delivers lectures in Vienna and becomes a regular visitor.

Publication of Schlick's *Problems of Ethics* (*Fragen der Ethik*).

Feigl studies at Harvard on a scholarship and meets Quine.

26 August: Gödel tells Carnap about his incompleteness theorems during a discussion at the Café Reichsrat.

September: Major gathering in Königsberg. Gödel indicates in conference that he has a proof for incompleteness of arithmetic (one of most important moments in the history of logic). He's basically ignored.

Vienna Circle takes over a journal, which they renamed *Erkenntnis*, for the publication of its ideas.

Waismann introduces verifiability criterion.

9 December: Wittgenstein meets Waismann and repudiates his initial book project.

1931   31 January: Carnap has fever. A vision comes to him in the night, which forms the basis of the *Logical Syntax of Language*.

Carnap moves to Prague.

Article introducing term *logical positivism* by Feigl and Blumberg, appears in *American Journal of Philosophy*.

Neurath publishes *Empirische Soziologie*.

1932   6 May: Wittgenstein writes letter to Schlick complaining that Carnap has plagiarized him.

W.V.O. Quine arrives in Vienna.

20 May: Dollfuss sworn in as Austrian chancellor.

November: Rose Rand starts a colored spreadsheet cataloging the philosophical opinions of some Circle members.

1933   30 January: Hitler becomes German chancellor.

February: Quine leaves for Prague.

7 March: Dollfuss announces he will govern Austria without a parliament.

A. J. Ayer attends the Circle.

22 March 1933: Susan Stebbing delivers a British Academy lecture on logical positivism. In the same year she is appointed professor, the first female professor of philosophy.

11 April 1933: Nazis close down Bauhaus.

May: Hans Reichenbach resigned from his professorship in Berlin.

September: Gödel leaves for nearly a year in Princeton.

First edition of *Analysis* published in the UK.

1934   12 February: Civil war erupts in Austria.

23 February: Ernst Mach Society disbanded.

24 February: The Viennese police commissioner summons Schlick to answer questions about the Ernst Mach Society.

February: Police raid Neurath's office. He's in Moscow, and decides not to return to Austria, traveling to The Hague instead.

6 March: Ernst Mach Society dissolved by government in a police action: the charge was that it had been politically engaged on the side of the Social Democrats.

24 July: Hans Hahn dies.

25 July: Dollfuss assassinated by Nazis. The new chancellor is Kurt Schuschnigg.

Popper's *Logik der Forschung* (*The Logic of Scientific Discovery*) published.

Carnap publishes *Logical Syntax of Language*.

October: Carnap invited by Susan Stebbing to lecture at the University of London.

Unity of Science movement launched. Showdown between the VC and nationalists at the International Philosophy Congress in Prague.

Hempel leaves Germany for Brussels.

1935   Tarski visits Vienna again.

Unity of Science Congress meets for first time at the Sorbonne in Paris.

3 October: Italy invades Abyssinia.

December: Hoare-Laval Pact exposed.

1936   January: Ayer publishes *Language, Truth and Logic*.

10 February: Waismann told he is to lose his job as librarian.

7 March: German troops move into the Rhineland.

12 June: death of Karl Kraus.

21–26 June: Unity of Science Congress meets in Copenhagen in the home of Niels Bohr.

22 June: Moritz Schlick murdered by Hans Nelböck. Meetings of VC discontinued.

11 July: Agreement between Schuschnigg and Hitler recognizing the full sovereignty of the Federal State of Austria.

Carnap moves to Chicago, begins teaching in October.

18 July: Outbreak of Spanish Civil War.

Gödel spends several months in a sanatorium, suffering from nerves.

Neurath visits New York to spread the word about the scientific-world conception.

1 November: Announcement that Germany and Italy have signed a Rome-Berlin Axis.

Popper resigns his teaching post.

1937   January: Wittgenstein reads a confession to various friends in England.

24–26 May: Trial of Hans Nelböck.

19–31 July: Congress meets in Paris.

20 July: Olga Hahn-Neurath dies.

Menger emigrates to the US (Notre Dame).

Waismann leaves for the UK.

Frank goes to Harvard.

Popper takes up post as lecturer in Canterbury, New Zealand.

Nelböck put on trial in early 1937 and sentenced to 10 years in jail.

1938   11 March: Schuschnigg broadcasts his resignation. "God protect Austria," he says.

14 March: Hitler arrives in Vienna: Anschluss.

23 March: Menger quits his university post.

10 April: 99.7 percent of Austrians vote in favor of Anschluss.

23 April: Gödel's *Lehrbefugnis* (authorization to teach) officially lapses.

Nelböck released from prison after serving only two years of his ten-year sentence.

May: Nuremberg Race Laws introduced in Austria.

14–19 July: Fourth International Unity of Science Congress held at Cambridge.

Publication of *International Encyclopedia of Unified Science.*

September: 10,000 Jews leave Vienna.

October: Frank arrives in the US.

9 November: Kristallnacht.

1939   14 April: Wittgenstein becomes British.

3 September: Start of World War II.

Zilsel to the US. August–September. Tarski goes to the US for the Unity of Science Congress in Harvard: this saves his life.

Carnap goes to Harvard as a visiting professor. Russell, Carnap, and Tarski were there together.

Otto Neurath publishes his classic Isotype work *Modern Man in the Making*.

1940   January: Gödel leaves for the US through Russia on the *Trans-Siberian Express*.

Erkenntnis ceases publication.

2 July: *Arandora Star* torpedoed off cost of Ireland; hundreds of internees lose their lives.

Feigl accepts a position at the University of Minnesota, where he will remain for the rest of his life.

1941   8 February: Neurath released from the Isle of Man.

26 February: Neurath and Marie Reidemeister marry, Neurath's third marriage.

2–6 September: Sixth and final Congress meets in Chicago.

1943   11 September: Susan Stebbing dies.

September: Rose Rand suffers nervous breakdown.

Neurath publishes *Foundations of the Social Sciences*.

Nelböck received a conditional release by Nazi government in 1938; his sentence is commuted in 1943.

1944   11 March: Zilsel kills himself. "If the janitor finds me, he may keep the $10 bill as compensation for the shock."

1945   8 May: VE day.

14 August: VJ day bringing World War II to an end.

Popper publishes *The Open Society and Its Enemies*.

Hempel publishes *Studies in the Logic of Confirmation*.

22 December: Neurath dies.

1946   January: Popper arrives in the UK to start a job at the LSE.

25 October: Popper waves a poker (or possibly not) at Wittgenstein at the Moral Sciences Club in Cambridge.

1947   Philipp Frank publishes his biography of Einstein.

1949   23 December: Felix Kaufmann dies in New York.

1951   4 March: Gödel (jointly) wins Einstein Award.

29 April: Wittgenstein dies.

Quine publishes his paper "Two Dogmas of Empiricism."

1952   13 August: Hoover writes to Pentagon about rumor Frank is a spy.

1953   Posthumous publication of Wittgenstein's *Philosophical Investigations*.
       Feigl founds The Minnesota Center for the Philosophy of Science.
       9 April: Reichenbach dies.

1954   4 February: Schlick's murderer, J. Nelböck, dies in Vienna.
       Rand moves to the US. Carnap moves from Chicago to UCLA.

1955   Goodman publishes *Fact, Fiction, and Forecast*.

1959   4 November: Waismann dies.

1960   Publication of Quine's *Word and Object*.

1962   Publication of Kuhn's *Structure of Scientific Revolutions*.

1965   Popper Colloquium in London: Popper, Carnap, Quine, Tarski present.
       The City of Vienna awards Popper the *Geistewissenschaften* prize.
       Posthumous publication of Waismann's *Principles of Linguistic Philosophy*.

1966   21 July: Frank dies.

1967   Bergmann publishes *The Metaphysics of Logical Positivism*.

1970   14 September: Carnap dies.

1971   27 May: Juhos dies.

1978   14 January: Gödel dies.

1980   28 July: Rand dies.

1981   21 April: Bergmann dies.

1983   26 October: Tarski dies.

1985   5 October: Menger dies.

1988   1 June: Feigl dies.

1989   27 June: Ayer dies.

1994   17 September: Popper dies.

NOTES

Preface

1. No relation, as far as I know, to Vienna Circle member Walter Hollitscher.

1. Prologue: Goodbye, Europe

1. Quoted in Reisch, p. 72; originally from *Time*, 18 September, 1939, 72–73.
2. Quine, p. 140.
3. Gilbert, p. 4.
4. Quoted in Stadler (2001), p. 198.

2. Little Rooster and the Elephant

1. Frank (1950), p. 1.
2. Neurath (1983), p. 230.
3. Popper (1976), p. 151.
4. Quoted in Allen, p. 249.
5. Nietzsche, pp. 181–82.
6. Einstein, p. 19.
7. Quoted in Gordin, p. 118.
8. Marx, Engels, and Lenin, p. 433.
9. Service, p. 193.
10. Carnap to Neurath, 23 August 1945, quoted in Uebel (1991), p. 5; and see Cat and Tuboly, p. 648.
11. Neurath (1973), p. 52.
12. Cat and Tuboly, p. 650.
13. Neurath (1973), p. 80, note 2.
14. Bergmann, p. 4.
15. Neurath to Josef Frank, 9 September 1945, quoted in Stadler (2001), p. 505.
16. Musil, p. 236.

3. The Expanding Circle

1. Spiel (2007), p. 51.
2. Popper (1976), p. 40.
3. Schilpp, p. 9.
4. Ibid.
5. Putnam (1988), p. xi.
6. The Circle in Prague discussed this topic. I am grateful to Ádám Tuboly for pointing this out to me.

7. Hume, p. 120.

8. Einstein to Schlick, 14 December 1915.

9. Ibid.

10. Einstein to Born, 1969, quoted in Stadler (2001), p. 173.

11. Frank (1948), p. 100

12. Ibid., p. 209.

13. Ibid., p. 210.

14. Feigl (1981), p. 2.

15. Ibid.

16. Popper (1976), p. 37.

17. Ibid.

18. Einstein to the French Philosophical Society, 6 April 1922, quoted in Gimbel, p. 1.

4. The Bald French King

1. Quoted in Monk (1996), p. 142.

2. Ibid., p. 153.

3. Quoted in Sigmund, p. 17.

4. Ibid.

5. In Creath (1990), pp. 247–248.

6. Russell (2009), p. 242.

7. Russell (1940), p. 6.

5. Wittgenstein Casts His Spell

1. Russell to Ottoline Morrell, 2 November 1911.

2. Russell (2009), p. 313.

3. Ibid.

4. Russell to Ottoline Morrell, 22 March 1912. He went on to live another six decades!

5. Russell (1978), p. 329.

6. Hermine Wittgenstein, quoted in Rhees (1984), p. 2.

7. Russell to Ottoline Morrell, 27 May 1913.

8. Russell to Ottoline Morrell, 5 March 1912.

9. Hermine to Ludwig, 10 June 1917, quoted in McGuinness (2019), p. 31.

10. McGuinness (2012), p. 89.

11. Wittgenstein to Russell, 6 May 1920: quoted in Moorehead, p. 309.

12. Engelmann, 24 April 1920, p. 31.

13. Russell (1988), p. 35.

14. Letter from Russell to Ottoline Morrell, 27 May 1912, quoted in Monk, p. 54.

15. Wittgenstein (1922), 6.41.

16. Ibid., 6.54.

17. Hermine to Ludwig, 23 November 1920, in McGuinness (2019), p. 85.

18. Ibid.

19. Letter of 17 November 1920, in McGuinness (2019), p. 79.

20. Paul, p. 109.

21. See Misak, pp. 423–25.

22. Ramsey to his mother, 20 September 1923.

23. Ibid.

24. Pittsburgh, Archives of Scientific Philosophy, Hans Reichenbach Collection, asp/HR-016-42-16.

25. Albers and Anderson, p. 319.

26. The crucial Ramsey role was pointed out to me by Cheryl Misak and is discussed in Misak (2019).

27. Frege, p. vii.

28. Hahn 1929/1988, pp. 55–56.

29. Ramsey makes the same move from logic to math. Misak argues that he was instrumental in the Circle's adoption of their position. See Misak, pp. 189–91.

30. Schlick to Wittgenstein, 25 December 1924.

31. Quoted in Monk, p. 242.

32. In Waismann (1979), p. 14.

33. Quoted in Monk, p. 242.

34. Engelmann, p. 118.

35. Feigl (1981), p. 8.

36. Schilpp, p. 25.

37. Feigl (1981), p. 8.

38. Schilpp, p. 26.

39. Feigl (1981), p. 64.

40. Schilpp, p. 25.

41. Ibid., pp. 25–26.

42. Wittgenstein to Russell, 29 October 1913.

43. This followed a row between Ramsey and Wittgenstein, to which we will soon come.

44. Although Menger writes that it was his idea that Feigl mention the lecture to Wittgenstein. Menger (1994), p. 130.

45. Ibid., p. 131.

46. Feigl (1981), p. 64.

47. Letter of 14 July 1929, quoted in Monk, p. 270.

48. The account of this viva is from Wood, p. 156.

49. Cambridge University Library/BOGS 2 1920–37/1925. I am grateful to C. Misak for sending me this correct quote, as opposed to the one often cited: "It is my personal opinion that Mr Wittgenstein's thesis is a work of genius; but, be that as it may, it is certainly well up to the standard required for the Cambridge degree of Doctor of Philosophy."

50. Letter to Schlick, 18 February 1929, quoted in Waismann (1979), p. 17.

6. Neurath in Red Vienna

1. Quoted in Lansdale, p. 11, from an unsigned article in *Harper's* 3 (1898).

2. H. Andics, *Der Staat, den keiner wollte* (Herder, 1962).

3. Hobsbawm, p. 9.

4. Correspondence with A. Hahn.

5. See Bottomore and Goode, p. 3.

6. Shangri-La was an imaginary haven in *Lost Horizon,* a 1933 novel by James Hilton.

7. Quoted in Gay (1988), p. 9.

8. Popper (1976), p. 32.

9. Ibid., p. 104.

10. Quoted in Neurath (1973), p. 76.

11. See Bright, p. 13.

12. Quoted in Burke, p. 258, and cited by Neurath in *Die pädagogische Weltbedeutung der Bildstatistik nach Wiener Methode* (1933), p. 241.

7. Coffee and Circles

1. Beller, p. 11.

2. Several attempts have been made to explain this phenomenon. See, for example, Schorske.

3. See, for example, Pentland.

4. 28 October 1935. Pittsburgh, Archives of Scientific Philosophy, Rose Rand Papers, US-PPiU-asp199001.

5. Popper (1976), p. 40.

6. A line, as we shall see, that also went through Karl Popper.

7. See Scheall and Schumacher, pp. 651–52.

8. Menger (1979), p. 237.

9. Ibid., p. 241.

10. Vogel, p. 174.

11. Crankshaw, p. 35. Crankshaw went on to become a journalist and Soviet specialist.

12. Zweig, p. 41.

13. Quoted in Ashby, Gronberg, and Shaw-Miller, p. 19.

14. Neurath to Kaempffert, 10 November 1944. Quoted in Eve, p. xvi.

15. In Stadler (1993), p. 16.

16. Beller, quoted in Ashby, Gronberg, and Shaw-Miller, p. 54.

17. Pinsker, p. 104.

18. From a speech delivered by Zionist Max Nordau at Second Zionist Congress in 1900. In Ashby, Gronberg, and Shaw-Miller, p. 80.

8. Couches and Construction

1. Letter reproduced in Jones, p. 474.

2. Letter of 11 July 1936, in McGuinness (2019), p. 208.

3. 4 June 1921, in McGuinness (2019), p. 105.

4. Quoted by Galison, in Sarkar, p. 78.

5. Quoted in Masheck, p. 205.

6. My thanks to Ed Harcourt for comments on this section.

7. Quoted in Stadler (2015), p. 227.

8. Bergmann, p. v.

9. Alan Hausman, in correspondence with author.

10. Quoted by Stadler, in Manninen and Stadler, p. 28.

11. For more on Ramsey and psychoanalysis, see Misak, chapter 7.

12. Letter to mother, probably 23 March 1924, Ramsey Papers. Quoted in Forrester, p. 14.

13. Misak, p. 163.

14. Ibid., p. 168.

15. Quoted in Paul, p. 168.

16. Quoted in Forrester, p. 15; from *Bloomsbury/Freud: The Letters of James Strachey and Alix Strachey*, ed. P. Meisel and W. Kendrick (Basic Books, 1986) p. 157.

17. Quoted in Galavotti, p. 3, in chapter by G. Taylor.

18. Misak, p. 166.

19. Ibid, p. 5.

20. In Ramsey, pp. 321–22.

21. For more about the Ramsey-Wittgenstein dispute, see Misak's excellent book on Ramsey.

22. Wittgenstein (1969), #255.

23. Wittgenstein (1966), pp. 22–23.

24. Ibid., p. 44.

9. Schlick's Unwelcome Gift

1. Quoted in Stadler (2001), p. 334.

2. Frank (1950), p. 38.

3. Ibid.

4. Ibid., p. 34.

5. Not much is known about Radakovic. He was a mathematician and not in Vienna for long.

6. In Waismann (1979), p. 18.

7. Wittgenstein (1967), #455.

8. Schlick, "Die Wende der Philosophie," *Erkenntnis* 1 (1930).

9. Ibid.

10. "Überwindung der Metaphysik durch logische Analyse der Sprache ("The Elimination of Metaphysics through Logical Analysis of Language"), *Erkenntnis* 2 (1931).

11. Frank (1941), p. 11.

12. The diary is available digitally at http://digital.library.pitt.edu/islandora/object/pitt%3A31735062213917/.

13. Quoted in McGuinness (1988), pp. 57–58.

14. Quoted in Feferman, p. 96.

15. In Ayer (1977), p. 156.

16. Lamont, p. 12.

10. Strangers from Abroad

1. Waismann (1979), p. 38.

2. Anthony Quinton in McGuinness (1985), p. 389.

3. In Waismann (1979), p. 24.

4. There is disagreement among Wittgenstein scholars about how much of Wittgenstein's later philosophy is foreshadowed in the *Tractatus*. Ishiguro, in Winch (pp. 20–21) is one of many commentators who argue that Wittgenstein's focus on "use" is present from the beginning, but in a less comprehensive way.

5. I am grateful to Josh Eisenthal for presenting the shift of Wittgenstein's philosophy to me in this way.

6. In McGuinness (2008), p. 199.

7. In McGuinness (2012), p. 213.

8. Wittgenstein to Schlick, 6 May 1932.

9. Wittgenstein (1922).

10. Quoted in Stadler (1993), p. 33.

11. In Waismann (1979), p. 26.

12. Quoted by Arne Naess in Stadler (1993), p. 12.

13. Menger (1979), p. 14.

14. Ayer (1977), p. 128.

15. Ibid., p. 131

16. Ibid., p. 133

17. Letter to Berlin, 11 January 1933, quoted in Rogers, p. 85.

18. Ayer (1977), p. 135.

19. Creath (1990), p. 465.

20. Ayer to Isaiah Berlin, 26 February 1933, quoted in Rogers, p. 94.

21. Ibid.

22. Quine (1985), p. 88.

23. Quoted in Stadler (1993), p. 14.

24. Ibid.

25. Janik and Veigl, p. 63.

26. He used both phrases but tended to prefer "empirically meaningful."

27. Carnap (1996), p. 16.

11. The Longest Hatred

1. In Fraenkel, p. 429.

2. In Hamann, p. 228, from O. Weininger, *Geschlecht und Charakter* (3rd ed., Vienna, 1905).

3. Roth, p. 122.

4. In Hamann, p. 286.

5. A. Hitler, "Monologue," 17 December 1941, p. 153; quoted in Hamann, p. 276.

6. Pulzer, in Fraenkel, p. 429.

7. Quoted in Timms, p. 28.

8. Quoted in Holmes, chapter 2, by John Warren, p. 37.

9. Freud to "Sehr geehrter Herr," 27 January 1925. Quoted in Gay (1987), p. 122.

10. Schnitzler, p. 13.

11. Mahler, p. 44.

12. Beller, p. 94.

13. In Gombrich, p. 11.

14. Bettauer, p. 77.

15. Hobsbawm, p. 21.

16. For more on implicit bias, listen to the BBC Analysis program at www.bbc.co.uk /programmes/bO8slvk8.

17. Mos, pp. 55–56.

18. In Hamann, p. 228, from O. Weininger, *Geschlecht und Charakter*, p. 418.

19. Quoted in Silverman, p. 3.

20. Wittgenstein (1980), p. 16.

21. LSE, Popper Archive, 313–10.

22. Popper (1976), p. 105.

23. Letter to his mother, probably 23 March 1924, Ramsey Papers. Quoted in Forrester, p. 14.

24. Quine, p. 32.

12. Black Days in Red Vienna: "Carnap Expects You"

1. Quoted in Wasserman, p. 38.

2. Menger (1994), p. 194.

3. Ibid., p. 196

4. Spiel (2007), p. 81.

5. This letter was begun on 10 February 1934, but this sentence was written on 13 February 1934. In McGuinness (2019), p. 192.

6. The three letters were Schlick to Hofrat Ganz, 2 March 1934, Schlick to the Bundes-Polizei-Direktion, 3 March 1934, Schlick to the *Sicherheitskommissär des Bundes für Wien*, 23 March 1934. In *Moritz Schlick Nachlass*, Vienna Circle Foundation (Amsterdam).

7. Menger (1994), p. 60.

8. An English translation of the manifesto can be found at www.manchesterism.com/the -scientific-conception-of-the-world-the-vienna-circle.

9. Carnap to Russell, 29 July 1922, quoted in Reisch, p. 50.

10. The speech was given by L. G. Tirala. Quoted by D. Hoffmann, in Richardson, p. 57.

11. Also known as Superfluous Entities, or Occam's Razor.

12. In McGuinness (1988), p. 112. My thanks to one of my (anonymous) readers for reminding me of this letter.

13. This summary is based on a translation by Christoph Limbeck-Lilienau, from a transcription by Brigitte Parakenings in shorthand.

14. In Menger, Karl, 1918–1919 *Tagebuch No. 1* (12/15/1918–12/31/1919). Durham, North Carolina, Duke University, David M. Rubenstein Rare Book & Manuscript Library, Karl Menger Papers, Box 33: Other Notebooks. Quoted in Scheall and Schumacher, p. 660.

15. R. Jeffrey in Buck, p. xxii. It should be pointed out that Carnap had little objection to religion being used as a practical or moral guide to how to live life. Where it failed was as a scientific description of the world.

13. Philosophical Rows

1. Bergmann, in Stadler (1993), p. 203.

2. Quoted in Critchley, p. 100.

3. See Yue-Ching Ho, pp. 1–5.

4. Naess, quoted in Critchley, p. 102.

5. *Erkenntnis* 2 (1932).

6. Ibid.

7. Scheffler, p. 66.

8. Carnap (1937), p. 52.

9. Frank (1941), p. 5.

10. Russell (2009), p. 444.

11. Neurath (1983), pp. 82–83; see also Cat and Tuboly, p. 640.

12. Ibid., p. 662

13. Putnam (1988), p. xii.

14. Neurath (1983), p. 92.

15. Ibid., pp. 100–114.

16. Ibid., p. 114.

17. Schilpp, p. 70.

18. See Monk, p. 277, quoting from *"Lecture on Ethics," Philosophical Review*, Jan. 1965, pp. 3–26.

19. Janik and Toulmin, p. 193.

20. Ayer (1958), p. 107.

21. See A. Tuboly, "Vacuum of Values and Different Philosophies: Ayer, Joad and the Charge(s) of Fascism," in Tuboly, ed., *The Historical and Philosophical Significance of Ayer's "Language, Truth and Logic"* (Palgrave Macmillan, forthcoming 2021).

22. Schlick in Ayer (1959), p. 247.

23. Ibid.

24. Quoted by Thomas Uebel in Creath (2012), p. 143.

25. See Bright (2017) for an excellent and longer discussion of logical empiricism and race.

26. See Tuboly chapter in Cat and Tuboly, p. 98.

14. The Unofficial Opposition

1. Popper (1976), p. 88.

2. Quoted in Sigmund, p. 238.

3. Popper (1963), pp. 37–38.

4. Ibid., p. 35.

5. Neurath (1983), p. 124.

6. Feigl (1981), p. 66.

7. Popper (1976), p. 82.

8. Quoted in Feferman, p. 94. Originally from L. Henkin et al., eds., *Proceedings of the Tarski Symposium*, American Mathematical Society (Providence).

9. Ibid.

10. And see Ter Hark for the link between Popper and German psychologist Otto Selz.

11. 1 November 1934, *Moritz Schlick Nachlass*, Konstanz, Philosophisches Archiv.

15. Now, You Damn Bastard

1. *Philosophical Review* 45, no. 4 (July 1936), p. 356.

2. Quoted in Stadler (2001), p. 869.

3. In Menger (1994), p. 197.

4. Crankshaw, p. 33.

5. *The Daily Telegraph*, 19 June 1936.

6. *Erkenntnis* 6 (1936).

7. 28 June 1936. Quoted in Wasserman.

8. Spiel (2007), p. 90.

9. Quoted in Janik (1999), p. 43.

10. Others, such as A. J. Ayer, took exception to this position. Ayer thought that talk of surviving the annihilation of one's body was self-contradictory.

16. The Inner Circle

1. See an interview with his son in Cohen (2014), p. 35.

2. Carnap to Neurath, 11 June 1936. Pittsburgh, Archives of Scientific Philosophy, Rudolf Carnap Papers 102-52-26.

3. In Tuboly (2021).

4. Quoted in Janik (1999), p. 44, and Monk (1990), p. 358.

5. Hermine to Ludwig, 11 July 1936. In McGuinness (2019), p. 209.

6. Wittgenstein to Rush Rhees, 13.7.1938.

7. Translation from a quote in Weg.

8. Ibid.

9. Quoted in Isaac, p. 148, from an unpublished manuscript.

10. 31 December 1935. Quoted in Rogers, p. 108.

11. See Rogers, p. 124.

17. Escape

1. Letter to Carnap, 16 June 1945, in Cat and Tuboly, p. 639.

2. *Daily Telegraph* correspondent, quoted in Faber, p. 146.

3. Quoted in Faber, p. 151; from N. Nicolson, ed., *Harold Nicolson, Diaries and Letters, 1930–1939* (Collins, 1966), p. 347.

4. For details, see Stember, p. 138.

5. Gutman, p. 455.

6. From a letter to his sister Hilda, 30 July 1939. Quoted in London, p. 106.

7. Freud, p. 217.

8. In Huemer, p. 13 in chapter by Fred Wilson—*The Vienna Circle and Freud*.

9. For a fuller account of this extraordinary episode, see Edmonds and Eidinow.

10. Quoted in Dawson, p. 91.

11. Draft of a letter of 27 November 1939. Quoted in Dawson, p. 141.

12. Dawson, p. 142.

13. Ibid.

18. Miss Simpson's Children

1. Quoted in Snowman, p. xiv, from E. Panofsky, *Meaning in the Visual Arts* (Peregrine Books 1970), p. 380.

2. See Beveridge.

3. *The Times*, 22 May 1933.

4. Beveridge, p. 6.

5. Cooper, p. 25.

6. Quoted in Cooper, p. 8.

7. Oxford, Bodleian Library, Society for the Protection of Science and Learning (hereafter SPSL), Neurath file.

8. Author interview with Michael Yudkin.

9. Cooper, p. 37.

10. LSE, Popper Archive (101–13). Quoted in Hacohen, p. 311.

11. SPSL, Popper file.

12. Popper to Kaufmann, 1 December 1936, quoted in Hacohen, p. 322.

13. 16 October 1936. SPSL, Popper file.

14. SPSL, Popper file.

15. SPSL, Waismann file.

16. Ibid.

17. Ibid.

18. Ibid.

19. Ibid.

20. Ibid.

21. Ibid.

22. Ibid.

19. War

1. Neurath (1973), p. 69.

2. Neurath to Carnap, 22 December 1942, quoted in Cat and Tuboly, p. 110.

3. 9 October 1939. Quoted in T. Kushner chapter in Ceserani, p. 87.

4. Sir Neville Bland, in a memorandum circulated in the Foreign Office. Quoted in Seabrook, p. 77.

5. 28 May 1940. Quoted in Matuschek, p. 327.

6. Kochan, p. 34.

7. F. Pierre to Colonel Wedgwood MP, 24 October 1941. Quoted in L. Burletson chapter in Ceserani, p. 104.

8. Kochan, p. 55.

9. From an unpublished diary of Wilhelm Hollitscher.

10. SPSL, Waismann file.

11. Ibid.

12. Letter of 5 August 1940. Ibid.

13. Quoted in Chappell, p. 84.

14. Kochan, p. 158.

15. SPSL, Neurath file.

16. Ibid.

17. Ibid.

18. Ibid.

19. Ibid.

20. Ibid.

21. Ibid.

22. Ibid.

23. Neurath to Carnap, 25 September 1943. Pittsburgh, Rudolf Carnap Papers.

24. Quoted in Neurath (1973), p. 64.

25. Neurath to Carnap. Ibid.

26. See Cat and Tuboly, p. 625.

27. Ibid., p. 636.

28. Neurath to Morris, 7 January 1942. Quoted in Reisch, p. 16.

29. Aydelotte, 10 November 1939. Quoted in Dawson, p. 145.

30. Dawson, p. 147.

31. Oskar Morgenstern, letter of 1965. Quoted in Sigmund, p. 343.

32. Quoted in Zilsel, p. 134.

33. Quoted in Zilsel, *Oakland Tribune*, Sunday, 12 March 1944, p. xxvi.

34. LSE, Rand file 5BFW/11/02/08.

35. SPSL, Rand file 1939/51 347/1.

36. Ibid.

37. Ibid.

38. Ibid.

39. LSE, Rand file.

40. Ibid.

41. SPSL, Rand file.

42. Simpson to Wittgenstein, 5 November 1943. SPSL, Rand file 347/1.

43. Simpson, letter of 30 April 1941. SPSL, Rand file.

44. SPSL, Rand file.

45. Ibid.

46. Ibid.

47. Ibid.

48. Ibid.

49. Letter from Wittgenstein, 19 January 1945. Pittsburgh, Rose Rand Papers.

50. Pittsburgh, Rose Rand Papers.

20. Exile

1. Dedication in Frank (1957) to his wife, Hania.

2. Schneider, p. 191.

3. Popper to Carnap, 23 June 1945. LSE, Popper archive.

4. The letter was written on 28 April 1946. In Wang, p. 45.

5. Author interview with Alan Hausman.

6. Clare, p. 123.

7. Popper (1976), p. 114.

8. Author interview with Miranda Hempel.

9. Versions of this story are recounted in several books including Clark, p. 510.

10. Quote from author correspondence with Laird Addis.

11. Quoted in Misak. Pittsburgh, Rudolf Carnap Papers 102-13-30.

12. Ceserani, p. 79, quoting historian Max Beloff.

13. Quoted by Hans Joachim Dahms in Stadler (1995), p. 58.

14. As told to Evan Fales: author interview.

15. Hoover, letter of 13 August 1952, quoted in Reisch, from Richardson (2007), p. 76.

16. Quoted in Reisch, p. 270.

17. This story is told in Holton, p. 49.

18. Nagel to Carnap, 5 January 1935. Quoted in A. Tuboly, "Carnap's Weltanschauung and the Jugendbewegung," in Stadler (2017), p. 141.

19. Feigl (1961), p. 16.

20. Ibid.

21. Ibid.

22. *News Chronicle*, 4 December 1945.

23. Author correspondence with Anthony Kenny.

24. Author interview with R. Harré.

25. Letter from Waismann, 13 January 1953. LSE, Popper archive.

26. Quoted in Waismann (1982), p. 10.

27. Reprinted in Waismann (2011), p. 29.

28. Carnap to Popper, 27 May 1947. LSE, Popper archive.

29. LSE, BFW 5BFW/11/02/08.

30. Pittsburgh, Rose Rand Papers.

31. Schilpp, p. 72.

32. 28 November 1956, quoted in Tuboly, "Carnap's Weltanschauung."

33. 27 February 1959. Pittsburgh, Rudolf Carnap Papers.

34. 7 March 1959. Ibid.

35. Quoted in Wang, p. 37.

36. Interview with author.

37. Quoted in Clark, p. 376.

38. Quoted in Wang, p. 34.

39. Author correspondence with William Hanson.

40. Quotes from Felix Rosenthal, Walter Goldstein, Richard Born in author correspondence.

41. Author correspondence with Rebecca Goldstein.

42. Peter Hempel in correspondence with author.

43. Hacohen, p. 524.

44. This is in a circular letter to Carnap, Frank, Hempel, Morris, and Nagel, 16 September 1954. Columbia University, Rare Books and Manuscripts Ernest Nagel Papers (Box 1).

45. Fetzer, p. 12.

46. Ralf Dahrendorf, quoted in Edmonds and Eidinow, p. 179.

47. The author's mother, on *Wittgenstein's Poker*, by David Edmonds and John Eidinow. Full disclosure, that David Edmonds stands in a one-to-one relation with the author of the book you are currently reading.

48. Carnap to Popper, 11 December 1959. LSE, Popper archive.

49. Quine, p. 337.

50. Malcolm, p. 100.

21. Legacy

1. Feigl (1981), p. 57.

2. Ayer (1958), p. 33.

3. Fred Hallberg in correspondence with author.

4. From a letter to his mother, 15 August 1946. In Wang, p. 70.

5. Wittgenstein (1953), para. 109.

6. There have been many attempts to come up with a single definition of "game": see Suits.

7. Author interview with R. Harré.

8. Ayer (1977), p. 132.

9. *Proceedings of the Aristotelian Society*, Supplementary Volume 19: 119–50.

10. This example is from *The Philosopher's Arms*, a BBC Radio 4 program presented by Matthew Sweet and produced by the author, which aired on 20 February 2017.

11. Author interview with David Papineau.

12. See Papineau's TLS review.

13. Edmonds and Eidinow, p. 230.

14. John Passmore in Edwards, pp. 52–57.

15. See Magee, p. 107.

16. Game theory is usually credited with having been launched by a book, *Theory of Games and Economic Behavior*, published in 1944 and written by Morgenstern and John Von Neumann.

17. As told to the author by A. Grünbaum, who himself became a very distinguished philosopher.

18. Quoted in Stadler (2001), p. 507.

19. See Ho.

20. Ibid.

21. Quote from Philip S. Marcus in correspondence with author.

22. David Chalmers in note to author.

SELECT BIBLIOGRAPHY

Of the books listed below, the following were particularly important resources: Hacohen (2000), Monk (1990), Stadler (2001), and Sigmund (2017).

Achinstein, P., and S. Barker, eds. *The Legacy of Logical Positivism*. Johns Hopkins Press, 1969.

Addis, L., G. Jesson, and E. Tegtmeier, eds. *Ontology and Analysis: Essays and Recollections about Gustav Bergmann*. Ontos Verlag, 2007.

Albers, D., and G. Alexanderson, eds. *Mathematical People*. Birkhauser, 1985.

Allen, G. *William James, a Biography*. Viking, 1967.

Antiseri, D. *Popper's Vienna*. The Davies Group, 2006.

Aschheim, S. *Beyond the Border: The German-Jewish Legacy Abroad*. Princeton University Press, 2007.

———. *Brothers and Strangers*. University of Wisconsin Press, 1982.

Ashby, C., T. Gronberg, and S. Shaw-Miller. *The Viennese Café and Fin-de-Siècle Culture*. Berghahn Books, 2013.

Ayer, A. *Language, Truth and Logic*. Victor Gollancz, 1958.

———. *Logical Positivism*. The Free Press, 1959.

———. *Part of My Life*. Collins, 1977.

Bauer, Y. *A History of the Holocaust*. Franklin Watts, 1982.

Beller, S. *Vienna and the Jews: 1867–1938*. Cambridge University Press, 1989.

Bergmann, G. *The Metaphysics of Logical Positivism*. University of Wisconsin Press, 1967.

Bettauer, H. *The City without Jews*. Translated by S. Brainin. Bloch Publishing House, 1926.

Beveridge, W. *A Defence of Free Learning*. Oxford University Press, 1959.

Bottomore, T., and P. Goode, eds. *Austro-Marxism*. Clarendon Press, 1978.

Bright, L. "Logical Empiricists on Race." *Studies in History and Philosophy of Biological and Biomedical Sciences*, 2017: 9–18.

Broda, P. *Scientist Spies*. Matador, 2011.

Buck, C., and R. Cohen. *Boston Studies in the Philosophy of Science: In Memory of Rudolf Carnap*. D. Riedel, 1970.

Bukey, E. *The Jews and Intermarriage in Nazi Austria*. Cambridge University Press, 2010.

Burke, C., E. Kindel, and S. Walker. *ISOTYPE*. Hyphen Press, 2013.

Burr, E. *Hitler's Austria*. University of North Carolina Press, 2000.

Butts, R. *Witches, Scientists, Philosophers*. Kluwer, 2000.

Caldwell, B. *Hayek's Challenge*. University of Chicago Press, 2004.

Canetti, E. *The Torch in My Ear*. Farrar, Straus and Giroux, 1982.

Carnap, R. *Intellectual Autobiography in the Philosophy of Rudolf Carnap*. Edited by Paul Arthur Schilpp. Open Court, 1963.

———. *The Logical Structure of the World*. Translated by R. George. Routledge and Kegan Paul, 1967.

———. *The Logical Syntax of Language*. Kegan, Paul, Trench Teubner & Cie, 1937.

———. *Philosophy and Logical Syntax*. Thoemmes Press, 1996.

————. *The Unity of Science*. Thoemmes Press, 1995.

Carr, G., and H. Mytum. *Cultural Heritage and Prisoners of War*. Routledge, 2012.

Carus, A. *Carnap and Twentieth-Century Thought*. Cambridge University Press, 2007.

Cat, C., and A. T. Tuboly, eds. *Neurath Reconsidered*. Springer, 2019.

Cesarani, D., and T. Kushner, eds. *The Internment of Aliens in Twentieth Century Britain*. Frank Cass, 1993.

Chalmers, D. *Constructing the World*. Oxford University Press, 2012.

Chappell, C. *Island of Barbed Wire*. Corgi, 1984.

Chapman, S. *Susan Stebbing and the Language of Common Sense*. Palgrave, 2013.

Clare, G. *Last Waltz in Vienna*. Pan Books, 1982.

Clark, R. *Einstein*. Hodder and Stoughton, 1979.

————. *Bertrand Russell*. Thames and Hudson, 1981.

Coffa, J. *The Semantic Tradition from Kant to Carnap*. Cambridge University Press, 1991.

Cohen, R. S., and I. K. Helling, eds. *Felix Kaufmann's Theory and Method in the Social Sciences*. Springer, 2014.

Cohen, R. S., R. Hilpinen, and R. Q. Risto, eds. *Realism and Anti-Realism in the Philosophy of Science*. Kluwer, 1996.

Cohen, R. S., and M. W. Wartofsky, eds. *Boston Studies in the Philosophy of Science. Vol 2: In Honor of Philipp Frank*. Humanities Press, 1965.

Cohen, S. *Rescue the Perishing*. Vallentine, Mitchell, 2010.

Cooper, R. M., ed. *Refugee Scholars: Conversations with Tess Simpson*. Moorland Books, 1992.

Crankshaw, E. *Vienna: The Image of a Culture in Decline*. Macmillan, 1936; reissued 1976.

Creath, R., ed. *Dear Carnap, Dear Van*. University of California Press, 1990.

————, ed. *Rudolf Carnap and the Legacy of Logical Empiricism*. Springer, 2012.

Critchley, S. *Continental Philosophy*. Oxford University Press, 2001.

Dainton, B., and H. Robinson, eds. *The Bloomsbury Companion to Analytic Philosophy*. Bloomsbury Academic, 2015.

Damböck, C., and G. Wolters, eds. *Young Carnap in an Historical Context: 1918–1935*. Springer, 2020.

Dawson, J. *Logical Dilemmas: The Life and Work of Kurt Gödel*. A. K. Peters, 1997.

De Waal, E. *The Hare with Amber Eyes: A Hidden Inheritance*. Chatto & Windus, 2010.

Eatwell, R. *Fascism: A History*. Chatto & Windus, 1995.

Edmonds, D., and J. Eidinow. *Wittgenstein's Poker: The Story of a Ten-Minute Argument between Two Famous Philosophers*. Faber and Faber, 2001.

Edwards, P., ed. *The Encyclopedia of Philosophy*. Volume 5. Macmillan, 1967.

Einstein, A. *Autobiographical Notes*. Translated and edited by P. Schilpp. Open Court, 1979.

Engelman, P. *Letters from Ludwig Wittgenstein, with a Memoir*. Blackwell, 1968.

Faber, D. *Munich*. Simon & Schuster, 2008.

Fergusson, A. *When Money Dies*. William Kimber, 1975.

Fraenkel, J., ed. *The Jews of Austria: Essays on Their Life, History and Destruction*. Vallentine, Mitchell, 1967.

Feferman, A., and S. Feferman. *Alfred Tarski: Life and Logic*. Cambridge University Press, 2004.

Feigl, H. *Inquiries and Provocations*. Edited by R. Cohen. D. Riedel, 1981.

Feigl, H., and G. Maxwell, eds. *Current Issues in the Philosophy of Science*. Holt, Rinehart and Winston, 1961.

Feigl, H., and W. Sellars, eds. *Readings in Philosophical Analysis*. Appleton-Century-Crofts, 1949.

Fetzer, J., ed. *The Philosophy of Carl G. Hempel*. Oxford University Press, 2001.

Feyerabend, P., and G. Maxwell. *Mind, Matter, and Method: Essays in Philosophy and Science in Honor of Herbert Feigl*. University of Minnesota Press, 1966.

Feyerabend, P. *Killing Time*. University of Chicago Press, 1995.

Fischel, J. *The Holocaust*. Greenwood Press, 1998.

Flanagan, O. "Wittgenstein's Ethical Nonnaturalism." *American Philosophical Quarterly* 48, no. 2. Wittgenstein and Naturalism (April 2011): 185–98.

Fogelin, R. *Wittgenstein*. Routledge, 1987.

Fölsing, A. *Albert Einstein*. Translated by E. Osers. Viking, 1997.

Forrester, J. "Freud in Cambridge." *Critical Quarterly* 46, no. 2 (2004): 1–26.

Frank, P. *Between Physics and Philosophy*. Harvard University Press, 1941.

———. *Einstein: His Life and Times*. Jonathan Cape, 1948.

———. *Modern Science and Its Philosophy*. Harvard University Press, 1950.

———. *Philosophy of Science*. Prentice-Hall, 1957.

Frankel, J., ed. *The Jews of Austria*. Vallentine, Mitchell, 1970.

Frascolla, P. *Understanding Wittgenstein's Tractatus*. Routledge, 2007.

Frege, G. *The Foundations of Arithmetic*. Blackwell, 1989.

Freidenreich, H. *Jewish Politics in Vienna: 1918–1938*. Indiana University Press, 1991.

Freud, M. *Glory Reflected*. Angus and Robertson, 1957.

Freund, F., and H. Safrian. *Expulsion and Extermination: The Fate of the Austrian Jews 1938–1945*. Translated by D. Rosenfeld and G. Biemann. Austrian Resistance Archive, 1997.

Friedman, M., and R. Creath, eds. *The Cambridge Companion to Carnap*. Cambridge University Press, 2007.

Gadol, E. *Rationality and Science*. Springer Verlag, 1982.

Galison, P. "Aufbau/Bauhaus: Logical Positivism and Architectural Modernism." *Critical Inquiry* 16 (1990): 709–52.

Galavotti, M. *Cambridge and Vienna: Frank P. Ramsey and the Vienna Circle*. Springer, 2006.

Gardner, S., and G. Stevens. *Red Vienna and The Golden Age of Psychology 1918–1938*. Praeger, 1992.

Gay, P. *Freud: A Life for Our Time*. J. M. Dent, 1988.

———. *A Godless Jew*. Yale University Press, 1987.

———. *Schnitzler's Century*. W. W. Norton, 2002.

Gibson, R., ed. *The Cambridge Companion to Quine*. Cambridge University Press, 2004.

Gilbert, M. *The Second World War*. Weidenfeld & Nicolson, 2009.

Gimbel, S. *Einstein's Jewish Science*. John Hopkins University Press, 2012.

Glock, H.-J. *A Wittgenstein Dictionary*. Blackwell, 1996.

Glock, H.-J., and J. Hyman, eds. *A Companion to Wittgenstein*. Wiley, 2017.

Goldstein, R. *Incompleteness: The Proof and Paradox of Kurt Gödel*. Atlas Books, 2005.

Gombrich, E. *The Visual Arts in Vienna*, vol. 1. The Austrian Cultural Institute London, 1996.

Gordin, M. *Einstein in Bohemia*. Princeton University Press, 2020.

Gower, B., ed. *Logical Positivism in Perspective*. Croom Helm, 1987.

Gruber, H. *Red Vienna: Experiment in Working Class Culture 1919–1934*. Oxford University Press, 1991.

Gutman, I. *Encyclopedia of the Holocaust*. Macmillan, 1990.

Hacohen, M. *Karl Popper: The Formative Years*. Cambridge University Press, 2000.

Hahn, H. *Empiricism, Logic, and Mathematics*. Edited by B. McGuinness. D. Riedel, 1980.

Hamann, B. *Hitler's Vienna*. Translated by T. Thornton. Oxford University Press, 1999.

Hanfling, O. *Logical Positivism*. Blackwell, 1981.

Harcourt, E. "Wittgenstein and Psychoanalysis." In *The Blackwell Companion to Wittgenstein*, ed. H.-J. Glock and J. Hyman. Wiley, 2017, 651–66.

Heidelberger, M., and F. Stadler, eds. *History of Philosophy of Science*. Kluwer, 2002.

Henning, M. "Isotypes and Elephants: Picture Language as Visual Writing in the Work and Correspondence of Otto Neurath." Chapter 6 in *The Art of the Text*, ed. S. Harrow. University of Wales Press, 2012, 95–114.

Hempel, C. *Science, Explanation, and Rationality*. Oxford University Press, 2000.

Herzog, H. *Vienna Is Different*. Berghahn Books, 2011.

Hickman, H. *Musil and the Culture of Vienna*. Croom Helm, 1984.

Ho, Y-C. "At 90, and Still Dynamic." *Intellectus* 23 (1992).

Holmes, D., and L. Silverman, eds. *Interwar Vienna*. Camden House, 2009.

Hobsbawm, E. *Interesting Times*. Pantheon, 2002.

Hollitscher, W. *Sigmund Freud*. Kegan Paul, 1947.

Holton, G. *Science and Anti-Science*. Harvard University Press, 1993.

Huemer, W., and M-O. Schuster, eds. *Writing the Austrian Traditions*. University of Alberta, 2003.

Hughes, R. *The Fatal Shore*. Vintage Books, 1988.

Hume, D. *An Enquiry Concerning Human Understanding*. Oxford University Press, 2007.

Hylton, P. *Quine*. Routledge, 2010.

Isaac, J. *Working Knowledge*. Harvard University Press, 2012.

Isaacson, W. *Einstein: His Life and Universe*. Simon & Schuster, 2007.

James-Chakraborty, K. *Bauhaus Culture*. University of Minnesota Press, 2006.

Janik, A., and S. Toulmin. *Wittgenstein's Vienna*. Touchstone, 1973.

Janik, A., and H. Veigl. *Wittgenstein in Vienna*. Springer Verlag, 1999.

Jones, E. *The Life and Work of Sigmund Freud*, vol. 3. The Hogarth Press, 1957.

Judson, P. *The Habsburg Empire*. Harvard University Press, 2016.

Kahane, G., E. Kanterian, and O. Kuusela, eds. *Wittgenstein and His Interpreters*. Blackwell, 2007.

Kandel, E. *The Age of Insight*. Random House, 2012.

Klagge, J., ed. *Wittgenstein: Biography and Philosophy*. Cambridge University Press, 2001.

Knittel, K. *Seeing Mahler*. Ashgate, 2010.

Kochan, M. *Britain's Internees in the Second World War*. Macmillan, 1983.

Kraft, V. *The Vienna Circle*. The Philosophical Library, 1953.

Kushner, Tony. *The Holocaust and the Liberal Imagination*. Blackwell, 1994.

Lamont, C. *Dialogue on John Dewey*. Horizon Press, 1959.

Landau, R. *The Nazi Holocaust*. I. B. Tauris, 1992.

Lanouette, W. *Genius in the Shadows*. University of Chicago Press, 1993.

Leonard, R. "Ethics and the Excluded Middle: Karl Menger and Social Science in Interwar Vienna." *Isis* 89, no. 1 (March 1998): 1–26.

Leonard, R. *Von Neumann, Morgenstern, and the Creation of Game Theory*. Cambridge University Press, 2010.

LeMahieu, M. *Fictions of Fact and Value*. Oxford University Press, 2013.

Le Rider, J. *Modernity and Crises of Identity*. Translated by R. Morris. Polity Press, 1993.

Lewy, G. *The Catholic Church and Nazi Germany*. Da Capo Press, 2000.

London, L. *Whitehall and the Jews 1933–48*. Cambridge University Press, 2000.

Lurie, Y. *Wittgenstein on the Human Spirit*. Rodopi, 2012.

Magee, B., ed. *Men of Ideas*. BBC, 1978.

Mahler, A. *Gustav Mahler: Memories and Letters*. Edited by D. Mitchell. John Murray, 1973.

Malcolm, N. *Ludwig Wittgenstein: A Memoir*. Oxford University Press, 1980.

Manninen, J., and F. Stadler. *The Vienna Circle in the Nordic Countries*. Springer, 2010.

Marks, S., P. Weindling, and L. Wintour, eds. *In Defence of Learning*. Oxford University Press, 2011.

Marx, K., F. Engels, and V. Lenin. *On Historical Materialism*. Progress Publishers, 1972.

Masheck, J. *Adolf Loos*. I. B. Tauris, 2013.

Matar, A., ed. *Understanding Wittgenstein, Understanding Modernism*. Bloomsbury Academic, 2017.

Matuschek, O. *Three Lives: A Biography of Stefan Zweig*. Translated by A. Blunden. Pushkin Press, 2011.

McEwan, B. *Sexual Knowledge: Feeling, Fact and Social Reform in Vienna, in 1900–1934*. Berghahn Books, 2012.

McGuinness, B., ed. *Wittgenstein in Cambridge*. Blackwell, 2008.

———, ed. *Wittgenstein in Cambridge: Letters and Documents, 1911–1951*. Blackwell, 2012.

———, ed. *Wittgenstein's Family Letters*. Bloomsbury, 2019.

———. *Young Ludwig*. Clarendon Press, 1988.

Medawar, J., and D. Pyke. *Hitler's Gift: Scientists Who Fled Nazi Germany*. Piatkus, 2001.

Menger, K. *Morality, Decision and Social Organization*. D. Reidel, 1974.

———. *Reminiscences of the Vienna Circle and the Mathematical Colloquium*. Edited by L. Golland, B. McGuinness, and A. Sklar. Kluwer, 1994.

———. *Selected Papers in Logic and Foundations, Didactics, Economics*. D. Reidel, 1979.

Misak, C. *The American Pragmatists*. Oxford University Press, 2013.

———. *Frank Ramsey: A Sheer Excess of Powers*. Oxford University Press, 2020.

———. *Truth, Politics, Morality*. Routledge, 2000.

Monk, R. *Bertrand Russell: The Ghost of Madness*. Jonathan Cape, 2000.

———. *Bertrand Russell: The Spirit of Solitude*. Jonathan Cape, 1996.

———. *Ludwig Wittgenstein: The Duty of Genius*. Jonathan Cape, 1990.

Moorehead, C. *Bertrand Russell*. Sinclair Stevenson, 1992.

Mos, L., ed. *History of Psychology in Autobiography*. Springer, 2009.

Musil, R. *Diaries 1899–1941*. Translated by P. Payne. Basic Books, 1999.

Naess, A. *Four Modern Philosophers*. Translated by A. Hannay. Phoenix Books, 1969.

Nemeth, E., S. Schmitz, and T. Uebel, eds. *Otto Neurath's Economics in Context*. Springer, 2007.

Neurath, O. *Empiricism and Sociology*. Edited by M. Neurath and R. Cohen. D. Riedel, 1973.

———. *From Hieroglyphics to Isotype: A Visual Autobiography*. Edited by M. Eve and C. Burke. Hyphen Press, 2010.

———. *Philosophical Papers 1913–46*. Translated by R. Cohen and M. Neurath. D. Riedel, 1983.

Nickles, T., ed. *Thomas Kuhn*. Cambridge University Press, 2003.

Nietzsche, F. *The Gay Science*. Translated and edited by W. Kaufmann. Vintage, 1974.

Oxaal, I., M. Pollak, and G. Botz, eds. *Jews, Antisemitism and Culture in Vienna*. Routledge and Kegan Paul, 1987.

Papineau, D. "Karl R. Popper: Knowledge and the Body-Mind Problem." *Times Literary Supplement*, 23 June 1995, https://www.davidpapineau.co.uk/uploads/1/8/5/5/18551740/popper-tls-complete.pdf [last accessed 16 March 2020].

Paul, M. *Frank Ramsey (1903–1930): A Sister's Memoir*. Smith-Gordon, 2012.

Pentland, A. *Social Physics: How Good Ideas Spread*. Penguin, 2014.

Pinsker, S. *A Rich Brew*. New York University Press, 2018.

Popper, K. *Conjectures and Refutations*. Routledge, 1963.

———. *Unended Quest*. Fontana, 1976.

Prater, D. *European of Yesterday: A Biography of Stefan Zweig*. Clarendon Press, 1972.

Pulzer, P. *The Rise of Political Anti-Semitism in Germany and Austria*. Harvard University Press, 1988.

Putnam, H. *Representation and Reality*. MIT Press, 1988.

Quine, W. "Russell's Ontological Development." *Journal of Philosophy* 63 (1966): 657–67.

———. *The Time of My Life*. MIT Press, 1985.

Ramsey, F. *Notes on Philosophy, Probability and Mathematics*. Edited by M. Galavotti. Bibliopolis, 1991.

Reeder, H. *The Work of Felix Kaufmann*. University Press of America, 1991.

Reichenbach, H. *Selected Writings 1909–1953*, vol. 1. Edited by M. Reichenbach and R. Cohen. D. Reidel, 1978.

Reisch, G. *How the Cold War Transformed Philosophy of Science*. Cambridge University Press, 2005.

Rentetzi, M. "'I Want to Look like a Lady, Not Like a Factory Worker': Rose Rand, a Woman Philosopher of the Vienna Circle." In *EPSA Epistemology and Methodology of Science*. Vol. 1: *Launch of the European Philosophy of Science Association*, edited by M. Suárez, M. Dorato, and M. Rédei. Springer, 2010, 233–44.

Rhees, R., ed. *Ludwig Wittgenstein: Personal Recollections*. Blackwell, 1981.

———. *Recollections of Wittgenstein*. Oxford University Press, 1984.

Richardson, A. *Carnap's Construction of the World*. Cambridge University Press, 1998.

Richardson, A., and T. Uebel. *The Cambridge Companion to Logical Empiricism*. Cambridge University Press, 2007.

Richardson, S. *Studies in History and Philosophy of Science* 40 (2009): 14–24.

Robbins, K. *Appeasement*. Blackwell, 1997.

Rogers, B. *A. J. Ayer*. Chatto & Windus, 1999.

Rose, A. *Jewish Women in Fin de Siècle Vienna*. University of Texas Press, 2008.

Roth, J. *The Wandering Jews*. Granta, 2001.

Rozenblit, M. *The Jews of Vienna: 1867–1914*. State University of New York Press, 1983.

———. *Reconstructing A National Identity*. Oxford University Press, 2001.

Runggaldier, E. *Carnap's Early Conventionalism*. Rodopi, 1984.

Russell, B. *Autobiography*. Routledge, 2009.

———. *An Inquiry into Meaning and Truth*. Spokesman, 2007 [first published 1940].

———. *The Philosophy of Logical Atomism*. Open Court, 1988.

Ryan, A. *Bertrand Russell—A Political Life*. Allen Lane, 1988.

Safranski, R. *Martin Heidegger*. Translated by E. Osers. Harvard University Press, 1998.

Sarkar, S. *Science and Philosophy in the Twentieth Century*. Volume 2: *Logical Empiricism at Its Peak*. Garland, 1996.

———. *Science and Philosophy in the Twentieth Century: The Legacy of the Vienna Circle*. Garland, 1996.

Sayre, K. *Adventures in Philosophy at Notre Dame*. University of Notre Dame, 2014.

Scazzieri, R., and R. Simili. *The Migration of Ideas*. Watson Publishing, 2008.

Scheall, S., and R. Schumacher. "Karl Menger as Son of Carl Menger." *History of Political Economy* 5, no. 4 (2018): 649–78.

Scheffler, I. *Gallery of Scholars: A Philosopher's Recollections*. Kluwer Academic Publishers, 2004.

Schilpp, P. *The Philosophy of Rudolf Carnap*. Open Court, 1963.

Schlick, M. "Die Wende in der Philosophie." *Erkenntnis* 1 (1930): 4–11.

———. *The Problems of Philosophy in Their Interconnection*. D. Reidel, 1987.

Schneider, G. *Exile and Destruction*. Praeger, 1995.

Schnitzler, A. *My Youth in Vienna*. Translated by C. Hutter. Weidenfeld & Nicolson, 1971.

Schorske, C. *Fin-de-Siècle Vienna*. Weidenfeld & Nicolson, 1980.

Seabrook, J. *The Refuge and the Fortress*. Palgrave, 2009.

Service, R. *Lenin*. Macmillan, 2000.

Sherman, M., ed. *Psychoanalysis and Old Vienna*. Human Sciences Press, 1978.

Sigmund, K. *Exact Thinking in Demented Times*. Basic Books, 2017.

———. "A Philosopher's Mathematician: Hans Hahn and the Vienna Circle." *The Mathematical Intelligencer* 17, no. 4 (1995): 16–29.

Silverman, L. *Becoming Austrians*. Oxford University Press, 2012.

Skidelsky, R. *John Maynard Keynes: 1883–1946*. Pan Books, 2003.

Snowman, D. *The Hitler Emigrés*. Chatto & Windus, 2002.

Spiel, H. *The Dark and the Bright*. Translated by C. Shuttleworth. Ariadne Press, 2007.

———. *Vienna's Golden Autumn 1866–1938*. Weidenfeld & Nicolson, 1987.

Spohn, W. *Erkenntnis Orientated*. Kluwer Academic Publishers, 1991.

Sprangenburg, R., and D. Moses. *Niels Bohr: Atomic Theorist*. Chelsea House, 2008.

Stadler, F., ed. *Integrated History and Philosophy of Science*. Springer Verlag, 2017.

———, ed. *Scientific Philosophy: Origins and Development*. Kluwer, 1993.

———, ed. *The Vienna Circle and Logical Empiricism: Re-evaluation and Future Perspectives*. Kluwer, 2003.

———. *The Vienna Circle: Studies in the Origins, Development, and Influence of Logical Empiricism*. Springer Verlag, 2001; rev. ed. 2015.

Stadler, F., and P. Weibel, eds. *The Cultural Exodus from Austria*. Springer Verlag, 1995.

Stember, C. H., et al. *Jews in the Mind of America*. Basic Books, 1966.

Suits, B. *The Grasshopper Games, Life and Utopia*. Scottish Academic Press, 1978.

Szaniawski, K. *The Vienna Circle and the Lvov-Warsaw School*. Kluwer Academic Publishers, 1989.

Ter Hark, M. *Popper, Otto Selz, and the Rise of Evolutionary Epistemology*. Cambridge University Press, 2004.

Timms, E. *Karl Kraus: Apocalyptic Satirist*. Yale University Press, 2005.

Timms, E., and A. Hammel. *The German-Jewish Dilemma*. Edwin Mellen, 1999.

Timms, E., and J. Hughes, eds. *Intellectual Migration and Cultural Transformation*. Springer, 2003.

Tuboly, Á., ed. *The Historical and Philosophical Significance of Ayer's "Language, Truth and Logic."* Palgrave Macmillan, forthcoming 2021.

———, ed. *Special Issue on the Life and Work of Philipp Frank* (*Studies in East European Thought*) 69, no. 3 (2017): 199–276.

Uebel, T. *Empiricism at the Crossroads*. Open Court, 2007.

———. "Learning Logical Tolerance: Hans Hahn on the Foundations of Mathematics." *History and Philosophy of Logic* 26 (Sept. 2005): 175–209.

———. *Overcoming Logical Positivism from Within*. Rodopi, 1992.

———, ed. *Rediscovering the Forgotten Vienna Circle*. Kluwer, 1991.

Urback, R. *Arthur Schnitzler*. Translated by D. Daviau. Frederick Ungar, 1973.

Verbaan, D. *Weg! Ontsnapt aan de Duitse besetting*. Scriptum, 2015.

Vogel, D. *Married Life*. Translated by D. Bilu. Peter Halban, 1988.

Von Neumann Whitman, M. *The Martian's Daughter*. University of Michigan, 2012.

Wagner, P., ed. *Carnap's Logical Syntax of Language*. Palgrave, 2009.

Waugh, A. *The House of Wittgenstein*. Bloomsbury, 2008.

Waismann, F. *Causality and Logical Positivism*. Edited by B. McGuinness. Springer, 2011.

———. *Lectures on the Philosophy of Mathematics*. Edited by W. Grassl. Rodopi, 1982.

———. *Philosophical Papers*. Edited by B. McGuinness. D. Reidel, 1977.

———. *The Principles of Linguistic Philosophy*. Edited by R. Harré. Macmillan, 1965.

———. *Wittgenstein and the Vienna Circle*. Edited by B. McGuinness. Blackwell, 1979.

Wang, H. *A Logical Journey*. MIT, 1996.

Wasserman, J. *Black Vienna*. Cornell, 2014.

Watson, A. *Ring of Steel*. Allen Lane, 2014.

Wimmer, A. *Strangers at Home and Abroad*. McFarland & Company, 2000.

Winch, P., ed. *Studies in the Philosophy of Wittgenstein*. Routledge and Kegan Paul, 1969.

Wistrich, R. *The Jews of Vienna in the Age of Franz Joseph*. Oxford University Press, 1989.

Wittgenstein, L. *Culture and Value*. Edited by G. H. von Wright. Blackwell, 1980.

———. *Lectures and Conversations*. Edited by C. Barrett. Blackwell, 1966.

———. *Philosophical Investigations*. Blackwell, 1969.

———. *Tractatus Logico-Philosophicus*. Kegan Paul, 1922.

———. *Zettel*. Edited by G.E.M. Anscombe and G. H. von Wright. Blackwell, 1967.

Woleński, J., and K. Eckehart. *Alfred Tarski and the Vienna Circle*. Kluwer, 1998.

Wood, A. *Bertrand Russell: The Passionate Sceptic*. George Allen & Unwin, 1957.

Zilsel, E. *The Social Origins of Modern Science*. Edited by D. Raven, W. Krohn, and R. Cohen. Kluwer: 2000.

Zimmerman, D. "The Society for the Protection of Science and Learning and the Politicization of British Science in the 1930s." *Minerva* 44 (2006): 25–45.

Zweig, S. *The World of Yesterday*. Atrium Press, 1987.

INDEX

AAC. *See* Academic Assistance Council

Abyssinia, 130–31, 174

Academic Assistance Council (AAC), 199–204

Adams, Walter, 200, 202, 214–15

Adler, Alfred, 167

Adler, Friedrich, 56

Adler, Mortimer, 240

Adler, Victor, 9, 121, 134

adult education, 135–36, 171

aesthetics, 43, 111–12

All Souls College, Oxford, England, 208

All-Union Institute of Pictorial Statistics of Soviet Construction and Economy (Izostat), 62–63, 132

Altenberg, Peter, 72

Am Steinhof psychiatric hospital, Vienna, 171

Analysis (journal), 185

analytic (Anglo-American) philosophy, vii, 34, 185, 251, 261

analytic truths, 24–25, 254–55

anarchy, 59

Andermann, Hermine (Mina), 68

Anglo-American philosophy. *See* analytic (Anglo-American) philosophy

Anglo-Iranian Oil Company, 195, 203

Annalen der Philosophie (*Annals of Philosophy*) (journal), 94

Anschluss, 2, 86, 124, 170, 188–89, 230

anti-Semitism: in Austrian politics, 118–19, 134; in Austria outside of Vienna, 118, 128; in Britain, 193, 212, 233; of Catholic Church, 58, 121; in educational institutions, 17, 67, 70, 71, 114, 117, 123, 129, 189, 199–200, 203, 205, 233; of Heidegger, 143; international, 126–27; Jewish instances of, 118, 124–25; of Nelböck, 190; postwar, 228; in US, 182, 192, 233; in Vienna, 82, 114–27, 249; Zionism as solution for, 120.

See also Jews and Jewishness: negative attitudes toward

a posteriori knowledge, 24–25

Apostles (intellectual circle), 84–85, 93–94

a priori knowledge, 24–25

Arandora Star (ship), 215–16

architecture, 78–81

Aristotle, 9, 32, 241

Army Service Corps, 12

Arntz, Gerd, 61, 183

Ataturk, 138

atoms, 9

Australia, 192

Austria, 55–56, 119, 129–31, 187–89

Austrian Federal Railways, 203

Austrian Freethinkers, 89

Austro-Hungarian Empire, 6, 27, 36, 55, 118–19, 127

Austro-Marxism, 9, 56–57, 67, 129, 133, 136

Axamit, Hilda, 182

Aydelotte, Frank, 219–20

Ayer, A. J.: conferences attended by, 98, 99; death of, 248; and ethics, 158; honors received by, 247; on immorality, 155, 285n10; Jewish origins of, 115; *Language, Truth, and Logic*, vii, 185–86, 251; and logical positivism, 185–86, 251, 259, 260; and Popper, 99, 202; and Vienna Circle, 106–8, 143, 251; and Waismann, 253

Bakan, David, 124

Bauer, Otto, 13, 56, 57, 67, 94, 136

Bauhaus, 79–80

Bavaria, 13

Bayes, Thomas, 156

Bayesian probability, 156

Beethoven, Ludwig van, 119, 125, 139, 141

Bell, George, 215

Beller, Steven, 121

A NOTE ON THE TYPE

This book has been composed in Arno, an Old-style serif typeface in the classic Venetian tradition, designed by Robert Slimbach at Adobe.